I0644703

Praise for *Speaking of Hebrew*

"*Speaking of Hebrew* is as timely as it is illuminating. Avni brilliantly unpacks a defining paradox—American Jews talk frequently about Hebrew while rarely speaking it—showing how discourse in and about Hebrew opens a window into American Jewishness, localized and repurposed to meet distinctive spiritual, cultural, and social needs."

—Kendall King, professor of multilingual education, University of Minnesota

"Avni has written a fascinating, creative book that explores what engagement with and talk about Hebrew can tell us about contemporary American Jewish life. Beautifully written in crisp, clear prose, this book will be of great interest to Jewish studies scholars and students, as well as sociolinguists and linguistic anthropologists. A must-read!"

—Ayala Fader, professor of anthropology, Fordham University

"Avni's lively, nuanced exploration of Modern Hebrew in America shows how it serves as a complex and dynamic resource intertwined with identity, sociality, and politics. Highlighting the importance of language ideologies and countering the notion of a single 'real' Hebrew, this insightful work illuminates how diverse speakers interact with Hebrew, reshaping it to build, sustain, and redefine contemporary Jewish belonging."

—Bambi B. Schieffelin, professor emerita of anthropology, New York University

"Sharon Avni has written a rare book that addresses scholars, educators, and students. Drawing on her special skills as a cultural anthropologist, she expertly unpacks what American Jews are doing when they study Hebrew and when they argue about it. This book will prompt scholars to think again about Hebrew's place in American Jewish life (Avni argues it is a defining feature). The book also might just inspire curious adults to invest in learning Hebrew themselves."

—Alex Pomson, principal and managing director, Rosov Consulting

"Avni's exploration of the world of American Hebrew enthusiasts is a remarkable accomplishment. *Speaking of Hebrew* offers a valuable, well-researched portrait of how American Jews think about, learn, and celebrate the language. Her affection for her interviewees rivals theirs for Hebrew, making her book both authentic and engaging."

—Nancy E. Berg, coeditor of *Exile and the Jews: Literature, History, and Identity* and *What We Talk About When We Talk About Hebrew (and What It Means to Americans)*

"In this thoughtful and interdisciplinary study, Hebrew is examined as a vital site through which American Jews negotiate authenticity, peoplehood, memory, and connection to Israel. *Speaking of Hebrew* is an important contribution to Jewish studies, sociolinguistics, and the study of religion and religious education."

—Leslie C. Moore, Ohio State University

"Sharon Avni asks a bold and innovative question: How does Hebrew function for a population of American Jews that do not really speak the language? As the book explains, Hebrew holds together so much of what American Jews think being Jewish is about. By listening carefully, Avni deftly weaves together an answer that is ingenious, insightful, and inspiring."

—Ari Kelman, Jim Joseph Professor of Education and Jewish Studies, Stanford University

"From Zoom rooms to children's books, synagogue decor to YouTube videos, Avni's engaging analysis shows how Hebrew animates so much activity and conversation among English-speaking Jews. We learn about the importance of language in minority communities—if we look for it in unconventional spaces."

—Sarah Bunin Benor, professor, Hebrew Union College, and director of the Jewish Language Project

SPEAKING OF HEBREW

Raphael Patai Series in Jewish Folklore and Anthropology

A complete listing of the books in this series can be found online at wsupress.wayne.edu.

SPEAKING OF HEBREW

What Language Does for American Jews

SHARON AVNI

WAYNE STATE UNIVERSITY PRESS
DETROIT

© 2026 by Sharon Avni. All rights reserved. No part of this book may be reproduced without formal permission.

ISBN 9780814352397 (paperback)
ISBN 9780814352380 (hardcover)
ISBN 9780814352403 (ebook)

Library of Congress Control Number: 2026937672

Cover design by Carrie Teefey

Published with support from the fund for the Raphael Patai Series in Jewish Folklore and Anthropology.

Wayne State University Press rests on Waawiyaataanong, also referred to as Detroit, the ancestral and contemporary homeland of the Three Fires Confederacy. These sovereign lands were granted by the Ojibwe, Odawa, Potawatomi, and Wyandot Nations, in 1807, through the Treaty of Detroit. Wayne State University Press affirms Indigenous sovereignty and honors all tribes with a connection to Detroit. With our Native neighbors, the press works to advance educational equity and promote a better future for the earth and all people.

Wayne State University Press
Leonard N. Simons Building
4809 Woodward Avenue
Detroit, Michigan 48201-1309

Visit us online at wsupress.wayne.edu.

CONTENTS

PREFACE

What can public discussions about Hebrew, its nature, its users, and its importance reveal about broader struggles and concerns in American religious life? How do these debates and polemics inform individuals' choices to learn and use an ethnoreligious language? How are Hebrew language educational initiatives instrumentalized for religious, political, and cultural objectives? These questions serve as the backbone to this book, whose primary aim is to provide a textured portrait of contemporary American Jewish life through American Jews' relationship with the Hebrew language. Casting a wide theoretical and methodological net, this book empirically explores a paradox that has captivated me for years: Why is it that Hebrew is a ubiquitous topic in American Jewish discourse despite American Jews not knowing Hebrew particularly well? I knew from the start that this question would require unpacking the intersections between Israel and American Jewry, Hebrew learning, and Jewish education. However, I had no idea when I started this project just how complex this exploration would become. Writing the chapters of this book in the winter and spring of 2024, only months after the October 7, 2023, attack put many of the themes explored here into stark relief and made me viscerally aware of the power of language to describe and make sense of our world, to express identity, draw people together, and fray boundaries with others.

I take the opportunity of this preface to put my scholarly cards on the table. This book does not directly speak to the events of October 7, 2023. Nor does it go into any great detail about the post-10/7 context in terms of American Jews' relationship to Israel, to each other, or to non-Jews. Based on data collected between June 2019 and June 2023, *Speaking of Hebrew* captures a particular time in American Jewish life before the seismic events of the Hamas terrorist attack and the ensuing war in the region. This is the nature of scholarly studies; academic manuscripts differ from journalistic accounts and are not built to respond to events happening in real time. Having said this, if you make it to the conclusion of this book, you will see that I offer a handful of examples in which American Jews have discursively and materially mobilized Hebrew in 2024. My position as a linguistic anthropologist and educator does not afford me any special powers to predict the future. Nor do I have any insider knowledge about how and when the conflict in the Middle East will be resolved or what the state of American Jewry will look like politically, religiously, or culturally as a result. Having said this, preparing this preface in 2025, I am well aware of the fraught nature of writing a book about American Jews, Hebrew, and Israel.

I am reminded of reading, in graduate school, how a linguistic anthropologist began her book on Latina youth gang language practices by observing that "one of the things that occurs to me as I introduce the book that you are about to read is that I cannot be certain of the publics that this text will encounter."[1] I, too, am uncertain about the publics that will engage with this book—or with particular parts of it—and I recognize that some readers may take issue with its focus or framing. Some may wish I had written more about teaching strategies, early childhood or higher education contexts, or the beauty and value of Hebrew fluency itself. Others may be disappointed that I have not centered Israeli Americans or non-Jews who engage with Hebrew, or that I refrain from taking a stronger political stance on Israeli leadership or American Jewish institutional life. Still others may wonder why I have not employed certain theoretical frameworks beyond those developed in these pages. Take my word for it when I say that, at one point or another over the course of this project, I have wrestled with each of these possibilities and weighed them carefully in relation to the arguments I aim to make. I believe, however, that the themes explored in the chapters that follow offer meaningful contributions to a range of readers. Those interested in critiquing Hebrew's role in nationalist and transnational projects, as well as those seeking evidence of Hebrew's enduring significance for American Jews, will find material here to support their perspectives. All of this is my way of saying that a book about Hebrew, American Jews, Israel, Jewishness, and Judaism speaks to a range of publics who come from different intellectual, personal, religious, political, and cultural viewpoints.[2] For the diverse reading public that encounters these pages, my hope is that this book deepens their understanding of the overlapping and divergent ways Hebrew continues to shape American Jewish life and imagination. While *Speaking of Hebrew* is a linguistic anthropological study of one community and its language beliefs and choices, it is also an analysis of key broader issues: struggles over the definitions of what it means to know a language and sound like an authentic speaker, debates over language knowledge as a site and symbol of group cohesiveness and dissension, and navigation of ethnoreligious identification at a time of rapid change.

That I am a Hebrew speaker or that I wrote a book about Hebrew in the United States was not an inevitability given my own background. I am not a native Hebrew speaker and did not grow up hearing much Hebrew at all. In many ways I fit the mold of the stereotypical American Jewish Hebrew learner. I was part of the generation of Jewish children who in the late 1970s–early 1980s could either belong to a Girl/Boy Scouts troop or attend "Hebrew School" at the local synagogue—an either/or choice due to the fact that both afterschool activities were scheduled at the same time on the same days. That I am unable to build a fire or use a compass for navigation says a lot about my parents' priorities. However, I dropped out of religious school in sixth grade, which meant that I was not eligible at my synagogue to become a bat mitzvah.

As a child, I did not learn to speak Hebrew, nor did I master the cantillation system used for chanting the Torah. What I did learn was how to decode Hebrew fluently and to write both block and script letters with ease. These early literacy skills would later prove invaluable when, as a young adult, I set out to acquire spoken Hebrew. They also sparked my fascination with language itself. During Friday night synagogue services I attended with my family, I often compared the Hebrew words on one side of the prayerbook with the English translation on the other, curious about the spaces between them. Even then I was captivated by transliteration—the way it mediated between languages and worlds. My Hebrew trajectory was also shaped by my family and by the place where I grew up: Cortlandt Manor, New York, a small town about fifty minutes north of Manhattan where most of my classmates came from Irish and Italian Catholic families. My father, Julius Reiss, often led services at our small, under-resourced synagogue made up of working-class members, especially during the frequent periods when it was without a rabbi. My father's Hebrew carried the distinct sounds of his Eastern European heritage—he recited prayers with a thick Ashkenazi accent. My mother, Irene Reiss (née Yoskowitz), by contrast, had no formal Jewish education and never learned to read Hebrew, like many women who grew up in the economic hardship of New York's Lower East Side in the 1930–40s. Yet her lack of Hebrew literacy did not define her Jewishness. If anything, she was the backbone of Jewish life in our home. She made monthly trips to the kosher butcher in Yonkers, lit Shabbat candles every Friday night, came to my elementary school to make latkes during Hanukkah, filled our home with Judaica, and led the synagogue sisterhood. Apart from synagogue services, my siblings and I probably heard more Yiddish than Hebrew, and Israel was not a frequent topic of conversation in our home. It was my mother, though, who decided to send my siblings and me to Jewish overnight camp so that we would have Jewish friends. I arrived at Camp Young Judaea Sprout Lake—a Zionist camp sponsored by Hadassah—in the summer of 1983. If I was apprehensive about leaving home for so long, that feeling quickly faded. Two months later I knew I would never spend another summer in Cortlandt Manor again. I returned year after year, first as a camper and later as a counselor, remaining part of the Young Judaea world well into college. Before long I was fluent in "Young Judaea-ese"—eating in the *chadar ochel* (dining room), visiting the *mirpa'ah* (health clinic), singing *chug* (group) cheers, and striving to be a *dugma* (role model) for younger campers.[3]

Knowing Young Judaea Hebrew, paradoxically, did not motivate me to learn more Hebrew. As a participant on a gap-year program in Israel prior to starting university, I placed into *ulpan aleph*, the lowest level in the immersive Hebrew learning program, and spent the entire year unable to say much of anything in the language. I attended Binghamton University, where, after taking the Hebrew placement test, I found myself again in Hebrew 101, where I received the lowest grade on my undergraduate transcript. After graduation I returned to Israel on Sherut La'am—a service-based yearlong program intended for university graduates. Arriving at Kibbutz Yagur, I was once again placed into *ulpan aleph*. While my Hebrew-speaking friends on the program got plum jobs working with children in the *gan* (nursery) or with other kibbutz members in the dining room, I worked six to eight hours a day by myself in the kibbutz laundry room ironing sheets. Eventually I made progress with the help of a small, nondescript book that showed me how the Hebrew verb system works, and the patience of many teachers, coworkers, and friends who graciously corrected my errors.

Living in Israel for nearly eight years—a period that included completing a graduate degree in language education at Tel Aviv University and working in both low-skill and professional positions—profoundly shaped my understanding of myself as a Jew, an American, a woman, and an English speaker. Those years deeply influenced my beliefs about language learning and teaching, my religious and political orientations, and my awareness that I am a product of a particular form of Jewish education situated within a specific moment in American Jewish history. I recount my Hebrew narrative at length to be transparent about my positionality and to underscore how my experiences with Hebrew have indelibly shaped the way I understand my own life, the society around me, and the complex world we inhabit. My story explains how I came to write a book about American Jews and Hebrew, but this book is not a language memoir. Rather, it is an effort to offer an empirical perspective on how Hebrew matters to American Jews and the varied forms this relationship takes.

In reflecting on my own life, as this preface does, I invite readers to think of this book as a kind of mirror—one that, when held up, not only reveals what American Jews' relationship with Hebrew looks like but also refracts dimensions of that relationship which have often gone unnoticed in discussions about the state of Hebrew in American Jewish life. My hope is that this book portrays more than what is in our immediate visual field when we are looking *at* or *for* Hebrew in the United States and, importantly, to consider how and when talk about Hebrew emerges, and what such moments tell us about the contours of the American Jewish experience. To be clear, my purpose in telling my story and writing this book is not to romanticize Hebrew, to celebrate those who learn it, to criticize those who do not, or to prescribe solutions to the challenges facing American Jews. Rather, I aim for the stories, discourses, and conversations presented here to illuminate what Hebrew *does* for American Jews, including how it functions, what it offers, and why it continues to matter so profoundly. Put differently, my goal is to draw on what language itself does best: to offer a portrait of our lived individual and collective selves, in all their richness and complexity.

ACKNOWLEDGMENTS

After working on this book for longer than I care to admit, it is a joy to finally thank the many people who, in one way or another, made its completion possible. My deepest gratitude goes to those who generously gave their time and agreed to participate in this project. Without their voices, this book would not exist. To the many scholars, public figures, and educators who spoke with me and allowed me to use their names, I thank you for your time, insight, and trust. A special note of appreciation goes to Arnee Winshall, Andrew Ergas, Vardit Ringvald, Avital Karpman, Barry Chazan, Sharon Feiman-Nemser, Shaul Kelner, and Lee Shulman (z"l), whose wisdom and expertise in Hebrew, Jewish education, and American Jewish life enriched this work in countless ways.

I am deeply grateful to those who read portions or the entirety of this manuscript and offered invaluable insights that strengthened it immeasurably. Special thanks to Jonathan Krasner, Sarah Bunin Benor, Arielle Levites, Omri Asscher, Ari Y. Kelman, Anastasia Badder, Jon Levisohn, Sivan Zakai, Laura Yares, and Ziva Hassenfeld. I cannot imagine realizing this project without Bambi Schieffelin. When I was a "lost" doctoral student seeking direction and first showed up at her NYU office more than two decades ago, she became, and has remained, a steady source of guidance, support, and inspiration.

I am blessed to be surrounded by wonderful colleagues who have become like family to me. Special thanks to Elana Shohamy, Ben Jacobs, Orly Haim, and Heather Finn. I owe a special debt to the CUNY gang that has stood by me over the years. Thank you to Kate Menken, John Beaumont, Christine Jacknick, M. Peregrine Balmat, and Sophie Maríñez. I am grateful to Ayala Fader and Jeffrey Shandler for their early encouragement and thoughtful conversations when this project was just beginning to take shape.

Several grant organizations funded different stages of the research and writeup of this book. Thank you to the Memorial Foundation for Jewish Culture, Mellon/ACLS Community College Faculty Fellowship, National Endowment for the Humanities (NEH) Summer Stipend, and PSC-CUNY Research Award program.

I am grateful for the opportunity to work with my editor, Sandra Korn, at Wayne State University Press. Special thanks to Mindy Brown, whose meticulous and thoughtful copyediting made this a much better book. I also extend heartfelt thanks to Howard Lupovitch and the two anonymous reviewers for their careful and constructive feedback.

Warm thanks and big hugs to my friends Allison and Tom Tam, Ayelet and Marc Miller, Dan Segal, Susan Kitzen, Mindy Israel, Frances Zelazny, Dave Spurr, Sharon and Dave Artz, Rachel Alter, Kim Van Naarden Braun, Josh Braun, Rebecca Moskowitz, and Gaby Hecht, who have patiently listened to my ramblings about my work for years. To Ayala, Isaac, Mika, and Danny Avni for embracing me into the Avni clan with open arms, and to Ira and Joanne Reiss and Marlene Hahitti for filling my life with laughter and reminding me of the importance of family.

My final thanks are reserved for the loves of my life—Yuval, Mia, and Gali. They may not have authored the words that make up this book, but their unconditional love and encouragement are present on every page. Yuval, thank you for your patience, sense of humor, and IT support—without which this book and so much more would not be possible.

1

WHY STUDY AMERICAN JEWS AND HEBREW?

For years I have relied on Google Alerts to notify me of new publications in online media about the topic of Hebrew education in the United States. I was not surprised, then, when I logged into my email on the morning of January 5, 2021, and was greeted with a notification about an op-ed in the *Jerusalem Post* entitled "Hebrew Language Day." Written by Ifat Ovadia Luski, then head of the Department for Hebrew and Culture at the World Zionist Organization,[1] this piece opened with a story about Ovadia Luski's high school–aged daughter completing a school assignment on the "Anglicism" of the Hebrew language—that is, the phenomenon of English language spreading into the Israeli vernacular. Regardless of this English encroachment, Ovadia Luski reassured readers that Hebrew usage in Israel "does not face any real threat, nor the danger of becoming extinct." Hebrew, however, she argued, faced a different threat: preserving "its status overseas to ensure that it continues to exist as a vital and important language for the Jewish communities in the Diaspora." To meet this challenge, she announced that the 38th World Zionist Congress had made a "historic decision" to "place Hebrew language at the forefront of its agenda." Practically speaking, this meant the establishment of a new department whose sole purpose would be strengthening the status of the language among diasporic Jews. Channeling Ze'ev Jabotinsky, a leader of Revisionist Zionism and a fierce proponent of the revival of Hebrew during the pre-state era, Ovadia Luski laid out the uncompromising steps to ensure the reality of a global pan-Hebrew-speaking populace:

> We must translate this national responsibility into action, and we must persist with determination. We must insist that Jewish educational institutions allocate significant time to teaching the Hebrew language. We must ask youth movements to hold events in Hebrew. We must provide teachers with the appropriate training and tools to instil [sic] the Hebrew language in their students. We must entrench the Hebrew language through Jewish and Israeli culture, and not surrender in the face of arguments of the lack of relevance of Hebrew in Jewish communities around the world.

Written at a time when much of the world was still in the throes of the COVID pandemic, Ovadia Luski ended her call acknowledging the difficulty all educational systems were undergoing at the time. "Throughout this challenging time" she wrote, "we must build connections with our brothers and sisters overseas and establish a common language with them."[2] As a bonding agent, Hebrew "unites us all, and we are required to help Diaspora Jews think in Hebrew, dream in Hebrew, feel an integral part of the Jewish people, and make the national language feel like their home." I read this article while I was in the midst of collecting and analyzing much of the data that makes up this book. Yet in many ways it encapsulated many of the motivations I had in the first place in undertaking a study about the role of Hebrew for American Jews.[3] In unambiguous terms, Ovadia Luski's piece explicitly articulates an ideological position of how Hebrew can activate particular forms of Jewish identities and interests. Though particular to Hebrew, her proposition reminded me of many of the nationalistic and ethnic projects around the world in which language is mobilized to create political, religious, and cultural aims. Already two years deep into this research study at the time when Ovadia Luski's op-ed appeared, I was nonetheless struck by the piece's tacit directive, its underlying assumptions, and its presumptuous tone that "no excuses" would be accepted anymore—"simple as that."[4] This was a directive to American Jews, but it lacked the voice of American Jews regarding their thoughts or needs. It also represented a genre I had come to recognize as discourse about Hebrew that was obliquely or directly about other broader Jewish concerns. This book, at its core, is a project to interrogate these discourses.

To be clear, nothing about this piece about teaching Hebrew to American Jews in order to reshape the connection between Israel and the Jewish diaspora was particularly new. Beyond breaking news about the "historic decision" of this new department in the WZO, this op-ed struck many familiar chords. To begin, it reiterated a reigning assumption that Hebrew was absent from Jewish communities outside of Israel and assumed that Hebrew was not a "central pillar in Jewish education." It also identified a litany of reasons why diasporic Jews need to know Hebrew, insinuating that this lack of knowledge comes at great risk to diaspora Jews' navigation of "assimilation, Jewish identity, combating antisemitism, and *Aliyah* [Heb: moving up, or permanent relocation to Israel]."[5] The remedy presented in this op-ed is for Israel to step in and to address the linguistic deficiencies plaguing the global Jewish community by providing more opportunities for Hebrew learning. On a discursive level, the repeated use of the modal "must" underscores the high stakes of this policy initiative.

Before going any further, it is crucial to make clear what Ovadia Luski is referring to when she writes about "teaching the Hebrew language." Which Hebrew is she referring to? Though it is commonly referred to in the singular, Hebrew actually comprises numerous temporal varieties—Biblical, Mishnaic, Medieval, Maskilic, and Modern—each linked to a distinct historical period.[6] Biblical Hebrew is the language of the Bible and was the language of political, religious, and cultural expression among the Israelites during the First Temple period (ca. 1000–586 BCE) through the early Second Temple period (538 BCE–70 CE). Following the Babylonian exile, Hebrew's role shifted from a spoken vernacular to a language of ritual, scholarship, and textual production. As Aramaic gradually supplanted Hebrew as the vernacular of many Jews, and Greek and Latin shaped the linguistic environment in which Jews lived, Mishnaic Hebrew survived as a learned language; it was the medium of the Mishnah, the liturgy, scholarly texts, and later rabbinic poetry (*piyyut*). Starting in the seventh century and continuing throughout the tenth century, Medieval Hebrew flourished as a language of liturgy, rabbinic literature, intra-Jewish commerce, and poetic literature, and, along with the incorporation of Ancient Greek and Arabic, encompassed the cultural vitality of Jewish communities living in the Islamic and Christian worlds. This diglossic condition of no longer being a vernacular yet still central to Jewish religious life is what allowed Textual Hebrew—a shorthand term I utilize in this book to refer to Hebrew used in Jewish study, prayer, and sacred canonical literature (which may also include Aramaic)—to function as a "portable homeland" and endure across centuries of diaspora.[7] Unlike other ancient "dead" sacred and religious languages that fell into disuse, Hebrew remained "alive." As such, it served as a touchstone of Jewish life throughout the centuries through the textual tradition of study, recitation, and reinterpretation.

The modern era introduced a new phase to Hebrew. From the sixteenth century onward, the rise of print expanded access to Hebrew texts and reinforced its centrality in Jewish life. The Jewish Enlightenment (*Haskalah*) of the eighteenth and nineteenth centuries elevated Hebrew as a medium for modern literature, journalism, and cultural expression, and it became a code for secular creativity and religious tradition. This literary renaissance of Maskilic Hebrew set the stage for the Zionist movement, in which revivalists consciously reengineered Hebrew and recast it into a spoken vernacular and national language. Revitalizing Hebrew in connection to its historical and religious sources, Hebrew advocates constructed a semiotic bridge between antiquity and the modern period—two eras in which Jews were sovereign in their own land.[8] With a shared linguistic heritage, Modern Hebrew was more than just a medium of communication in Mandatory Palestine (and later in the State of Israel); it became an emblem of modern Jewish identity. This abbreviated history is important for the historical and linguistic records. For our purposes it also contextualizes Ovadia Luski's initiative. When she speaks about diasporic Jews learning Hebrew, she is talking about Modern Hebrew.

Ovadia Luski's depiction of a diasporic community at risk of losing its long-term vitality is not exceptional in the long history of Israel–diaspora thought. Anyone familiar with the history of the Zionist movement's central assumption of *shlilat ha-golah* (rejection of the diaspora) can recognize in her initiative an echo of an ideology that both privileged Israel as the authentic site of Jewish life and dismissed the diasporic existence. Semantically, this ideology explains the preference for the adjective *Ivri* (Hebrew) instead of *Yehudi* (Jewish) to describe the arts (e.g., Hebrew dance, Hebrew theater), names of sports and cultural events, language, literature, youth clubs, and other civic spaces and activities that emerged in the Jewish community living in Mandatory

Palestine and later in the State of Israel. Over time, Hebrew culture became known as Israeli culture.[9]

Reading Ovadia Luski's piece in 2021, I recognized an Israel-centric concern about the future vitality of diasporic Jewish communities. It prioritized spoken Modern Hebrew over other varieties of the language used in Jewish study or prayer, activities in which American Jews have greater exposure through synagogal and ritual practices. Thus her lack of acknowledgment of these uses suggests a lack of faith in the ability of other forms of Hebrew to ensure the future of American Jews. Instead her op-ed reads as a moral imperative to "entrench" Modern Hebrew so that diasporic and Israeli Jews will have a common language and diasporic Jews can thus "feel an integral part of the Jewish people."[10] As such, this Hebrew initiative can be understood as a case study of centripetal language policy that mobilizes language education to shape the minds and hearts of those living outside the State of Israel.

I open this book with this example because it reaffirms the understanding that any discussion about American Jews and Hebrew can never be wholly untethered from American Jews' relationship to Israel and Israelis. In this sense the story of the nationalist imaginary that underwrites Hebrew education in the diaspora is not all that unique. Indeed, the connection between language and nationalism has been central to the development of modern nation-states since the eighteenth and nineteenth centuries, when thinkers such as Johann Gottfried Herder emphasized that a national language binds people together. Hebrew's revival, as one example of language and nationalism, demonstrates the extraordinary power of language to mobilize ethnoreligious pride and construct national identity. Israeli leadership calls for American Jews to learn Hebrew illuminate how language, far from being a neutral medium, is a contested terrain on which the struggles over Jewish identity are debated and navigated.

Understood in this perspective, Ovadia Luski's piece brings into stark relief a set of unresolved tensions between Israel and the United States—the two dominant Jewish centers that offer opposing trajectories of authentic Jewish life—and the place of Hebrew in this dynamic. Often at odds with one another, Israeli and American Jewish communities jostle over authority and status in the Jewish world. What is less understood, and what this book sets out to explore, is the American Jewish viewpoint of this complex and contingent relationship. Understanding what American Jews think about Hebrew, uncovering what they actually do with the language, and interrogating how Hebrew animates or drives American Jewish educational policies encapsulate many of the reasons I wrote this book. Broadly speaking, the book offers a nuanced exploration of what American Jews say *in* and *about* Hebrew as a crucial dimension of American Jewishness which includes its cultural, religious, and national-political dimensions. Born out of my strong conviction that an individual or group's attachment to a language is actuated and materialized by sociological dynamics as much as linguistic ones, this book shifts the focus away from questions of linguistic competence and what American Jews can linguistically do in Hebrew. Rather, it takes a functionalist approach, asking what Hebrew does for American Jews as they think of themselves as individuals and as a collective. Countless hours spent interviewing hundreds of American Jewish adults about their experiences learning and using Hebrew in a variety of informal and formal settings, speaking with communal leaders, educators, and policy makers, and poring over an extensive corpus of discourse about the role of Hebrew in the United States disabused me of many of the reigning assumptions about the relationship between American Jews and Hebrew. Finding out that there was a Hebrew meetup group that had been gathering at a café in Manhattan for more than a decade (stopping briefly only during the COVID pandemic), and that had spun long-lasting friendships (and even resulted in a marriage between two participants) refuted the idea that Hebrew is completely missing from the American scene. Hearing from active Hebrew learners that linguistic mastery—that is, being a fully competent Hebrew speaker—was not always their primary goal forced me to reckon with the varying aspirations and desires people attached to the language. It also made me take seriously what American Jews were saying about Hebrew in public discourse. These "sitings" of where Hebrew appears in American Jewish discourse and what is said about the language stand at the heart of this book.

To say that I set out with the explicit goal of challenging prevailing assumptions about Hebrew in the United States would not be entirely accurate. In truth, the first spark for this project came about somewhat accidentally. One day in late 2019, I realized that the digital folder where I had been saving opinion pieces, surveys, speeches, and articles about Hebrew in the United States had grown to include hundreds of documents. As I began sorting through them, I was struck by a curious paradox. Despite the widespread belief that American Jews are indifferent to Hebrew, community leaders, philanthropists, educators, journalists, and scholars were in fact talking and writing about it constantly. Unpacking this paradox became a central motivation for undertaking this book. As I discuss in Chapter 2, much of this discourse is framed through a discourse of deficiency, a pattern that highlights American Jews' failure to learn Hebrew and attributes their poor outcomes to a lack of effort, inadequate pedagogy, or both. Many of these writers also assert that American Jews simply do not view Hebrew as a meaningful part of their lives.

This book takes a different approach. It argues that perhaps we have been looking in the wrong places or asking the wrong questions when trying to understand the ways Hebrew becomes meaningful in the American Jewish context. This is not to dismiss the value of Hebrew acquisition or dismiss the work that Hebrew educators do to cultivate both literacy and fluency. On the contrary, I devote considerable attention to how people learn Hebrew as a leisure activity, an affective pursuit, a social practice, and a cognitive endeavor. However, the fascination with American Jews' linguistic competence, while important in its own right as a pedagogical matter, is too myopic a focus if we want to better understand the relationship American Jews have with Hebrew and what these practices can tell us about American Jewish life. What this book seeks to do, therefore, is to shift the focus from pedagogy to ideology—from *how* Hebrew is taught to *what* people say and believe about learning and knowing it. By attending to the perspectives of community leaders, educators, scholars, and everyday learners, I aim to reveal what Hebrew *does* for those most invested in its study and use, and how these engagements illuminate the broader meanings of Jewish life in America. Providing an interpretative reorientation to the nature and value of Hebrew for American Jews, this book argues that metalinguistic commentary (that is, talk about Hebrew) is itself a defining practice of modern American Jewish culture, though it is often not recognized as such.

With this framework in mind, the book proceeds from several core premises. First, Hebrew is far from absent in the American context if we understand Hebrew engagement not only as what is expressed *in* the language but also as what is said *about* it. Public figures, scholars, communal leaders, and individual learners all participate in discourses that imbue Hebrew with meaning at the collective and personal levels. A crucial part of this premise is recognizing how such discourse often collapses the language's multiple historical layers—Biblical, Mishnaic, Medieval, Maskilic, and Modern—into a single, undifferentiated category of "Hebrew." This conflation, I suggest, is not incidental; it advances particular understandings of why Hebrew matters to American Jews. Conversations about Modern Hebrew in American Jewish life therefore frequently invoke Textual Hebrew, and it is precisely this slippage between varieties that reveals how Hebrew functions ideologically within American Jewish culture. Second, Hebrew is commonly understood as a Jewish language that unites Jews across space and time. In this sense it operates as a proxy for Jewish peoplehood and solidarity. Yet Hebrew can also produce disunity and mark symbolic boundaries that separate rather than connect. This book seeks to unpack this paradox and show how the language simultaneously unifies and divides. Third, what American Jews say *about* Hebrew is as revealing as what they say *in* Hebrew. From the perspective advanced here, the debates, polemics, and reflections surrounding Hebrew are never far removed from deeper anxieties, uncertainties, and aspirations about the future of American Jewry itself. With these three premises as a foundation, each chapter examines this argument through a different lens: public discourse, the lived practices of Hebrew learners, and the educational curricula that structure Hebrew instruction in the United States.

Diverging Language Paths

In his seminal work *Hebrew in America: Perspectives and Prospects*, literary scholar Alan Mintz asked, "What would it mean for Hebrew to play a significant role in the life of American Jewry?"[11] That Mintz felt the need to ask this question implies a recognition that the language is adjuvant to their Jewish engagement. The question also implies that the reality of Hebrew occupying a meaningful place in American Judaism is an unlikely proposition. While noting the "sources of hope" of students studying Hebrew in day schools or on college campuses, Mintz did not believe that these learners would alter the peripherality of Hebrew in the American Jewish landscape. Mintz's prognosis is reflective of a general malaise surrounding the state of American Jews' knowledge of Hebrew. Others have referred to the role of Hebrew in the United States as "obscure and talismanic, at best liturgical but never transparent or normal"[12] and "relegated primarily to the religious sphere, secondarily to the arena of Jewish culture, and marginally to the dedicated Israelophiles who have learned the language on the street."[13] This book takes these misgivings as a reflection of an unresolved tension regarding what it would mean for Hebrew to have a significant role for American Jews.

Understanding expressed unease about Hebrew requires some historical context regarding the divergent paths that Hebrew took in the American and Israeli Jewish communities. In Mandatory Palestine (and later in the State of Israel), cultural Zionist leaders saw the revival of Hebrew as the *sine qua non* of Jewish nationalism. Creating a Hebrew-speaking Jewish collective identity required discrediting diasporic Jewish languages, turning Yiddish, for example, into nothing more than a "historical detour."[14] In contrast, the sociolinguistic trends looked much different in the United States during the nineteenth and early twentieth centuries. The large number of European Jewish immigrants who arrived in the United States between 1880 and 1920 sought to navigate their Jewish faith within American openness and opportunity. Historian Hasia Diner notes that in seeing themselves as permanent immigrants to a new promised land, American Jews balanced Jewish particularism with American universalism, leading them to "constantly think about how to be Jewish and American at the same time."[15] Integration was recognized as critical to American Jews' success. So too was being heard as English speakers. Jewish immigrants to the United States underwent language shifts in workplaces, public schools, and homes as they embraced English as their ticket to civic belonging and upward mobility. Outside of the ultra-Orthodox Jews who continued to use Yiddish as a spoken language, American Jews became an English-speaking community. When the second and third generations of American Jewish immigrants left the city centers for the suburbs in the post–World War II period, the synagogue became the center of American Jewish life and to varying degrees adapted itself to American Jews' monolingual English patterns. English became the primary language of American Jewish religious and cultural life, delimiting textual Hebrew to home rituals, congregational worship, and sacred text study. Over the following decades, this trend away from Hebrew accelerated as denominational institutions continued to rely on English translation and transliterated Hebrew in synagogue prayerbooks.[16]

The period of rapid linguistic and cultural transformation among Jewish immigrants coincided with the emergence of American Hebraism in the early twentieth century. Made up of a small group of highly educated Jewish (predominantly male) immigrants from Odessa and other European centers, the progenitors of American Hebraism saw Hebrew as a dynamic force in the cultural revival of the Jewish people and a vital element in retaining their distinctiveness and Jewish authenticity in the United States.[17] With roots in the Enlightenment—a liberal movement that looked to integrate Judaism with modern, secular Western thought—the Hebraists, many of whom were religiously learned, sought to repurpose Textual Hebrew to guide American Jews through the choppy waters of "identity-annihilating absorption" and the assimilative forces of diasporic life in modernity.[18] For American Hebraists, Hebrew was not solely a liturgical language. It was a vehicle for cultural renewal, a link to the historical canon of Jewish texts, an expression of nationalistic aspirations, and a bulwark against assimilatory forces. Though deeply committed to Hebrew revitalization projects, the American Hebraists did not always agree on the purpose and character of the language for American Jews.[19] While some advocated for a literary resurgence and established journals, institutions, and publishing houses that promoted Hebrew literature, others focused on promoting cultural Hebrew activities centered on spoken language.[20] They also disagreed on whether to cater to the elite or to the masses, with most distancing themselves from their fellow Jewish immigrants who spoke Yiddish—a language they pejoratively associated with working-class radicalism and immigrant ghettos.[21] American Hebraists also had complicated perspectives about their connection to America. Crucially, they saw themselves as productive citizens of their newly adopted homeland and were never fully removed from American Jewish institutional structures. At the same time, though they dreamt of a revived Jewish nation in the Land of Israel, many were ambivalent about leaving the States. As journalist Adam Kirsch notes, "To be an American Hebraist meant rejecting the language of America, while also refusing to leave it."[22] The American Hebraists' critique was not directed at becoming American per se. Rather, they worried that wholescale American integration would erase Jewish distinctiveness.

In this way American Hebraists occupied a paradoxical position: They embraced the opportunities American civic culture offered but feared that a full embrace of these English-centric opportunities would sever Jews from their textual and literary traditions. They also struggled with their lack of broader appeal among American Jews. Underestimating the pull of American social and civic incorporation, they miscalculated their own influence on the broader American Jewish community and its lack of support for a Hebrew revival. They failed to understand that "the cultivation of the Hebrew language and literature had little or no appeal to a bright boy who had his eyes on New York's tuition free City College."[23] Additionally, they suffered from other countervailing forces. The creation of Hebrew culture (e.g., Hebrew literature, music, dance, theater, art) in Mandatory Palestine undermined their efforts to create an American Hebrew culture.[24] At the same time, they faced resistance from the American Jewish reading public who gravitated to Jewish literature written in English—a genre that was gaining wider recognition as an essential part of the American literary canon. By the 1960s American Hebraism was mostly an aborted movement, as many vanguard American Hebraists had either moved to Israel or passed away.[25] Literary scholar Michael Weingrad aptly summarizes that "theirs was a brief flourishing, with a heyday from roughly 1915 to 1925 that was always based more on hopes and aspirations than on solidity and permanence."[26]

We can better understand the impulses of American Hebraism by looking at a handful of American Jewish intellectuals in this time period who promoted Hebrew as a prerequisite for a robust Jewish life in the United States.[27] One of the most significant twentieth-century Jewish thinkers, Simon Rawidowicz (1896–1957), argued that Hebrew was not merely a linguistic medium but the very lifeblood of Jewish continuity. For Rawidowicz, Hebrew embodied the transhistorical and transnational links bridging Jews across time and space. With a strong belief that the Jewish future hinged on maintaining Hebrew as a living, dynamic language, he rejected its relegation as a sacred and fixed code, thinking instead about Hebrew as a "most treasured possession—and main connective tissue—of the Jewish cultural nation."[28] Because he recognized the particular challenges of Hebrew serving as an everyday language for Jews in the United States, he urged American Jews to cultivate Hebrew not only for prayer and ritual but also as a medium of culture, education, and intellectual life. Only by doing so, Rawidowicz argued, could Jewish identity in the United States avoid becoming shallow and unsustainable.

Another significant figure in American Judaism, Mordecai Kaplan (1881–1983), the founder of Reconstructionist Judaism, envisioned Judaism not only as a religion but as an evolving civilization with language, land, and culture as its foundational pillars. Within his theological and sociological framework, Hebrew was indispensable. It was the historic language of Jewish peoplehood, the medium of classical texts, and the code of Jewish nationalism. As the first principal of the Teachers Institute at the Jewish Theological Seminary, Kaplan maintained high standards for Hebrew educators and pushed for schools where Hebrew would be taught as a living language. Crucially, Kaplan argued that American Jews needed a grounding in written and spoken forms of Hebrew in order to connect to the Jewish tradition and the wider Jewish world. In his words, Hebrew "supplied the elements of historic continuity and present solidarity" and was indispensable to the "fostering of the Jewish consciousness."[29] However, he was also a pragmatist. Self-identifying as a "compromiser and a syncretist by nature," he differentiated himself from those Jewish educators who prioritized promoting Hebrew over other forms of Jewish content.[30] As a result, he often emphasized Hebrew's symbolic and cultural value even when fluency was unattainable.

Finally, Samson Benderly (1876–1944), the first director of the New York Bureau of Jewish Education, placed Hebrew at the center of his pedagogical reforms to modernize Jewish education for American Jews. As director of the Bureau of Jewish Education in New York, he rejected the translation-based approach that had long dominated Hebrew education and dismissed rote memorization of texts used in ritual and sacred spaces. Instead Benderly, along with a cadre of educators referred to as the Benderly Boys, promoted the natural method of language acquisition—*Ivrit b'Ivrit* (Hebrew in Hebrew), a progressive educational methodology that required Hebrew educators to use Modern Hebrew as the medium of instruction. This methodology, Benderly believed, reframed the language as a modern cultural resource rather than a liturgical artifact. Doing so, Benderly argued, would cultivate a new generation of American Jews who could participate in a broader Jewish cultural renaissance in the United States.

What is worth noting is that each of these men held strong beliefs about the importance of Hebrew as a living language for American Jews, framing this imperative in philosophical and existential (Rawidowicz), pragmatically cultural (Kaplan), or pedagogical (Benderly) terms. While these perspectives shaped the discourse on Hebrew's role in American Jewish identity, they also reveal the tension in American Jewish life between broader societal integration and Jewish distinctiveness, and the challenge of turning Hebrew into a site of identity for diaspora Jews. In the case of Kaplan and Benderly, who shared an unwavering belief in the promise of America and a conviction in the role of Hebrew in revitalizing Jewish life in America, realities on the ground shaped their beliefs and determined the success of their Hebrew projects. When Jewish supplementary schools took on the moniker of "Hebrew schools" in the mid-1900s, many saw this "semantic vagary" as a reflection of the success of American Hebraism.[31] Yet Benderly's ambitious goal of widespread Hebrew fluency among American Jews was never realized, though as historian Jonathan Krasner notes, many of his pedagogical initiatives did shape Jewish camping and education for decades to come. Kaplan, for his part, took an ambivalent position, recognizing that it would be futile to expect Hebrew to function as a vernacular for diasporic Jews. Emphasizing accessibility and integration, Kaplan espoused a vision of Jewish civilization that could flourish in English while retaining Hebrew for symbolic, liturgical, and cultural purposes.

This partial and abbreviated account of the history of the American Hebraist movement and the intellectual and religious leaders who espoused theories of Hebrew as a living language and a vehicle for Jewish identity in the diaspora underscores the complicated relationship between American Jews and Hebrew—a relationship shaped by broader sociocultural dynamics. Importantly, a historical perspective shows that American Jews mobilizing Hebrew to navigate American Judaism is not a new phenomenon. Religious and communal leaders have grappled with the role of Hebrew in the American contexts in their writings, in the institutions they create, and in the methodologies they develop. Though American Jews by and large have never fully embraced Hebrew, public discourse and educational efforts about the importance of Hebrew have been an enduring catalyst in shaping thoughts, expressing religious identification, and projecting a vision of a community. Early American Hebraists saw their dogged efforts as deeply intertwined with, and informed by, how they understood their condition as an ethnoreligious minority in the American setting. Their effort to clarify not so much the separate terms "Jewish" and "American" as the dash that connects them is as relevant today as it was more than a hundred years ago, though it may take on a different register and vocabulary.

A historical framing also reveals a sociolinguistic reality: The divergent linguistic paths American and Israeli Jews took in their embrace of Hebrew (or lack thereof) continue to inform the complex dynamics between these two large Jewish communities. Hebrew occupies markedly different roles in Israel and the United States. In Israel it is both the language of national renewal and revival—central to the state's founding narrative—and the primary language of everyday life, education, and culture, though other languages are present in Israeli society.[32] For most American Jews, by contrast, Hebrew remains a language encountered as a foreign tongue learned to various degrees. Yet it is not wholly absent from American Jewish experience, and as this book sets out to explore, it does important work for American Jews. As such, American Jews' relationship to Hebrew must be understood as unfolding within the dialogical tensions between two interconnected yet distinct Jewish centers. In Israel Hebrew is a living vernacular and signifier of Jewish nationhood; in the United States it primarily functions as a ritual, educational, and symbolic resource. Within this transnational dynamic, Hebrew is a site of divergent understandings of Jewish identity and belonging.

Speaking of Hebrew builds on the premise that this dynamic and American Jewish life can be better understood by examining what American Jews say about Hebrew and how they engage with it. Situating contemporary discourse within its historical lineage reveals how communal and religious leaders continue to frame Hebrew around themes of Jewish vitality, resilience, diaspora, and survival—mobilizing language as a cultural touchstone and a strategy of collective continuity. This discourse does important cultural work in that it demonstrates the persistent pull of Hebrew as a site where questions of Jewish knowledge, authenticity, and continuity coalesce. At the same time, this book centers what literary scholars Naomi Sokoloff and Nancy Berg aptly call "Hebraists by choice": individuals who voluntarily and deliberately integrate Hebrew into their daily lives.[33] These "Hebrew enthusiasts," as I describe them throughout the book, are not heirs to the centralized, elite American Hebraists of the early twentieth century. They are not founding journals, organizing societies, or cultivating a Hebrew literary renaissance. Rather, they are decentralized, grassroots individuals whose passion for Hebrew is deeply personal and identity-driven. They embody what sociologists of religion describe as elective forms of religiosity, in which participation is driven by personal meaning-making rather than institutional or religious obligation. Their choice to learn and speak Hebrew invests the language with new meanings, transforming it from a solely liturgical or symbolic artifact into a practice of Jewish self-fashioning. Studying Hebrew enthusiasts reveals what Hebrew does for American Jews as they engage in identity work that links their personal engagement to the understanding of their Jewishness. While they do not constitute a mass movement, their efforts shed light on the enduring power of Hebrew and the possibilities it continues to hold for American Jews. If Mintz asked what it would mean for Hebrew to play a significant role in American Jewish life, my argument in this book is that Hebrew enthusiasts offer some compelling answers.

Hebrew in the Time of Jewish Turmoil

This book is not the first attempt to think about American Jewish life through the lens of language.[34] It follows in the footsteps of compelling studies that explore how other American religious communities imbue everyday language practices with symbolic, ideological, religious, and cultural meanings.[35] Many of these explorations of religious life share the perspective that language practices are a form of "lived religion"—a term that captures everyday religious life beyond the doctrine of written texts, outside of institutional settings, and experienced by people in loosely organized activities.[36] While many uses of Hebrew occur in synagogues and Jewish educational settings, it also occurs in "secular" spaces like cafés, in virtual learning communities, and on language-learning apps. For this reason, as tempting as it is to think about Hebrew language acquisition in the abstract as many linguists do, this book intentionally prioritizes the improvisational and creative ways people engage with Hebrew in all sorts of ways. Watching Israeli television shows with or without the English subtitles, translating the lyrics of a popular Israeli song, or meeting up with other Hebrew enthusiasts online or at a café may lie outside of traditional Jewish settings, but as this book argues, these spaces are equally generative spaces for Jewish life. Taking a cue from scholars who explore contemporary American Jewish life beyond the synagogue, this book asks what people do with Hebrew in everyday activities that are not always considered "religious" in nature.[37] My exploration of Hebrew enthusiasts challenges us to look beyond the ritualistic and synagogal uses of Hebrew and consider discourse as part and parcel of American Jewish life.

At the same time, this book places a lot of attention on the broader context in which Hebrew is being spoken about and used. Anyone who reads the American Jewish press, spends any time at a synagogue or Jewish community center, or scrolls social media knows that navigating American Jewishness is more complex than ever. American Judaism is arguably in a "time of dissensus" as it grapples with what it means to be Jewish in an increasingly destabilized world.[38] In many ways the disruption and discontinuity are similar to what other American religious groups are experiencing. With a nod to Leo Tolstoy, American religious communities are alike; each anxious about its future in its own way. Religion remains an important aspect in American life today, but it has taken on new shapes and different forms, especially in regard to organized religion and a broader decline in social cohesion. American Jewry is not immune from these shifts.[39] American Jews increasingly eschew religious authority, denominational affiliations, and legacy communal institutions. They no longer feel limited by inherited and ascribed traditions, and increasingly see their Jewishness as distinctively personal, fluid, and elective. They reject the structures and identifications that long grounded and guided American Jewish life. They feel connected to a sense of Jewish heritage, but their Jewishness is viewed as only one dimension of their intersectional identities.[40] They fear a surge of antisemitism coming from the political left and right. When taken together, these dynamics create an unsettling moment in which many American Jews find themselves grappling with the orientations and practices that comprise their Jewishness, while navigating the imminence of change.[41]

Perhaps no topic galvanizes greater concern than the endangered relationship between American and Israeli Jews, as the two largest Jewish communities in the world grapple with political, theological, and cultural differences around a range of issues.[42] As products of their particular histories and memories, American and Israeli Jews can, at times, act like estranged siblings. Jewish studies scholar Gil Ribak writes, "Both American Jews and Israelis see themselves as leaders of the Jewish world, and both populations live in a country that they think of as the Promised Land."[43] Ribak's analogy that American Jews are from Venus and Israeli Jews are from Mars[44] (borrowed from John Gray's popular 1992 book about gender differences) underscores not only the two communities' contrasts, but how these two entities revolve around each other in a symbiotic, relational, and gravitational dynamic that does not allow one to ever wholly separate from the other.[45] In more recent decades the relationship between American Jews and Israel, including to the land, the state, its people, and its government, has undergone dramatic shifts, particularly among the liberal and non-Orthodox groups that make up American Jewry and particularly among younger generations. At the same time there are fissure points within American Jewry outside of anything connected to Israel. Indeed, the idea of an American Jewish community as a monolithic group belies the heightened polarization and heterogeneity across political, religious, or cultural orientations. Journalist Dan Schnur puts these vexing internal divisions into stark relief, writing that "as the political, generational and cultural divisions within our own community continue to grow, it may be that the most important bridge-building that needs to happen is actually between [American] Jews."[46]

This turmoil informs American Jews' relationship to Hebrew. Most noticeably, as this book explores, the topic of Hebrew has a curious way of popping up when other high-stakes topics impacting American Jews are being discussed. As American Jews debate Hebrew practices and policies, they also engage in conversations about Jewish values, about different visions of Jewishness, and, in some respects, what kind of Jewish community they wish to be part of. This is particularly evident in discussions around Hebrew as a component of Jewish education, in which Hebrew is called upon to meet American Jews' divergent concerns. Yet what is most interesting in these discussions is how Hebrew literacy is situated as the scapegoat of an endangered community, as well as a panacea for its survival. When Jewish educators talk about Hebrew, they address questions about the goals of Jewish education in preparing the next generation of Jewish leaders. Examining how Hebrew education takes on broader concerns about American Jewish life, as this book does, shows how Hebrew education does important work in shaping definitions of what it means to be an educated Jew—a concern that is widely seen as key to ensuring Jewish communal vitality.

Hebrew Language Ideologies

Conceptualizing Hebrew as a site of reflexivity and self-determination necessitates a departure from conventional metrics of language acquisition. Rather than assessing Hebrew knowledge primarily through the lens of linguistic mastery, that is, the ability to communicate fluently with native speakers, this book asks a different set of questions: What does Hebrew *do* for American Jews? How is the language mobilized in expressive, religious, political, ideological, and discursive practices? This approach is grounded in the view that understanding the relationship American Jews have with Hebrew requires attention not only to language use itself but also to the ways Hebrew is discussed and imagined. The analytical shift from assessing what individuals know about Hebrew to examining why they engage with it is central to this inquiry. I make this shift through the lens of language ideology, a construct rooted in linguistic anthropology that examines the beliefs, values, and assumptions people hold about language(s), how they act on those beliefs, and what those actions reveal about broader social and cultural formations.[47] By foregrounding language ideologies, this book highlights the symbolic and affective dimensions of Hebrew and offers insight into how Hebrew operates as a resource for meaning-making, identity negotiation, and communal belonging in American Jewish life.

A language ideological framework foregrounds *metalinguistic discourse*, defined as people's explicitly and implicitly stated beliefs and assumptions about language usage and language communities. In her influential analysis of the public battles about linguistic prescriptivism, politically correct language, and language standards, linguist Deborah

Cameron demonstrates that disputes over language usage frequently reflect deep societal anxieties.[48] According to Cameron, the impulse to regulate language is rarely about language alone. Rather, it serves as a proxy for broader concerns about cultural change, social order, and collective identity. A seemingly glib remark about bad grammar, for instance, can operate as a symbolic act of control or as a coded indictment of responsibility. At first glance, public conversations among American Jews about Hebrew, including critiques of Hebrew illiteracy, debates over the authentic Hebrew accent, and the best methods of Hebrew instruction, may appear to be far removed from the types of linguistic debates Cameron discusses. Nonetheless they follow strikingly similar cultural logics connecting language usage to broader social concerns. We can see how, for example, why positions about Hebrew literacy and translation ideologies reflect communal fears about continuity, authenticity, and Jewish survival. Indeed, the discourse around the role of Hebrew in the United States frequently takes on what Cameron describes as an "obsessive, moralistic, and alarmist manner."[49] It becomes clear that disputes about the proper Hebrew accent, pedagogical priorities, or the decline of Hebrew fluency function to shine attention on uncertainties about the direction of American Jewish life. As I argue throughout this book, such highly charged debates about Hebrew can be read as attempts to assert communal norms and mitigate anxieties about identity, belonging, and future viability. Cameron's insights help illuminate the stakes involved when people discuss what it means to "know" Hebrew and for what purposes such knowledge should be cultivated. Examining Hebrew language ideologies therefore goes a long way in revealing the underlying expectations, priorities, and fears of the contemporary American Jewish community.

These dynamics are especially evident in the often unspoken assumptions that undergird Hebrew education in the American Jewish context. One prevailing belief is that American Jews should be fluent in Hebrew, particularly given the time and resources devoted to the language in day schools and supplemental education programs. Putting aside the question of whether this expectation is realistic or achievable, this belief that communicative fluency is a desirable goal of Hebrew learning underscores its ideological import and raises important questions about what counts as valuable or legitimate Hebrew knowledge. Should the focus be on Biblical Hebrew or Modern Hebrew? Is the ability to recite liturgy and navigate the prayerbook as important as conversational proficiency with Israelis? A language ideological approach enables us to interrogate these questions not merely as curricular decisions but as reflections of deeper communal visions and concerns. Doing so provides a powerful analytic lens for understanding how American Jews imagine and negotiate their relationship to Hebrew and, by extension, to Jewish identity itself.

The second underlying assumption shaping discourse about Hebrew in American Jewish life is the belief that a lack of Hebrew linguistic competence renders American Jews outsiders to Jewish authenticity. This notion rests on a widely held, though rarely interrogated, idea that language proficiency functions as a marker of communal insiderness. The origins of this idea can be traced to the early conceptualization of speech communities first introduced in the 1930s.[50] Initially defined as bounded groups, such as nations, neighborhoods, or other socially cohesive collectives, speech communities were understood as members who possessed a shared set of linguistic norms as well as full communicative competence. Within this framework, native speakers emerged as the arbiters of linguistic legitimacy. Their fluency conferred authenticity, establishing them as the "real" speakers of the language and, by extension, the rightful bearers of cultural identity. This native-speaker ideology exerts particular force when applied to Modern Hebrew. For American Jews situated outside the linguistic and national boundaries of the State of Israel, their relationship to Hebrew is often characterized as non-native, a categorization that raises a host of complex and politically charged questions. Can American Jews claim authenticity as Hebrew speakers if they lack fluency? What status is accorded to non-native or hybridized forms of Hebrew? Is Hebrew a shared Jewish inheritance, accessible to all, or is it the cultural property of Israelis alone? Who holds the authority to determine what real Hebrew sounds like, and which forms should be prioritized in diasporic educational settings?

These questions connect directly to a third prevailing assumption, that American Jews, as a whole, lack substantive Hebrew knowledge beyond the mechanical decoding of sacred texts for ritual participation. Despite the increasing visibility of Hebrew in American media through Israeli television series streamed across global platforms, the international prominence of Israeli celebrities like Gal Gadot, and the proliferation of Hebrew in public signage and visual culture, the dominant narrative remains one of Hebrew deficiency.[51] This narrative is bolstered by findings from major demographic studies. The Pew Research Center's 2013 *A Portrait of Jewish Americans*, for instance, revealed that while 52 percent of respondents reported being able to decode Hebrew phonetically, only 13 percent indicated they could understand most or all of what they read.[52] Notably, the survey did not ask respondents about their spoken Hebrew proficiency, and the 2020 follow-up report omitted questions about Hebrew entirely—an omission that speaks volumes about the language's perceived relevance in American Jewish life.[53] It is rare, indeed, to come across media depictions of American Jews joyfully or confidently using Hebrew. Instead, the language is more frequently depicted as a source of embarrassment—an object of unremitting critique and communal shame.[54] In this context, Hebrew knowledge is understood not just as a difficult goal but as a kind of unachievable chimera. Hebrew in this way signifies a Jewish pipedream marked by dwindling interest and longstanding institutional neglect.

One of the central aims of this book is to show that such narratives operate as powerful language ideologies. They function as discursive formations that not only describe a sociolinguistic condition but actively shape communal priorities, perceptions, and policies. Public debates over Hebrew learning and use, in this framework, do not merely reflect a crisis in Jewish education; they constitute it by imbuing Hebrew with moral, political, and cultural urgency. At the same time, this book brings into view an often overlooked counterpoint of American Jews who actively and enthusiastically pursue Hebrew learning. These individuals, whom I refer to as Hebrew enthusiasts, complicate the dominant discourse of Hebrew decline. Their stories offer valuable insights into individuals who enact language ideologies through elective and often leisure-based learning practices. Unlike communal leaders or public figures who speak in intellectual or policy-driven terms, these learners articulate personalized understandings of Hebrew, grounded in their friendships, personal experiences and memories, and affective connections to Jewishness. Though they may represent a relatively small subset of American Jews, Hebrew enthusiasts offer important alternative narratives. Many of them are engaged in processes of reconnection. That is, they are reclaiming a relationship to Hebrew that may have been marked by frustration or alienation in earlier periods of their lives. When seen in this light, Hebrew enthusiasts' language beliefs and practices speak to a more expansive understanding of Jewish identity in which Hebrew serves not only as a tool of ritual or national belonging but as a medium of personal meaning-making. By foregrounding these voices, this book offers a rejoinder to the dominant assumption that American Jews are uninterested in or ambivalent about Hebrew. Instead it reveals a quieter but no less significant movement of individuals who are finding in Hebrew not a burden or failure but a source of joy, purpose, and renewed Jewish connection.

Book Organization

Readers of this book will not find a typical organization that tells the story of one specific Hebrew-learning context or a specific usage of the language. Instead, each chapter offers a distinct analytical intervention framed by its own conceptual parameters. Crucially, each chapter focuses on a set of questions that collectively illuminate the broader theme of the book: the social, cultural, religious, and ideological work that Hebrew does in American Jewish life. While each chapter stands on its own, there is a deliberate progression that moves across contexts and scales, from the abstract to the lived, from institutional discourse to personal practice.

Chapter 2 lays the theoretical foundation for the book, offering a conceptual mapping of Hebrew-language ideologies in the American Jewish context. Drawing on the discourse of communal leaders, educators, journalists, and intellectuals, this chapter explores how Hebrew is imagined in relation to Jewish authenticity, knowledge production, peoplehood, and the complex dynamics of Israeli-American Jewish relations. It frames Hebrew not simply as a language but as a site of ideological contestation and symbolic investment.

Chapter 3 shifts focus from elite and institutional discourse to the lived experiences of adult Hebrew learners referred to here as Hebrew enthusiasts. Through an analysis of more than one hundred language biographies, this chapter presents a textured account of individual learning trajectories, motivations, and aspirations. It argues that, for many learners, Hebrew is not merely a project of linguistic mastery but a vehicle for self-exploration and Jewish meaning-making. Language acquisition, in this context, is deeply entangled with questions of identity, memories, and Jewish expression.

Chapter 4 continues this ethnographic focus by examining how Hebrew enthusiasts engage explicitly and implicitly with American-Israeli relations. The chapter investigates how Hebrew learning spaces serve as sites where individuals navigate political ambivalence and communal expectations surrounding Israel. While dominant language ideologies often posit Hebrew as a conduit for deepening affective ties to the State of Israel, this chapter complicates that assumption. It reveals a discursive strategy of selective avoidance, whereby Hebrew learners engage in nostalgic and uncontroversial discussions about Israel that circumvent the complexities of the country's politics.

Chapter 5 builds on this theme by exploring the sociolinguistic significance of the Hebrew accent. Situating contemporary concerns about the American Hebrew accent within the longer history of Zionist language ideology, the chapter analyzes how pronunciation operates as a symbolic boundary between Israeli and American Hebrew speakers. For American learners, accent becomes a site where authenticity, legitimacy, and national belonging are navigated. Through their reflections on accent, Hebrew enthusiasts articulate what it means to be Jewish in America in relation to Hebrew-speaking counterparts in Israel.

Chapter 6 turns to the instrumentalization of Hebrew education in American Jewish life. It examines how Jewish day schools, synagogue-based programs, and public school Hebrew initiatives have mobilized Hebrew curricula to teach Jews and non-Jews about Jewish life. Focusing on the past two decades, the chapter analyzes the ways Hebrew instruction has addressed concerns about continuity, prioritized particular aspects of Jewishness, and ensured Jewish vitality in the United States.

The conclusion synthesizes the book's central arguments by highlighting how discourse in and about Hebrew opens a window to see the contours of American Jewishness. It considers how Hebrew has been localized and recast in American terms and tones to meet American Jews' distinctive spiritual, cultural, and social needs. A brief coda addresses the shifting ideological terrain following the events of October 7, 2023. It reflects on how American Jews have mobilized Hebrew in both familiar and novel ways in response to the profound challenges facing Jewish communities globally and locally, reaffirming the enduring, if evolving, role of Hebrew in American Jewish life.

The approach taken in this book is deeply informed by analytic frameworks and methodological tools drawn from a range of disciplines, including sociology, religious studies, education, anthropology, and linguistics. Conceived as an intentionally interdisciplinary project, the book embraces theoretical eclecticism as a strength, even if it raises questions about its primary audience. Quite simply, my hope is that this book resonates with a wide spectrum of readers, including scholars of contemporary American Jewish life and Israel–diaspora relations, religious studies scholars interested in language, linguistic anthropologists working at the intersection of language and religion, language instructors, Jewish educators and Hebrew teachers, communal leaders and policy-makers and, importantly, Hebrew learners themselves who may find in these pages conceptual tools to better understand their own experiences and emotions around the language. The data that inform this study were collected between June 2019 and June 2023 and include a diverse array of sources. This corpus includes recorded interviews with hundreds of individuals, ethnographic participation and observation in both in-person and virtual Hebrew classes and meet-up groups, and content analysis of media articles, pedagogical materials, and curricular documents related to Hebrew language use and instruction.

To the existing literature that celebrates the beauty of Hebrew and traces its historical and philological development, this book provides a different contribution. I offer a sociocultural snapshot of the Hebrew language ideologies shaping American Jewish life in the early 2020s. My hope is that the perspectives articulated in these chapters prompt further inquiry into what a language *does* for a minority ethnoreligious group as it negotiates the religious, political, and cultural pressures of modern-day society. American Jews are uniquely positioned to contribute to broader conversations about language, identity, and belonging in diasporic and transnational contexts, and it is my hope that what they say about Hebrew becomes part of that wider and ongoing conversation.

2

HEBREW LANGUAGE IDEOLOGIES

Writing in 1967 in the *Journal of Jewish Education*, Shlomo Shulsinger—executive director of Massad summer camps and a leading promoter of spoken Hebrew in the United States—articulated a vision regarding the importance of Hebrew for American Jews: "Any language serves not merely as the vehicle for the transmission of knowledge but also stamps its own image and character on the culture which uses it. This is an even greater truism for the Hebrew language; it is unique that literally every word serves as a reservoir of cultural and historical content." He went on to add, "If there is any hope of the American Jewish community preserving its identity as an ethnic sub-community, it must be through transmitting to the younger generation—or at the very least to a select portion of it—the 'key' to the Jewish treasure house furnished by the Hebrew language."[1] Almost thirty years later, in a piece that decries the inability of American Jewish literature written in English to create a Jewish cultural identity, literary scholar Ruth Wisse was unambiguous in her call for "the Hebrew imperative." Arguing that "Hebrew alone can give children unmediated access to their heritage," she adds that "English leaves them forever at the mercy of second-rate interpreters."[2] Notwithstanding the different professional roles of two leading American Jewish voices or the distinct sociohistorical contexts in which their thoughts were penned, Shulsinger and Wisse share a set of beliefs that Hebrew is indispensable to American Jews' identity. Both carried strong convictions about the importance of Hebrew for American Jews, and what its absence would portend for American Jewry. For Shulsinger, Hebrew words contain the essence of Jewish history and culture; for Wisse, Hebrew is the sole vehicle for expressing and conveying Jewish heritage. Taken together, these two influential Jewish thinkers espouse a cultural logic about what Hebrew "does" for American Jews, which in this case revolves around the intersection of Hebrew knowledge and Jewish communal survival. Knowledge of Hebrew is not simply additive to American Jewish identity; without Hebrew, ongoing authentic and Jewish life in a diasporic context is at risk.

I chose Shulsinger's and Wisse's commentaries to open this chapter because they speak to three paradigmatic beliefs about Hebrew: (1) The language holds the essence of Jewish heritage; (2) the language is an essential component of Jewish education; and (3) lack of Hebrew knowledge portends a diminished American Jewish future. Yet I could have easily picked from a cast of public intellectuals, community leaders, rabbis, journalists, educators, and scholars of American Jewish life who have expressed similar concerns. The discourse around the necessity of American Jews' knowledge of Hebrew and the imputed price they pay for not having this knowledge can be thought of as a hobbyhorse of American Jewish discourse. Crucially, this discourse reveals how language is mobilized for broader goals beyond its communicative functions. With this in mind, the chapter examines how Hebrew is talked about and how these public discussions spotlight, frame, and perpetuate particularistic concerns about American Jewish communal life. If the belief that Hebrew knowledge shapes Jewish life runs deep in Jewish discourse, it also aligns with scholarship that demonstrates that metalinguistic talk—that is, talk about language, whether it is describing a language's role in a community, commenting on people's (mis)use of the language, or recommending educational language policy—is an important social practice that reveals people's desires, fears, and hopes. At its core this chapter sets out to show that ruminations about Hebrew are never solely about language, and that they are never simply background "noise." Rather, this chapter underscores that American Jews navigate their relationship to Jewishness on the terrain of Hebrew learning and usage.

It is a well-accepted principle that public debates about language are rarely solely about language. More often than not they coexist and overlap with other cultural beliefs about social relations. The construct of language ideologies helps to untangle this connection. Defined as "the cultural system of ideas about social and linguistic relationships, together with their loading of moral and political interests," language ideologies are the beliefs that individuals and groups have about languages and their speakers.[3] Language ideologies explain why some languages and ways of using them are deemed better, more authentic, or more legitimate in comparison to others. What people hold in their minds regarding a language is often assumed to be *a priori*. However, in practice these beliefs are always in the process of being constructed, reaffirmed, and challenged. Thus when people believe that French best allows for romantic thoughts to be expressed or that gender pronoun changes are antithetical to English, they are attaching ideological beliefs to linguistic codes, along with attendant beliefs about their speakers and how language works in the world. It is this presumptive nature that makes language ideologies such a powerful analytic construct. In this chapter I explore Jewish writers', educators', leaders', and thinkers' Hebrew language ideologies to reveal how beliefs about Hebrew take on political, moral, and social weight. As Jewish communal stakeholders discuss the state of Hebrew in the United States, they also speak to beliefs about Jewish collectivity, resilience, creativity, knowledge, history, and Jewish survival.

Before doing so, the methodology of content analysis of public discussions used in this chapter needs to be carefully unpacked. In citing a wide range of scholars, journalists, communal figures, and thinkers, my objective is to focus on what they are saying about Hebrew. It is clear that many of these individuals are more widely known for their political and religious positions beyond those that are explicitly about Hebrew. Some are academics better known for work in entirely different fields. Readers may question why some of those cited live in Israel while others live in the United States. I included both; the criteria for inclusion focused on the intended reading public. Hence, I include any piece that was written for American Jews and was written in English. I make no claims that I have identified every item that has been written about Hebrew. Clearly, some authors are more well known than others; and some may be considered more controversial than others. I do not include this background when I write about any individual; rather, I describe their professional role (e.g., head of an organization, scholar of a field, journalist, etc.). This choice is intentional. My aim is not to judge any of these individuals or to take sides. Rather, it is to reinforce my argument that Hebrew shows up in a wide array of public discussions by a wide range of people, even when the person speaking is not primarily known as a Hebrew educator or sociolinguist. Indeed, that so many choose to write about Hebrew goes a long way in proving my point that Hebrew is integral to many of the most important discussions happening in American Jewry. Whether the topic of Hebrew shows up in a sentence or two, in a full paragraph, or as the organizing theme of an entire article, my purpose is to examine what these "sitings" of Hebrew are doing, and how the topic of American Jews and Hebrew gets implicated in discussions about American Jewish religious and cultural vitality.[4]

Starting from the position that talk about Hebrew is a window into American Jews' understandings of themselves as an ethnoreligious community, this chapter poses a set of questions: How do thought and communal leaders marshal Hebrew to define and address communal goals? How do beliefs about Hebrew (il)literacy connect to discourses of community deficiencies? And how do Hebrew language ideologies threaten core narratives in Jewish thought? To answer these questions, I present Hebrew language ideologies that emerge in public discourse in public media.[5] While some of these ideologies emerged in texts specifically about Hebrew language, many others were found in pieces covering a range of topics about American Jewry.[6] For the sake of clarity in this chapter, I differentiate Hebrew language ideologies into distinct categories. In practice, however, these categories are dynamically interconnected, overlapping, and even, at times, contradictory. Tying all these categories together is the premise that public discussions about Hebrew serve as a platform on which educational, cultural, political, and religious concerns and hopes can be expressed. Derivative to this, a second theme is that talk about Hebrew is not random or inconsequential. It is a recurring motif in American Jewish discourse, and as such constitutes an important feature of American Jewish life.

Hebrew Ideologies of Peoplehood

The iCenter, a leading Jewish organization in North America working to advance the field of Israel education, highlights Hebrew as a core principle in their mission.[7] According to a piece by Jewish educator Lori Sagarin posted on its website, "Hebrew is more than the language of Israel—it is in many ways one of the core threads of Jewish peoplehood, connecting the Jewish people through time and space."[8] By no means is Hebrew the first or only language that has been imputed with this agentive role. Indeed, the assumption that language constructs the essence of group identity underwrites a central plank throughout the social sciences.[9] This conceptual prevalence notwithstanding, Jews are arguably focused on the trope of Hebrew's vehicular role in connecting Jews across the generations and geographic space. Metaphorically, Hebrew is often spoken of as the linguistic thread, connective tissue, or bridge among Jews. Other Jewish languages have served similar roles, yet none is seen as capable of fulfilling this unifying function with the same force. As Ruth Wisse contends, Yiddish, despite its prevalence among Ashkenazi Jews in pre–World War II Eastern Europe, was never "the language of *all* the Jews in space and time." It is "the deeper logic of peoplehood" that requires "the generative powers of Hebrew, for it alone could provide for the Bnei Israel of India and the Jews of Morocco as well as for the Hasidim of Belz."[10] This type of statement does not dismiss the importance of other Jewish languages; rather, it amplifies the notion that Hebrew is singularly distinct.

Indeed, a core Hebrew language ideology links Hebrew with the notion of Jewish peoplehood. Yet its ubiquity requires unpacking, if for no other reason than to understand what this strong bond reveals about the depth and reach of this belief. A good place to start is the emergence of the term *peoplehood* and its signification in American Jewry. Coined in the 1930s by the founder of Reconstructionist Judaism, Mordecai Kaplan (1881–1983), the term *peoplehood* was revolutionary when it was initially introduced into American Jewish parlance. Relatively quickly it was widely adopted as a popular concept, both as a descriptor and a desideratum of Jewish life in modern society. As historian Noam Pianko argues, American Jewish leaders in the late 1940s and 1950s marshalled the term to "navigate the status of American Jews, negotiate a new set of parameters for the American-Jewish synthesis and translate Jewish nationalism into an American context."[11] The notion of peoplehood therefore offered American Jews a palatable way to display Jewish collectivity "while avoiding the highly charged language of nation," even after the State of Israel was an established reality.[12] Crucially, the term allowed American Jews to navigate a course between the Scylla and Charybdis of Jewish distinctiveness and American belonging at a time when their loyalty to the

United States was being questioned. If, as Pianko argues, the term was born out of feelings of "Jewish insecurity in America" in the mid-1900s, it has since become an article of faith in American Judaism—a "key term" in philanthropic, educational, and religious discourse.[13] It is no longer a "back door" to talk about Jewish nationalism, but seen as a highly visible welcome sign that connotes a shared sense of Jewish belonging and kinship, regardless of difference in religious expression and practice, educational standing, political and cultural orientation, class, or nationality.[14]

Peoplehood's uncritical and widespread adoption is particularly noteworthy for its appearance in discourse centering anxieties about the irreparable disruptions in modern Jewish life. Much of the word's use reflects a fervency in the belief that Jewish sharedness is necessary to safeguard and ensure Jewish life in the future. As a signifier and catalyst of peoplehood, Hebrew is positioned as one of the last remaining commonalities among disparate Jewish communities. Rabbi Andrew Ergas, writing as then chairman of the Council for Hebrew Language and Culture in North America, made this juxtaposition clear: "The two animating forces that have long united the Jewish people—Israel and the Holocaust—are weakening." Facing this new reality, he contends that Hebrew remains the "one thing that can connect all Jews." Part bulwark and part savior, "Hebrew may be our last resort to revive ourselves as one people."[15] In a time of great uncertainty, Ergas evinces an ideology that Hebrew can overcome incommensurability.

The language ideology of Hebrew's indispensability comes through clearly in Alan Mintz's article entitled "Seven Theses on Hebrew and Jewish Peoplehood":

> Hebrew, finally, is a point of consensus among the contentious and divergent parties in Jewish life. It is protean in its prestige, being not necessarily religious and not necessarily secular and definitively fused with Israel. Even if this prestige is often only lip service, the unexploited potential of this moral capital is enormous. For there are so very precious few sancta of Jewish life that cut across so many boundaries and maintain such a high level of acceptability. The protean nature of Hebrew is no conceit. Hebrew is the joystick of Jewish life, and it can be pushed in a number of directions to enrich and accelerate substantive Jewish identity.[16]

Mintz's analogy of Hebrew as a critical lever takes on heightened resonance in light of contemporary Jewish diversity that is marked by competing religious, political, and social movements as well as particularistic and local conditions. These differentiations are most evident in the relationships between the American and Israeli communities, which constitute the world's largest Jewish populations.[17] As these communities experience "substantive" different Jewish lives as a result of historical circumstances, metaphors of "hugging," "wrestling," and "distancing" have emerged to describe a relationship that is increasingly fraught over political, partisan, and religious grounds.[18] As is well documented, the relationship between American Jews and Israel, including to the land, the state, its people, and its government policies, has undergone dramatic shifts in recent decades, particularly among the liberal and non-Orthodox groups that make up American Jewry, as well as across the divide.[19] Sociologist Bethamie Horowitz talks about the evolving and deteriorating nature of this union using the language of a wound in the body politic of Jewish life: "What was once more simply 'blue and white' has become 'black and blue.'" If in the past the Israeli flag (a metonym for the Jewish state) was firmly located at the center of Jewish life with all its attendant meanings, this standing is now in a "more bruised mode" as "the otherwise taken-for-granted virtue accorded to it by American and other diaspora Jews" is undergoing scrutiny.[20]

These changes have profound implications for beliefs about the role of Hebrew in the United States. Literary scholar Omri Asscher convincingly shows that historical, religious, and sociological factors led the two Jewish communities to take dissimilar directions in regard to Hebrew. While Hebrew ideologues of the late nineteenth century and early decades of the twentieth century assigned great ideological and practical import to the revitalization of Hebrew as part of the Zionist mission, early American Jewish intellectuals in the mid-1900s did not see Hebrew as a prerequisite for a robust Jewish life in the States. Indeed, for Jews to be accepted as an ethnoreligious minority group in the United States and part of a Judeo-Christian framework, they had to achieve two sociolinguist moves: They had to reject the secularized and nationalistic Hebrew ideology being espoused in nationalist revival efforts, and they had to delimit Textual Hebrew to the religious domain. As they embraced the United States as their home, American Jewish leaders firmly believed it was possible to construct a productive American Jewish culture in English. Over the following decades they endowed English with a "note of confidence" that it could ensure "Jewish cultivation, survival and creativity."[21] American Jews made crucial decisions about Hebrew to define themselves and manifest their religious, national, and civic identities.

Throughout the early decades of the 2000s, fears of a waning collective spirit between American and Israeli Jews led to calls to promote Hebrew education as a corrective to this rupture, based on the logic that Hebrew knowledge could provide American Jews with a deeper (and more positive and empathetic) understanding of Israeli society. Mintz noted:

> Hebrew is a potential bridge between Israel and the Diaspora. The asymmetry is stark: Almost all literate Israelis know English; very few literate American Jews can manage a sentence in the Jewish national language. Yet anyone who has learned even some Israeli Hebrew knows that it goes a long way toward granting access to the inner struggles of Israeli society beyond the media—and fundraising—images. There are possibilities of reciprocity, as well. The Hebrew of American Jews tends to be a mixture of the Hebrew of the prayerbook and Torah study and Israeli conversational practices—so that when we speak our Hebrew, however haltingly, we enact the richness of our Jewish identities in conversation with our Israeli brethren.[22]

A similar theme of transnational connection underlies American-born Israeli writer and editor David Hazony's sentiment that American Jews learning spoken Hebrew can repair the "cultural disconnect between Israeli and American Jews." Looking at the cultural advancements that Israeli society has made in defense, architecture, science, and medicine, Hazony contends that American Jews neither know about nor participate in these success stories. This disconnect—what Hazony refers to as the failure of American Jews to "get on the Israeli-civilization bus"—is "quite simple to solve" but only "if American Jews decide they want to solve it." As Hazony puts it, the "only way forward if this peoplehood thing is going to work" is that "American Jews have to learn Hebrew."[23]

Other leading thinkers have espoused this proposition. Historian James Loeffler's *cri de coeur* entitled "Should American Jews Speak Hebrew?" insists that a lack of Hebrew knowledge not only disadvantages American Jews but is also the cause of a "fraught kinship" between American Jews and Israel.[24] According to Loeffler, a root of the scission between these Jewish communities can be attributed to a linguistic divide:[25] "The largest Jewish community in the world outside of Israel lives out its relationship to the Jewish State entirely in English."[26] David Gedzelman, CEO of the Steinhardt Foundation for Jewish Life, likewise espouses a belief in the capacity of Hebrew to better connect American and Israeli Jewish cultures. "For Americans," he writes, "a Jewish Peoplehood that connects them to the culture of Israel cannot be achieved if they remain ignorant of the basic element of that culture, the Hebrew language." Gedzelman suggests that, more than a matter of communication, a lack of Hebrew knowledge poses a wider risk to American Jews' religious authority: "It is hard to imagine American Jewish expressions making serious inroads in gaining legitimacy in Israeli eyes unless those expressions are made in Hebrew by Americans who can speak, write, read and understand the language." Accordingly, the stakes of American Jews' Hebrew deficiency extend into the authoritative voices in Jewish religious life: "Israelis justifiably cannot understand why they should respect an American rabbi's claim to Jewish legitimacy if that rabbi stumbles in Hebrew."[27]

The idea that American and Israeli Jews lack a common language of communication is not uncommon. An article in the Jewish press describes a conference in early 2023 that brought together American Jewish organizational leaders, donors, and members of the Israeli-American Council (IAC)—an organization that supports Israeli Americans and builds connections between the United States and Israel.[28] When participants sitting at tables displaying pictures of Theodor Herzl and the Statue of Liberty were asked to consider how the bond between these two groups could be strengthened and how Israeli Americans could be better integrated into American Jewish communal leadership roles, a reporter at the event noted that "the literal language barrier was one of several issues that came up."[29] American-born Israeli journalist Dmitri Shufutinsky makes a similar argument in his piece. While he acknowledges the friction between American and Israeli Jews over Israel's military occupation in the West Bank and the rejection of liberal Judaism by the Chief Rabbinate (the rabbinic authority in Israel), he identifies this schism as a "language and communication barrier." The solution, he writes, is simple: "Hebrew proficiency or fluency," he argues, "will allow American (and other diaspora) Jews to better understand Israelis and communicate with them—seeing us as their brothers, not some distant far-off family you almost never talk to."[30] Hebrew, in other words, can mitigate familiar estrangement.

Daniel Gordis, an influential writer on American-Israeli Jewish dynamics, responded to the 2020 pieces written by Peter Beinart—a once staunch defender of Israel turned critic.[31] Gordis argues that Beinart's position on Israel is misguided in part because of his lack of Hebrew knowledge. As Gordis argues, Beinart is wholly dependent on English-translated Israel media or the English-language press and therefore cannot fully understand Israeli society.

> If Beinart could read the Shabbat culture sections of either [newspapers] *Ha'aretz* on the left or *Makor Rishon* on the right, he would see the celebration of Hebrew poetry each week, the preoccupation with newly published Israeli books, interviews with philosophers and public intellectuals. Yes, there are articles about Bibi and corruption and annexation and the pandemic and poverty and the demise of America and much more—but nowhere would he find fretting about annihilation. It is obviously not Peter's fault that he cannot read those newspapers or Israeli literature until it is translated (and most of it is not), or mine Israeli op-ed pages of all sorts for a sense of what animates us. He is not to blame for the fact that he only "knows" what animates Israel by listening to the sales pitches of the very American Jewish institutions that he wishes to dismantle. But it's a reality he would do well to acknowledge.[32]

The question of translation as a Hebrew language ideology is fully discussed later in this chapter. However, it is important here to underscore how much of the discourse revolving around Hebrew and Jewish peoplehood identifies American Jews' lack of Hebrew knowledge as a cause of the widening rift between American and Israeli Jews. When understood in this way, the religious, social, and political stakes of language ideologies about the role of Hebrew in fostering Jewish peoplehood take on a new level of meaning. More than simply a vehicle of cohesion that, when activated, can bring together disparate Jewish communities under one roof, Hebrew becomes embedded in broader debates about the nature of the relationship between American and Israeli Jews. Hebrew knowledge, in this sense, is never merely a linguistic question. It is a referendum on what kind of collectivity American and Israeli Jews are, or aspire to be.

Ideologies of Adaptability

In his book *The Mystique of Hebrew: An Ancient Language in the New World*, Jewish education scholar Alvin Schiff writes about the "tightrope existence" of the Jewish people. Explaining the precarious need to balance Jewish particularism with universalist demands, Schiff describes this "bi-polar adjustment" as "keeping the constants" while simultaneously "keeping up with the times."[33] For Schiff, Hebrew provides a solution to this tension by drawing on the language's capacity to be contemporary while maintaining its history. As the quintessential *altneuschprache* (an old-new language), Hebrew has transformed from the language of Jewish sacred texts to the vernacular of the "businessman, the scientist, the *yeshiva bohur* [student], the farmer, the housewife, and the university professor alike." It is this unique "adaptive mechanism"—to be simultaneously classic and modern—that has allowed Judaism to evolve into a modern religion, as well as become one of its defining characteristics.[34] Ideologies of peoplehood imagine Hebrew as a force that bridges internal Jewish difference. Hebrew ideology of adaptability, in contrast, highlights beliefs in the singularity of Hebrew to signify Judaism's distinctiveness to preserve the "sacred past of eternal Jewish values" as well as serve as "a major expression of contemporary Jewish vitality."[35] The dichotomy this language ideology espouses offers an interpretative frame to constitute Jewishness around themes of survival and continuity. Being perceived as old and new enables Hebrew to function as a metonym for Jewish resolve, renewal, and adaptability.

Analyzing the workings of this ideology requires a basic understanding of the evolution of the Hebrew language. Hebrew's roots trace back to a Semitic dialect developed in the latter half of the second millennium BCE in the area between the Jordan River and the Mediterranean Sea—the area making up the State of Israel today. While we refer to Hebrew as a singular category, in actuality it is an umbrella term that comprises temporal varieties. The earliest is Biblical Hebrew, the language some Jews and Christians believe is the language in which the divine created the world. This form evolved into Mishnaic Hebrew, used by the rabbis in the second and third centuries for scholarly texts and liturgy. Starting around the seventh century and continuing throughout the tenth century, Medieval Hebrew functioned as a language of liturgy, rabbinic literature, intra-Jewish commerce, and poetic literature. In the eighteenth century, European Jewish writers influenced by the Jewish Enlightenment (*Haskalah*) developed Maskilic Hebrew as a literary vehicle for Jews living in modern European nations. This repurposing was taken up by Zionist ideologues, who aimed to revitalize Hebrew into a spoken vernacular that could meet the communicative, aesthetic, and ideological needs of Jewish nationalism. Doing so required the Hebrew revivalists to draw on themes of the language's adaptability to evolve and meet its needs as a secular and modern language.

This is not to say that the pursuit of adaptability has always been welcomed.[36] Linguist Benjamin Harshav shares an excerpt of a lecture by Yosef Klausner, himself a proponent of Hebrew revival and literature in the early 1900s, in which he lamented that the new form of Hebrew was becoming a "linguistic ragout or vinaigrette," which led to the creation of a bastardized language "yoking an elephant and a mastodon together."[37] The purists notwithstanding, a common trope about Hebrew has been that its adaptability is not a defect but rather a defining characteristic of its survival over time and across space. Perceived as a palimpsest in which new expressions coexist with ancient meanings, Hebrew is endowed with "symbolic power far beyond normal language."[38] Unlike other sacred languages whose sole presence remained fixed on the pages of sacred texts, revitalized Modern Hebrew was symbolically understood as a resuscitated language that could carry the weight of the future and breathe renewed vitality into Jewish life.[39]

Hebrew's derivational nature enabled this life-affirming evolution. Users can generate infinite numbers of words with different but related meanings due to its three- or four-letter root system (*shorashim*), to which prefixes and suffixes can be added. Numerous writers have celebrated the language's morphological generativity. Its root system has been called "a stunning mechanism."[40] Part of the lore of Hebrew's generativity includes stories of Eliezer Ben-Yehuda and other Hebrew revivalists creatively mining the root system for words in the Jewish canonical sources and from foreign languages to coin neologisms. If French is often considered the language best equipped to express romance, and German is thought to be overly erudite with its unnecessarily long words, Hebrew is touted for its prolificacy and its capacity for regeneration.

The effusiveness about Hebrew goes beyond admiration for its morphological structure to encompass broader claims about the characteristics of its speakers. Linguistic anthropologists have long debated the relationship between linguistic features and the social identities of language users. Going back to the development of the influential albeit highly controversial linguistic relativity hypothesis (also known as the Sapir-Whorf hypothesis), there is a tradition of thought that views the structure of a language as inseparable from speakers' perceptions of the world and their place in it. Applied broadly, this logic helps illuminate how enthusiasm for Hebrew's morphological dynamism is undergirded by a language ideology in which Hebrew is not just a vehicle of expression but a marker of Jewish distinctiveness. This was certainly the case in the formative years of statehood, when Zionist leaders mobilized Hebrew as central to their nation-building project and anchored the emerging Israeli identity in ancient roots while projecting a modern, future-oriented Jewish collectivity. A similar dynamic is visible in contemporary American Jewish discourse, such as Joseph Lowin's long-running "About Hebrew" column in *Hadassah Magazine*, where he explores the semantic and cultural richness of three-letter Hebrew roots across biblical, rabbinic, medieval, and modern Israeli usage. Here the language is not merely functional but laden with ingenuity, resourcefulness, and creativity.[41]

Once Hebrew is linked with qualities such as resourcefulness, adaptability, and endurance, its indexicality, that is, its capacity to point to and embody Jewishness, becomes apparent. This linkage is especially potent in discussions of Jewish continuity and survival. For example, scholar Alvin Schiff refers to the "mystique of Hebrew" as a measure of "the miracle of Jewish durableness," part of "the mystery of the

Jewish people's stubborn existence."[42] Similarly, linguist Lewis Glinert contends that "the story of Hebrew is much like the story of the Jews: misty origins, ancient splendor, sudden eclipse followed by centuries of alien domination, staunched somehow by an infinite ability to adapt and survive—and culminating, in our century, in a dramatic paradox of ruin and rebirth."[43] Jeremy Benstein echoes this framing, contending that Hebrew's evolution reflects a Jewish narrative that tries to "reconcile tradition with change" in the service of "growing the Jewish future."[44]

Across these accounts, Hebrew's morphological flexibility is not simply a linguistic feature. It becomes a metaphor for Jewish resilience and cultural perseverance. What makes Hebrew extraordinary—its linguistic secret sauce—is that in integrating the old and new it fights discontinuity with continuity and ensures Jewish vitality. Its ability to absorb and transform ancient roots to express modern, even secular or heretical, concepts is seen as an inherently Jewish act of synthesis. As Benstein puts it, when figures like Eliezer Ben-Yehuda repurposed biblical roots for modern usage, they were "committing a deeply Jewish act."[45] Glinert adds that Hebrew's "zest for change among constancy" reflects a defining characteristic of Judaism itself.[46] In this cultural logic, revitalized Hebrew and Judaism are imagined as mutually reinforcing. They are co-constitutive and codependent and symbolize the vitality, endurance, and adaptive capacity of the other. This ideology positions Hebrew as more than a language. It becomes a metonym for Jewish life, with its capacity for infinite renewal standing in for the perceived durability and evolution of the Jewish people. What begins as commentary on linguistic structure ultimately serves as a powerful narrative about identity, continuity, and cultural survival.

Ideologies of Hebrew Primacy

Hebrew ideologies of adaptability derive from an understanding that Hebrew constitutes a distinctive Jewish characteristic. Thus, it obliquely espouses a belief about the capacity of other languages to meet this challenge. This set of Hebrew language beliefs raises questions about the use of translation. In a world in which an app on a smart phone can provide an increasingly accurate translation of almost any text in less time than it takes to look up a single word in a dictionary, ideologies about Hebrew primacy (that is, the necessity of using Hebrew over other languages) shape ideas about literacy, Jewish identity, and Jewish continuity.[47]

The topic of Hebrew translation is not new to Jewish life. One might argue, indeed, that it is constitutive of Jewish multilingualism, a core feature of the Jewish experience in the diaspora as well as in the Land of Israel.[48] Educational linguist Bernard Spolsky describes this multilingual reality as a phenomenon resulting from the historical conditions impacted by Jews' expulsion and their need to interact with their non-Jewish neighbors:

> By force of circumstances, ever since the Babylonian exile in the sixth century before the Common Era, and even more since the destruction of the Temple and the Jewish state by the Romans and the dispersion of Jews throughout the ancient world, exacerbated by regular expulsions by Christians and Muslims alike, resulting in even wider geographical spread and contact with even more languages, Jews have been individually plurilingual and collectively multilingual, held together over these three millennia by their devotion to and the use of the original Jewish language: Hebrew.[49]

Jewish multilingualism notwithstanding, translation of Jewish sacred texts and liturgy also constituted diasporic Jewish life.[50] Outside of the (male) intellectual elite, the ability to comprehend the Bible and liturgical texts was rare, especially among women and children. Geographically dispersed Jewish communities with only a partial grasp of the original Hebrew turned to translated texts as a lifeline to stay connected to their sacred textual history.[51]

Debates about translation are fraught with contradictory impulses, especially in regard to accessing sacred texts. On one hand, translation is often upheld as essential to Jewish continuity in the diaspora. Many religious authorities historically acknowledged the necessity of translating scripture and liturgy into vernacular languages as a precondition for Jewish survival.[52] In this view, translation functions as a pragmatic and even sacred act. Understood as such, it enables ongoing access to tradition in new cultural and linguistic contexts. On the other hand, a competing ideology casts translation as a harbinger of rupture and disconnection from Jewish authenticity. Most notable, the Septuagint—the translation of the Hebrew Bible into Greek in the third century BCE—is frequently invoked as a diasporic-demise morality tale. According to this narrative, as Alexandrian Jews attained a considerable degree of political, economic, and social status, they doomed themselves to extinction when they "attempted to transfer the 'content' of Judaism into a Greek 'vessel.'"[53] Fearing that American Jews will eventually suffer the same fate as Hellenized Jewry, Hebrew literary scholar Gershon Shaked issued a proleptic elegy for American Jewry: "Jewish New York seems to me like a strange transformation of Jewish Alexandria: its sages are brilliant Hellenistic sages, Jews who read Scripture in translation, for the Hebrew language is forgotten, and, if it is remembered in certain circles, it is considered only a secondary ancient foreign language, which must be interpreted in the vernacular—the quotidian English that rules the roost."[54] Such views frame translation not as a bridge but as a slippery slope, pulling diaspora Jews away from the linguistic core of Jewish identity toward the shoals of irreparable harm.

Other Hebrew language ideologies amplify these anxieties, particularly around the perceived sanctity and untranslatability of the Hebrew text. For those who regard the Hebrew Bible as the literal word of God, translation becomes not just a practical compromise but a theological risk that threatens to mediate, dilute, or distort a direct relationship with the divine. We can also see the potency of the idea of the written Hebrew word as immutable and untranslatable in debates over definitions of Jewish authenticity. Ruth Wisse points out that a reliance on translation underlies perceptions that individuals who can read the Torah in Hebrew are "recognized by those who cannot as 'authentically' Jewish."[55] The Reform and Conservative movements' "acceptance of English as a substitute for Hebrew . . . has had a cumulatively weakening affect" and "ensures that they will remain forever marginal, unable to become full participants in prayer and study."[56] Similar concerns appear in Alan Mintz's analysis of the proliferation of translated Jewish texts, in which he shares concerns about the scope of translated Judaism, rationalizing that the "enormous outpouring of translations from classical Hebrew sources is cause for both celebration and consternation." If the "phenomenon represents an admirable democratization of Jewish learning," it also "conduces to a belief that the Hebrew original is simply an obstacle to be overcome as well as a medium for messages that can be better, or at least more rapidly, understood in English."[57] Author and translator Hillel Halkin similarly laments that the "down side of the boom in Hebrew-English translation" will result in reaching a "point that one soon won't have to know Hebrew at all to consider oneself Jewishly literate."[58] These beliefs extend to contemporary Hebrew speakers who are often valorized for their ability to "open a three-thousand-year-old chapter of biblical prose and understand it almost unaided," a powerful, if idealized, image of linguistic and religious continuity.[59]

Debates about Hebrew-English translation go beyond sacred texts to include Modern Hebrew literature. Shaked notes that "just as ancient Hebrew literature is being translated into English to make it part of the cultural heritage of American Jews, so also modern literature is being translated for the same purpose."[60] Arguing against translated contemporary Hebrew literature, others raise doubt that English translation can capture Jewish authenticity.[61] Halkin argues that translation "has involved accepting, and in a sense even legitimizing, the disappearance of Hebrew as the international language of the Jews." Among the indicators of the extent of these developments, Halkin laments that a "scholarly conference in Jerusalem on S. Y. Agnon, Hebrew literature's sole Nobel Prize winner," was "held in English, too."[62] One can assume that it is not solely the endangerment of the Hebrew word that Halkin fears in the increased reliance on English translation, but a devaluation of Israeli cultural production as a part of Jewish life. American authors have added an interesting dimension to discussions of Jewish literature written in English and Jewish authenticity. American novelist Dara Horn acknowledged that her fictional 2013 book, *A Guide to the Perplexed*, was "a little contrived in English, since most contemporary English fiction doesn't concern itself with . . . time and memory, and modernity and ancient belief, and state and free will." In contrast, Horn describes the Hebrew translation of her book as "a much less artificial book than the one I had written in English, one whose words and phrases and references and travels through time felt entirely ordinary, natural, and authentic." With a postmodern twist, Horn concludes that the novel she had written in English "was the translation" and that "in Hebrew, I was reading the original."[63]

Ideologies about Hebrew translation also extend to spoken language. Contending that the Hebrew spoken in Israel is the "single, true embodiment of Hebrew" and the "most highly authentic Jewish form of communication," Benstein attests that "anyone cut off from that source—that is, Jews who don't speak Hebrew—are somewhere off in Babylon, far from the wellsprings of vitality."[64] English and Jewish studies scholar Julian Levinson takes a similar stance that American Jews' lack of spoken Hebrew knowledge contributes to intra-Jewish irreconcilable differences and incommensurable values: "Whether due to our belatedness in history, lack of training, geographical displacement, or mere ignorance, we [American Jews] find ourselves stranded on the far side of meaning, deaf to some message, suggestion, question, demand, warning." American Jews are in "a recurrent experience of standing in the presence of impenetrable words that seem to contain some important, even decisive matter" without any ability to decipher them in a meaningful way.[65]

If much of the scholarship on Jewish languages has focused on the multilingual achievements that have enabled diasporic Jews to integrate into their host societies while remaining distinctively Jewish through religious rituals, there is a countervailing sentiment that links English translated texts with Jewish discontinuity. "Whatever language Jews spoke—Greek, Aramaic, Arabic, Yiddish, Ladino," Loeffler argues, "Hebrew remained at the core of their spiritual and cultural lives, especially for educated elites." In contrast, he argues, American Jews have rejected multilingualism and elevated "the embrace of English to the level of an exclusive, ideological choice."[66] Similar concerns about language choice and the survival of American Jewry permeate literary critic Leon Wieseltier's unambiguously titled piece, "Language, Identity, and the Scandal of American Jewry." Unsparing in his critique, Wieseltier fustigates that American Jews are "the spoiled brats of Jewish history," and that American Jews' "illiteracy is nothing less than a variety of blindness"—a self-harming and enfeebling choice that if left untreated will lead to a figurative and literal death: a community with no future. "If the Jews of America do not make the commitment to replete ourselves by recovering our language, to bring to an end, if not in ourselves then in our children, this absurd helplessness before our own tradition, then we may dream of only a limited greatness, not only in our literature but also in our lives."[67] To many who fear English replacing Hebrew as the language of Jewish knowledge and authenticity, the problem is unequivocally clear. So too is the solution. Rather than blaming the translators, Halkin argues that the guilty party is "the lack of Hebrew education in America."[68] Mark Charendoff, editor of *Sapir*, shares this perspective: "We have all but given up on teaching Hebrew, making American Jews a historical anomaly—a Jewish community without a distinct language."[69] When seen in this way, Hebrew learning is not only an educational corrective; it is framed as an efficacious and moral act to protect American Jewry.

While pedagogical and curricular problems get a fair share of blame in Hebrew education (a topic that I explore in depth in Chapter 6), sociopsychological reasons also explain American Jews' Hebrew illiteracy. Dara Horn, for example, contends that the reason American Jews do not know Hebrew is "because they think they can't"—by which she means that they do not feel entitled to claim the language as their own. Recalling her own Hebrew-learning experiences as a child, Horn thought that there were "only three kinds of American Jews" who were allowed to learn Hebrew: the Orthodox, those who had lived in Israel, and those who had attended a Jewish day school.[70] Not belonging to one of these entitled groups, she denied herself the right to claim Hebrew as her own. It was not until she was in her thirties, when she attended a keynote talk delivered in Hebrew at a Jewish writers' conference in Jerusalem, that she recognized she was, much to her own surprise, a Hebrew speaker.

Literary scholar Michael Weingrad also looks to sociopsychological reasons to explain why American Jews do not learn Hebrew. It is not, he argues, a matter of insecurity in their ability. "After all," he writes, "American Jews are hardly known for their lack of confidence when it comes to intellectual pursuits." He notes, "We are surrounded by American Jews who learn languages and expect their children to learn languages: Spanish, Mandarin, JavaScript."[71] Looking beyond a lack of "confidence or resources," Weingrad finds his answers in the "American Jewish psyche" and specifically American Jews' need to embrace alterity: "American Jewish identity is based on feeling outside, on the threshold knocking at the door of Jewishness but never quite entering. To enter fully would be to lose one's identity and become something different, unthinkable for most American Jews. For them, the front stoop has become home."[72] Underlying Weingrad's logic is the idea that Hebrew illiteracy affords American Jews a sense of outsiderness, which is indispensable to their maintaining a distinctive American Jewish identity. It is "this odd, ironclad commitment to ambivalence—to that eternal door-knocking" that keeps American Jews from embracing Hebrew.[73] This reason explains why American Jews prefer to keep Hebrew "obscure and talismanic, at best liturgical but never transparent or normal."[74] Anything else would be an existential threat to their American Jewish identity.

Hebrew Ideologies of Jewish Endangerment

Ideologies about the status and role of Hebrew in American Jewry shape broader discussions about the future vitality of the community. While there are convincing claims that discussions about Jewish identity and continuity elide alternative ways of thinking about American Jewish life, it is a safe bet that whenever the topic of Jewish vitality and survival surfaces, enumerating data describing changes in American Jewish life are never far behind.[75] Arguably, American Jews are a number-conscious group.[76] To be sure, Jews are not the only social group that looks to numbers and quantification to better understand themselves and hypothesize about directions and trends impacting their demographics. Indeed, social scientists have long recognized counting practices as a crucial indicator of the health, cohesion, and future trajectory of nations. Scholars have also long noted that it is the perception of numbers and figures as neutral and objective that endows them with heightened rhetorical and predicative powers for explaining demographic and communal change.[77] In the field of linguistics, for example, the vitality of a language is frequently measured by the number of fluent speakers or new learners. Language loss or growth is thus numerically tracked and evaluated, with these data points often used as proxies for assessing cultural sustainability or decline. Sociolinguists Alexandre Duchêne and Monica Heller highlight the power of these numbers, arguing that discourses of language endangerment are fundamentally discourses about "some threat from outside (from some Other) to the social order" that are in need of intervening forces to prevent or remedy.[78] Language inventories, in this sense, are invaluable not only for what they describe linguistically but for how they are put to use in policies and practices. Like other forms of enumerating discourse, they put a picture of complex social dynamics into concise data points that construct and legitimize broader narratives of communal vitality or decline.[79]

I offer this background to look at the use of enumeration in discussions about Hebrew learners and the strength of the American Jewish community. Jewish organizations, educators, and communal leaders routinely collect and circulate numerical data on community members' engagement with religious and cultural practices, their participation in Jewish institutions, and their attitudes toward a range of Jewish and secular issues. These figures of Jewish school enrollment, summer camp attendance, Birthright participation, philanthropic giving, synagogue affiliation, participation in cultural art venues, and more populate the landscape of American Jewish discourse. Leaders of American Jewry would likely make the case that these inventories, demographic studies, and quantifications of Jewish behaviors are vital tools to help identify areas of concern, track trends, and guide strategic planning. While this may be true, their prevalence creates the illusion they have always existed. Cultural scholar Jeffrey Shandler, however, dates the emergence of this practice of making inventories to after World War II, when, after the catastrophic decimation of Jewish life in Europe, American Jewish leadership felt a profound responsibility to monitor and safeguard Jewish life. Statistical and demographic surveys became central to this project.[80]

Building on this insight, anthropologist Michal Kravel-Tovi examines how social scientists, public intellectuals, and lay leaders infuse numerical figures, charts, tables, and graphs with emotions, turning these dry demographic data into "wet numbers" full of potent narratives of crisis and metaphors of calamity and social illness. Kravel-Tovi argues that, "framed with affect-laden discourses," wet numbers are often uncritically taken as objective, straightforward, and irrefutable, used to shape perception, provoke response, and drive action. In her analysis, this dynamic is a key feature of "Jewish biopolitics," wherein demographic data undergird discourses of continuity, inform institutional priorities, and drive investment.[81] This phenomenon was evident in the discourse surrounding the release of the Pew Center's 2020 survey of American Jewish life—a highly esteemed collection of demographic data of American Jewish life.[82] Days before the release of the report, journalist Andrew Silow-Carroll presciently anticipated the response the publication of this report would create. "If history is any guide," he wrote, "the results will launch a thousand internal Jewish debates about who is a Jew, who gets to decide and what's the future for a diverse, splintered, assimilated and persistent community of communities."[83] His prediction proved accurate. The study's release monopolized Jewish communal discourse, with social scientists and communal leaders using its numerical findings to highlight communal success, stress concerns, debate trends, and chart new policies. Ultimately, enumerative discourse does more than measure. It functions as a speech act that effects change in a community.

In the case of Hebrew and American Jewish life, these narratives often reflect deeper ideological commitments and anxieties about identity, continuity, authenticity, and cultural survival. If enumerated data are taken as a sign of American Jewry's health (or lack thereof), what can be made of the numbers collected about Hebrew usage and learning? How do these figures constitute language ideologies about Hebrew's role in present and future American Jewish life? How are numbers of Hebrew learners infused with emotion and social meaning? Critically, it is important to note that the "dry" data about Hebrew knowledge are not readily abundant. The 2013 Pew report, as one example, provided only limited data on the strength of Hebrew among American Jews. We learned that, at the time of the report, 60 percent of those who identified as "Jews by religion" claimed to know the Hebrew alphabet, compared to 24 percent of those who identified as "Jews of no religion." Among all Jews in the survey sample, 13 percent said they could understand all or most Hebrew words, while 12 percent said they could hold a conversation in Hebrew.[84] It is notable that the survey did not define "understanding" and whether it referred to decoding or comprehension. Tellingly, the follow-up 2020 report removed all questions about language—Hebrew or otherwise. Nonetheless, the 2013 survey still provided some fodder for moralizing and speculating about the health of the American Jewish community. James Loeffler made a tacit connection among the Pew survey data, Hebrew illiteracy, and Jewish communal enfeeblement:

> What we do learn from the study is that half of American Jews claim to value, as essential to their Jewishness, the quality of intellectual curiosity and/or a good sense of humor. Half also know the letters of the Hebrew alphabet—but not much more than that.

> Obviously, none of this so much as begins to add up to a Jewish cultural identity in its classical sense, and little in the Pew Study seems even to entertain the possibility, so central to the vision of a hundred years ago, of a secular Jewishness immersed in a coherent, historically rooted world of sounds, ideas, rituals, emotions, texts, and affiliations.[85]

Loeffler points to a profound change over time in what a Jewish cultural identity encompasses, with Hebrew illiteracy as a dimension of this change.

Statistics about the declining numbers of American Hebrew learners are also interpreted as a leading indicator of broader communal decay. The 2021 American Jewish Committee survey pointed to a generational trend. While more than half of the respondents over sixty were able to read and speak Hebrew, that percentage declined to only 35 percent among respondents between eighteen and thirty-nine years old.[86] In her 2019 piece, journalist Aviya Kushner hones in on the downward enrollment patterns in university Hebrew courses, which she claims "may soon have profound effects on the American Jewish community." Specifically, Kushner notes that enrollment dropped 17.6 percent in Modern Hebrew and almost 24 percent in Biblical Hebrew courses between 2013 and 2016. Citing an array of figures to underscore the severity of these trends, Kushner notes that whereas 9,620 college students enrolled in a Modern Hebrew course in 2006, this number fell to 6,698 in 2013 and further decreased to 5,521 in 2016—an almost 40 percent decline in fewer than ten years. Biblical Hebrew fared no better, as its enrollment numbers decreased from 14,000 students in 2006 to 9,587 in 2016. If the absolute numbers were not dire enough, Kushner looks at comparative data, showing that Modern Hebrew had "the dubious distinction of having one of the five lowest percentages of enrollments of advanced language students." In simpler terms, there were more introductory Hebrew 101 students than advanced-level Hebrew students, indicating a decrease in the pipeline of continuing Hebrew students. Concluding, Kushner calls for "extensive discussion on the crisis in Hebrew-language enrollment," arguing that the decrease in the numbers of students taking university Hebrew classes is a canary in the Jewish vitality coalmine.[87] Almost fifteen years earlier, the linguist Bernard Spolsky reached a similarly grave conclusion about the sustainability of the American Jewish community when he noted the diminutive numbers of opportunities to be exposed to Hebrew in the American context. He noted that "where once there were 10 teacher colleges using Hebrew as a language of instruction and several Hebrew speaking camps . . . now it is considered appropriate to conduct Hebrew teachers' conferences in the co-territorial vernacular." This decline led Spolsky to declare: "Clearly, in the United States Hebrew is now an endangered language."[88]

Dwindling numbers of American Hebrew learners not only provide a relational framing of past and present conditions but also rhetorically link this threat to a fear of communal discontinuity. The discourse takes on the shape of a moral panic—a public discourse defined as "an obsessive, moralistic and alarmist manner, as if it betokened some imminent catastrophe."[89] To be sure, the numbers do not portend optimism, but what, in fact, is endangered? With almost nine million Hebrew speakers worldwide and a growing Jewish population in Israel, Hebrew is not at risk of disappearing. What is at stake, then, is something else entirely. Duchêne and Heller help us to understand the stakes of this discourse by reminding us to turn our attention away from the actual numbers and toward the mobilization of numbers in policy and practice. Crucially, they claim that "discourses of language endangerment are discourses about other kinds of threats which take place, for specific reasons, on the terrain of language."[90] Thus we can see how enumerated data about declining numbers of American Jewish Hebrew learners capture fears about eroding Jewish commitments and shifting priorities.

Numbers tell us something about the counted. However, they tell us even more about the counters. Statistics about Hebrew learners function not merely as descriptive data but as tools through which rabbis, educators, communal leaders, social scientists, and journalists express alarm, take stock of initiatives, coalesce around priorities, advocate for change, and implement small and large communal interventions. In this way, enumeration about Hebrew learning readily converges with broader discourses of communal vulnerability, especially anxieties about the sustainability of a vibrant American Jewish collective. When evidence points to a decline in Hebrew use, seen in the proliferation of English translations, the drop in university Hebrew course enrollment, and a general sense of growing illiteracy, Hebrew becomes a mechanism of cultural preservation and resistance to these trends. When translation and illiteracy are cast as threats to American Jewish identity, Hebrew knowledge is mobilized as the antidote. The result is a potent language ideology that positions Hebrew as essential to safeguarding American Jewish identity and securing its future. These overlapping concerns about translation, illiteracy, and the perceived endangerment of Hebrew fuel the urgency around Hebrew education. If Hebrew is imagined as the key to Jewish vitality, then debates over its teaching, learning, and usage become charged sites of both hope and anxiety—a topic taken up at length in Chapter 6.

Ideologies of Decontextualization

The Hebrew ideologies discussed so far have been grounded in what we might think of as broad connections among Hebrew, Jews, and Judaism. Whether Hebrew shapes interpretations of Jewish peoplehood, resilience, or vitality, these beliefs share an understanding that Hebrew is central to Jewish life. This section takes a different tack, exploring what happens when a linguist, fiction author, and head of an educational organization untether and decontextualize Hebrew from its Jewish associations and frame it in ways that challenge its most foundational identity as a Jewish language. Attending to these processes, I seek to show that Hebrew language ideologies are mobilized in ways that challenge core beliefs about the ontology of Modern Hebrew, its rootedness in the territorial and national life of Israel, and Hebrew as a constitutive dimension of Judaism and Jewish life.

One area in which fundamental beliefs are put in stark relief is in scholarly discussions about whether the Hebrew spoken today is a derivative of Biblical Hebrew or if its roots can be traced to other non-Semitic languages.[91] Linguist Ghil'ad Zuckermann, a leading proponent of the latter "mixed language" school of thought, espouses the view that the vernacular Hebrew spoken in Israel is a semi-engineered Semito-European hybrid language and not, as many believe, a Semitic language spoken by populations in the Middle East, Northern Africa, and Southwest Asia.[92] While acknowledging that older forms of Hebrew contributed to Israeli Hebrew, Zuckermann argues that other languages, including Yiddish, Arabic, Russian, Polish, German, Ladino, and English, were also foundational. More precisely, he claims that Israeli Hebrew's "phonetics, phonology and syntax are primarily European, while its morphology and basic vocabulary are mainly—albeit not exclusively—Semitic."[93] Proposing that Israeli and Biblical Hebrew are typologically and genetically different and that Israeli Hebrew is not a proto-Jewish language, Zuckermann's research challenges the idea that Israeli Hebrew derives from Biblical Hebrew.[94] Doing so, it disputes a core tenet in Zionist thought that revitalized Hebrew is a modern iteration of the Hebrew used in Jewish antiquity.

Not surprisingly, Zuckermann's scholarship has provoked trenchant critiques.[95] Writing under the pen name Philologos, Hillel Halkin, for one, attributes a political agenda to Zuckermann's scholarship, insisting that his "attitude toward modern Hebrew is less that of a professional linguist than of someone driven by the agenda of post- (if not anti-) Zionism." According to his perspective, Zuckermann's findings are a critique of Zionism.

> It is not so much about Hebrew as it is about Jewish history. If one believes that the Hebrew-speaking state known as Israel is not an organic outgrowth of Jewish history—that it is in some sense foreign to it, perhaps even a distortion, usurpation, or overthrowing of it—then there is a logic to calling CVI [Contemporary Vernacular Israeli] "Israeli" as a way of stressing its non-continuity with the Jewish past. If one doesn't believe it, there's every reason to call CVI Hebrew. In the end, you might say, it boils down to a question of Zionism.[96]

Questions about Hebrew etymology touch a nerve because they push against bedrock connections among Hebrew, Jews, and Israel, thereby putting other core beliefs at risk. If the Hebrew spoken in Israel today is not etymologically related to the Hebrew used by the Jews of antiquity, what does this mean for claims connecting Jews to a homeland in the region in which the State of Israel was established?

Other forms of decontextualization call into doubt the connection between Hebrew and Jewishness. In 2021 novelist Sally Rooney joined a collection of authors who refused to have their novels translated into Hebrew as part of a symbolic boycott of Israel because of its policies toward Palestinians.[97] As Rooney put it, “I simply do not feel it would be right for me under the present circumstances to accept a new contract with an Israeli company that does not publicly distance itself from apartheid and support the U.N.-stipulated rights of the Palestinian people.”[98] In response, the largest book sellers in Israel removed all of her novels from their online and brick and mortar stores.[99] Similar to reactions to other Boycott, Divestment, and Sanctions (BDS) demands, Rooney's protest led to strong rebuttals. Ari Rudolph, then planning executive for UJA-Federation's Commission on the Jewish People, decried attempts to disconnect Hebrew from Judaism as a gross misreading of history: “The writer sees Hebrew as the language of the State of Israel, not of the Jewish people.” For Rudolph, Hebrew, Israel, and Jews are inseparable; they are co-constituted categories, defined in relation to one another, with Hebrew being the “only language that has any formal standing in Judaism.”[100] Others questioned the hypocrisy of Rooney's refusal to have a Hebrew translation for an Israeli reading public given that the “Hebrew-language publishing industry is centered in Israel, the only country where Hebrew is an official language.”[101] Jewish public figures denounced Rooney's decision as antisemitism, asserting that while she claimed to be making a political statement about Israel, she was defaming Jews more broadly. They rejected the stance that Hebrew could symbolize Israel's policies but not represent its Jewish readers or be separated from its Jewishness.

Efforts to disassociate Hebrew from Jewishness were also apparent in the discourse around the opening of Hebrew language charter schools in the United States in the early 2000s.[102] While a discussion of Hebrew charter schools is presented in Chapter 6, here I focus on some of the statements that sought to universalize the language beyond its signification as a Jewish language. As an indicative piece, I look at an article published in a local Connecticut newspaper, in which journalist Paul Bass reports on the intention of Hebrew Public, a charter management organization, to launch a Hebrew charter school in New Haven, Connecticut, in the fall of 2024. In this piece Bass quotes Jon Rosenberg, president and CEO of Hebrew Public, who lauds Hebrew's universality to help students become successful global citizens and promotes Hebrew charter schools as “diverse by design.”[103] In other words, schools operating in the Hebrew Public network intentionally include students from all religious, ethnic, and linguistic backgrounds. Rosenberg's appeal to Hebrew's universalism are appeals to liberalism and societal advancement. "There's a need for what we do," Rosenberg explains in Bass's article. Schools like this one can open students' eyes to "all sorts of issues of difference," a goal desperately needed given "what's happening in our country and in our world where people are talking past each other, where people are in isolated ideological bubbles, where segregation is increasing in public schools in the United States."[104] By reframing Hebrew education in the parlance of the progressive educational discourse of equal opportunity and inclusivity, Rosenberg refashions what was once a sectarian mission into a larger public good.[105]

Rosenberg's appeal to Hebrew's universalism also refutes accusations that Hebrew charter schools are doing Jewish education on the public dime. "Our schools are public schools," he affirms. "They're not Jewish schools." Preempting any misgivings about the schools' intentions, he adds, "People often get confused when they see the word Hebrew in the name and hear that we teach modern Hebrew. They get confused in a way that they don't if they see Mandarin or Spanish or French. They get more confused with Hebrew because they have heard of things like 'Hebrew School' or the natural tendency to conflate Hebrew with Judaism."[106] If the default is to associate Hebrew with Judaism, Rosenberg is taking a different position, pointing to other world languages commonly taught in American public schools. Any confusion about this matter is also addressed on the Hebrew Public website's FAQs. In response to the question "How is it possible to have a Hebrew language charter school that is not a religious school?," the answer notes that while some languages may be affiliated with a religion, they are not inherently religious: "Hebrew is a distinct language and culture that stands on its own. It is naturally associated with Judaism, but it is not inherently religious—much the same way that Greek is not inherently Greek Orthodox, Arabic is not inherently Muslim, Italian is not inherently Roman Catholic, or English is not inherently Anglican. The best proof of Hebrew's secular nature is the fact that it has long been taught and studied at public schools and colleges across America without raising any First Amendment issues."[107]

Finally, in Bass's article Rosenberg touts the additional benefits of learning Hebrew without any explicit mention of Jewishness or Judaism. Specifically, Rosenberg notes that Modern Hebrew is "a unique language with ancient roots in Near East culture, as well as a fascinating case of an ancient language that was revived in modern times, and is today at the heart of a culture that bridges Europe and Asia, East and West." Additionally, "Hebrew is also an entry point to other Semitic languages, including Arabic. And it is the language of a burgeoning number of technology and innovation companies founded in Israel or by Israelis."[108] Thus Hebrew Public resignifies Hebrew as a secular, social, and cultural resource for American youth regardless of their religious, ethnic, or communal identifications, and not for the chosen few. Part of this resignification derives from identifying Hebrew as the authentic voice of Israeli culture while minimizing the Jewish *raison d'être* for the existence of the state in which that culture exists.[109]

On the surface, a linguist challenging the semitic roots of Israeli Hebrew, authors banning Hebrew translations of their literary works, and a Hebrew charter management organization may appear to have little in common. They operate in distinct spheres (academia, publishing, and education), espouse different rationales for their actions, and hold divergent views on Israel. Yet when examined together, these cases illuminate how beliefs about Hebrew become entangled with broader positions about Jewish history, Israel, and Jewish culture. Arguably, they are all playing in the same proverbial Hebrew sandbox as they disentangle and decontextualize Hebrew from its associations with Judaism, Jews, and Israel. Zuckermann, using the tools of his scholarly discipline, contests a Hebrew language ideology that underwrites narratives of Hebrew and Jewish revival. For Rooney and other authors who disavow Hebrew translation, disentangling Hebrew from Judaism while maintaining its attachment to Israel offers a public forum to criticize Israel's policies toward Palestinians and engage in Boycott, Divestment, and Sanctions activities while avoiding being seen as antisemitic. And for Hebrew charter school leadership, detaching Hebrew from Judaism while promoting a connection with Israel reimagines Hebrew as a modern universal language that is similar to other world languages taught in American public schools. Notably, these three positions challenge the *a priori* link among Hebrew, Judaism, and Israel that other Hebrew ideologies work assiduously to create and preserve. The decontextualization at work here demonstrates the symbolic malleability of Hebrew and, more broadly, the flexibility of language ideologies themselves. As symbolically fungible resources, they can be mobilized to advance a wide range of scholarly, educational, political, and cultural agendas.

Zooming In

This chapter maps a set of Hebrew language ideologies circulating within contemporary American Jewish discourse. What may initially appear as surface-level debates about language often function, on closer examination, as proxies for broader anxieties and aspirations—concerning Jewish peoplehood, homeland–diaspora relations, communal continuity, and perceived deficiencies in Jewish knowledge and education. Exploring these ideologies reveals the symbolic power of talk about Hebrew as a defining characteristic of American Jewish identity. While a dominant narrative suggests that Hebrew is largely absent from American Jewish life, the sheer volume of discourse devoted to lamenting this absence suggests otherwise. Indeed, it may be more accurate to say that discussions about the lack of Hebrew are among the most prominent conversations shaping American Jewish communal discourse. Surveys that document declining Hebrew literacy, debates over the cultural and political risks of translation, critiques of Hebrew education, and claims of American Jewish uninterest in the language contribute to a discursive ecosystem in which Hebrew serves as a touchstone for emotive, moral, and political judgments about the state of American Jewry. Talk about Hebrew, when seen in this way, does not merely reflect communal concerns. It actively produces and sustains them. This understanding expands on the notion of Hebrew as a "flexible signifier" by showing how discourse about the language helps constitute what it means to be Jewish in twenty-first-century America.[110]

While these broader ideological frameworks are essential for understanding communal discourse, they raise a second, equally important, question. How do individual American Jewish adults experience and understand Hebrew in their everyday lives? It is one thing to analyze abstract and institutional narratives about Hebrew. It is quite another to explore how individuals engaged in Hebrew activities internalize, negotiate, and understand these ideologies. Recognizing the force of Hebrew language ideologies makes it all the more necessary to examine the lived experiences of American Hebrew users. Do they perceive themselves as combatting Hebrew illiteracy? Do they view their efforts as contributions to Jewish peoplehood or as part of a broader project of diaspora–Israel repair? Do they approach Hebrew primarily through spiritual, cultural, political, or affective lenses? The next three chapters take up these questions by focusing on Hebrew enthusiasts, defined as adults who engage with Hebrew learning across a range of settings. This closer examination complicates prevailing narratives that American Jews are uninterested in Hebrew or that the language holds only ritual or ceremonial value. Instead, it reveals a wide array of personal meanings that individuals attach to their Hebrew pursuits and that speak directly to how they understand their Jewish identities.

3

CHOOSING TO BE A HEBREW ENTHUSIAST

On a cold weekday evening during the winter of 2020, I sat down in front of my computer screen in my home and logged on to the Cheder Ivrit (Hebrew Room) Zoom call, where I was greeted by twelve other participants joining from their homes in Long Island, New York City, and Florida.[1] Cheder Ivrit originated as a Hebrew adult education class offered at a New York City synagogue. Years later, it had evolved into an independent group, affiliated with the synagogue but open to anyone who wanted to participate in monthly Hebrew meetups. Run by a professional Hebrew teacher for many years, the free weekly classes were at the time of my participation organized by a long-time member who scheduled the dates and sent out reminders. Though the group had at one time used a coursebook, they now relied on ad hoc material including YouTube videos, stories, songs, and newspaper articles. Rotating responsibility, members of the group took turns preparing and running the class. During the COVID pandemic, the group met over Zoom, where once a month anywhere between six and fifteen members gathered for approximately ninety minutes to speak and improve their Hebrew.

While all the participants self-identified as Jewish, this was a diverse group of individuals with different levels of Jewish education, Hebrew learning, and religious affiliation and observance. The majority of the participants in Cheder Ivrit were mostly between fifty and seventy years old, though occasionally a twenty- or thirty-year-old participant would join. Many had been part of the group for years, some since its inception in the early 2000s. Others had heard about it through word of mouth, which is how I became aware of it. Like many people looking to take advantage of online learning opportunities that the pandemic afforded, I appreciated the balance of formality and informality that characterized these monthly meetings. One tacit rule was a Hebrew-only policy; if participants started using English, others in the group would gently rebuke them and remind them to speak in Hebrew. The meetings also followed a pattern, usually starting with about five minutes of small talk while everyone logged on. Once everyone had chit-chatted for a few minutes, the volunteer organizer presented a Hebrew text, which included short stories, dialogues, song lyrics, poetry, and simplified news articles. Participants took turns reading out loud and clarifying new words or expressions for each other.

On this particular night in December, Sarah, a woman in her sixties from Manhattan, shared a stanza of Hayyim Nahman Bialik's "Ha-Brekha" (The Pool).[2] Though we had read several contemporary poems in the past, reading Bialik was difficult—a fact that should not be surprising to anyone who has ever tried to read his poetry. Written in 1905, when Bialik was living in the Russian empire and the revival of Modern Hebrew was still in its infancy, "The Pool" did not use contemporary Israeli Hebrew. Rather, it was written in a literary form Bialik developed based on his extensive knowledge of the Jewish canon of sacred texts and folklore.[3] In addition to the complex form in which the poem was written, the content of "The Pool" was conceptually challenging. Presenting a prelapsarian world untouched by modernity, the poem grapples with the notion of innocence, the wonder of childhood, and the perplexity of beauty. It is, in short, not a poem for the weak of heart. Even for the Cheder Ivrit highly motivated learners, reading "The Pool" proved to be a daunting endeavor.

Sarah nonetheless was undeterred. Speaking in what could be described as intermediate-advanced Hebrew, she provided a short biography of Bialik, which included his title as the "national poet of Israel." She then called on someone to begin reading the first line of a stanza out loud.[4] We continued in this fashion, taking turns reading each line in Hebrew and translating the words into other known Hebrew words. Once we had gone over each individual word, we moved on to making sense of the stanza as a whole. However, the transition from decontextualized reading to holistic analysis was tough. At one point when we were struggling over the meaning of one line, I thought it might be helpful to ask my spouse, Yuval, who had been raised and educated in Israel, to assist us. Had I put on my educator hat (from my days of teaching English to immigrant populations) and thought about all the times I had argued that simply knowing a language does not make a person into a language teacher, I probably should have seen the folly of this plan. But my excitement got the better of me. Yuval, to his credit, saw red flags as soon as he learned we were reading Bialik. While he was game to help, very quickly we realized that his Israeli Hebrew was not going to help us unlock the poem's meaning. Yuval corrected a few of our translation errors but also struggled with the meaning of some of the archaic Hebrew words, and at some point left us to our own devices.

Despite these challenges, we persisted for about another thirty-five minutes until we had reached some semblance of understanding of this poem. If nothing else, we retained a sense of humor. One participant riposted, "That was great. I didn't really understand the poem, but I now know the Hebrew word for *spawn*, which I am sure one day will come in handy." With only a few minutes left in the class, we discussed the logistics of the next meeting and parted at around 8:30 PM. Immediately after logging off, I was surprised by my own feelings about what had transpired. Most noticeably, I was exhausted but felt I had participated in a meaningful, rewarding, and enjoyable activity. At the same time I was struck by the structure of the activity we had engaged in. The methodology we had utilized was a traditional—some may even say old-fashioned—approach to language learning which had us translating each word individually. It reminded me of the *lernen* (Yiddish: ritualized study of sacred texts) that anthropologist Samuel Heilman richly described in his research at an adult Talmud study circle in New York.[5] Observing how the all-male study partners followed a pattern of recitation, translation, explanation, and discussion, Heilman noted that this interactional routine created a Jewish fellowship. When I reached out to one of the participants to hear her thoughts several days after the Cheder Ivrit class, she noted that learning about this poem had entailed a strong social dimension. After joking that neither of us could recall the word for *spawn*, she expressed a strong appreciation for the sense of bonding she had experienced. "I don't know what others thought," she said, but "this is my way of being Jewish, and it brought up all kinds of feelings and memories of being part of Jewish tradition and heritage."

What on the surface may have encompassed Hebrew learning focused on the acquisition of vocabulary words revealed itself as a space in which individuals could connect to their Jewish selves *through* and *in* Hebrew. Success determined by the comprehension of the poem and the retention of new words was secondary to the affective response that evoked a feeling of Jewish collectivity.

What would Bialik have thought of Cheder Ivrit? Perhaps a poet like Bialik, who was deeply concerned with representations of the real and imaginary, might have been tickled by a technology like Zoom, which blends the virtual and the actual. Perhaps he might have been perplexed seeing his words taken so literally, given that he prioritized the form of poetry over prose. Perhaps he would have been fascinated by a group of non-Orthodox Jews grappling with the tension between the Jewish religious tradition and the encroachment of the modern and secular world—a theme of many of his poems.[6] Or maybe seeing American Jews electively choosing to read an Israeli cultural figure would have flummoxed him, given his fears of assimilation in the diaspora. This is, after all, the person who lambasted diaspora Jews who thought they could live outside Israel and still be Zionists.[7] Yet here was a group of diaspora Jewish adults valuing the Hebrew language, the only language he believed could "serve as the foundation and root" of Jewish life.[8] Perhaps as someone who moved at the age of fifty-one to Tel Aviv (in 1924) and who wrote in a language not his own, Bialik would have found fellowship with other adult diasporans reading and talking about literature in a language not their own and intentionally avoiding the use of an English translation.[9] I would like to think that, if nothing else, his belief that language was the "only replacement for religion in a post-religious world" may have led him to appreciate that a group of self-guided and self-motivated American Jews came together around Hebrew.[10]

These speculations aside, my Cheder Ivrit peers provided a new lens for thinking about American Jews' relationship to Hebrew. While so much of the scholarship on language learning focuses on the goal of acquisition for instrumental purposes, this was not the motivating force here. These learners had electively chosen to take on this activity. Nobody was forcing them to take on this challenge, especially when outside of this classroom these efforts offered them minimal, if any, social or linguistic capital. Captivated by their efforts, I set out to explore their and other adult Hebrew learners' personal stories that propelled them to learn Hebrew and understand how they did it and why. Simply put, I wanted to know who they were, why they were doing this, and what it meant to them as American Jews (if anything at all). Examining their learning trajectories, motivations, and aspirations could, I believe, help me to better understand what Hebrew language ideologies looked like on the ground and to better see what type of work Hebrew did for them as American Jews. It is one thing for a Jewish communal figure, journalist, or educator to say that Hebrew is the language of Jewish peoplehood or connects American Jews to Israeli culture. It is quite another to explore how (and if) these ideologies manifest in individuals' everyday Hebrew practices. At the same time, analyzing individual adults like those I met in Cheder Ivrit offered a refutation of the dominant assumption that American Jews are not interested in Hebrew and that the language is widely absent from the American context. The Cheder Ivrit participants that winter evening could have been binging a new television series, cleaning their houses, scrolling their social media feeds, or simply doing nothing at all. But they made a different choice. With this affirmative choice in mind, this chapter carves out a new way of thinking about the meaning Hebrew holds for those who choose to learn and practice it.

Defining the Hebrew Enthusiast

This chapter spotlights a broad array of American Jewish adults who actively, intentionally, and voluntarily facilitate and seek out opportunities for Hebrew engagement. I think of the individuals I depict in this chapter as a subset of the "Hebraists by choice" that literary scholars Naomi Sokoloff and Nancy Berg refer to in their smartly titled edited collection, *What We Talk About When We Talk About Hebrew (and What It Means to Americans)*.[11] In contrast to Sokoloff and Berg's focus on scholars, intellectuals, and writers, this chapter centers people I refer to as Hebrew enthusiasts. Importantly, they are not culture makers or brokers. They are not Hebraists in the mold of the Hebraist movement of the early twentieth century. Rather they are ordinary people involved in a range of individual and group-centered Hebrew advancement activities. For the sake of cohesiveness, I define a Hebrew enthusiast in this book as an individual over the age of twenty-one who does not need to know Hebrew for work-related purposes; who is studying Hebrew outside a university credit-bearing undergraduate or graduate program; who is not being raised in Israel or by Israeli Hebrew-speaking parents; and who is not planning to move to Israel.[12] When I described these criteria to others, I was often told that I was searching for *meshugayim l'devar*, a term that roughly translates as people who are overly crazy about something. This classification did not go unnoticed by those who were identified as such. One interviewee gleefully admitted that "you have to be a bit crazy to decide to do this," especially because he identified as a "non-observant and not religious Jew." Humor notwithstanding, this individual's comment underscores a point that Sokoloff and Berg emphasize with their semantically loaded modifier "by choice." While an argument can be made that some knowledge of Textual Hebrew is needed to participate in Jewish religious rituals, it is much harder to claim that American Jews must know Modern Hebrew to participate in American Jewish life. A driving goal of this chapter is to unpack the meaning of choice by putting the spotlight on ordinary American Jewish adults' lived experiences with and beliefs about Hebrew. Taking up Sokoloff and Berg's call to uncover the "challenges and joys of being a Hebraist in America in the twenty-first-century," I center my analysis on choice—how and why people decide to make Hebrew a meaningful part of their lives.[13]

Taking this approach aligns with historian Riv-Ellen Prell's call for a qualitative approach to the study of Jewish identity that turns "away from the great social categories of social science inquiry and toward the specificity of local and life course experience." Doing so, I looked to "the study of the construction of Jewishness in personal narratives."[14] Language narratives (also called language memoirs) serve as a window into seeing individuals' Hebrew engagement as a form of religious life, which includes textual and cultural dimensions of Judaism. If social scientists of religion have tended to define their object of study in terms of religious traditions and rituals (especially those occurring within houses of worship), frameworks of "lived religion" demonstrate how individuals imbue the routine and unexpected aspects of their lives with religious and spiritual meaning through everyday actions, interactions, and language. Crucially, while people may identify some Hebrew actions as explicitly religious, this perspective also makes space for routine or unanticipated practices that might not immediately be recognized as such, lending a more capacious definition to what counts as Jewish experience and practice. In this way, their talk about their relationship with Hebrew places them "as narrators and interpreters (and reinterpreters) of their own experiences and histories"—which include their connection to textual and modern forms of Hebrew and different components of Judaism.[15]

Importantly, I make no claims that the people with whom I spoke are representative of all the adult Hebrew learners in the United States today. Nor do I believe that my study reached all adult elective Hebrew classes or meetups. I am under no illusions that the Hebrew enthusiasts featured in this book represent a majority of American Jews. To be clear, I believe they represent a small subset of what is already a minority group in the United States. Indeed, the people I got to know think deeply and self-consciously about the Hebrew language as a component of their lives, which makes them distinct from the majority of American Jews who spend little to no time learning or using Hebrew. Nonetheless, exploring their Hebrew narratives is revelatory and important because their lived Hebrew experiences emerge out of their relations with institutions, personal histories and experiences, and the times and contexts in which their learning is experienced. Shining a spotlight on these individuals offers a more nuanced picture of American Jewish adults' needs, interests, and concerns, and pushes us to attend to the elective, leisurely, and, at times, messy and unstructured ways in which they learn and find Jewish meaning in their lives.[16]

With this in mind, this chapter gives voice to individuals' Hebrew experiences as an expression of their Jewishness—as they define it. Doing so, it offers a textured representation of what Hebrew does for individuals who seek to learn and engage with the language, and how this relationship has changed over the course of their lives. Centering language narratives proved beneficial in several ways. First, the open-ended nature of the interviews gave people an opportunity (often for the first time) to articulate their Hebrew ideologies. Many welcomed the opportunity to talk about a topic they loved, but one they often felt was not of interest to others. Second, talk about how and why they chose to learn Hebrew led to discussions about the people who came in and out of their lives, including parents, roommates, spouses, teachers, rabbis, friends, children, romantic partners, and colleagues, as well as trips they took, institutions they encountered, and experiences they had. What emerged clearly from these conversations is that Hebrew learning is embedded in a web of relationships, encounters, and social worlds that shape its meaning and significance for the learner. Their stories reveal that they think deeply about the Hebrew language, despite previous less-than-ideal experiences with the language in their youth and despite the low status of Hebrew in the broader American context and specifically among American Jews. They are the exceptions to the rule in many ways, but also show how a language can become meaningful at different points of one's life. Finally, Hebrew language narratives surfaced alternative perspectives regarding definitions of Hebrew learning success. When they spoke about their desired Hebrew goals, they did not always prioritize fluency or mastery. Rather, they identified a host of nonlinguistic goals that were equally if not more important in the spiritual, religious, and social role of Hebrew. Understanding people's practices and overlapping objectives helps to build a more robust picture of what Hebrew means to them.

In Search of Hebrew Enthusiasts

I would like to be able to say that the idea to study adult Hebrew learners was always in the cards, but in fact the impetus to this project started with a selfish desire to maintain the conversational Hebrew I had acquired when I lived in Israel in the 1990s. Simply put, I wanted to halt my Hebrew attrition and started to search out Hebrew enrichment opportunities. My first course of action was to purchase a bunch of novels by popular Israeli authors; however, the sense of guilt I got when I stared at these books was similar to how I felt when I looked at the collection of *New Yorker* magazines amassed in my living room: I felt good about having them but was aware that I would most likely not make full use of them. I then turned to listening to Hebrew podcasts on high- and lowbrow topics and watching Israeli television shows and movies. Yet I still missed interacting with others. Going online to see if there were any Hebrew classes nearby, I ended up speaking with Doron Friedman, a professor of Hebrew education at Hunter College (CUNY), who invited me to audit his advanced Hebrew class in the fall of 2019. At first I was so focused on my learning that I did not pay attention to my classmates or what they were doing during the lessons. However, I slowly noticed there were two types of students in the class. The first category consisted of the matriculated undergraduates—mostly young adults who came to class with enormous cups of coffee and earbuds in their ears. They peppered Doron with questions about assignments, due dates, and grades. The second category of students were the "auditors"—people mostly over the age of fifty who were taking the class for no credit. When they sat down, they took out their hard-copy dictionaries and notebooks and diligently wrote down every word Doron put on the board. They also insisted on speaking only in Hebrew.

As I was leaving Doron's classroom one afternoon, I walked to the stairs with Marjorie, a woman in her early sixties, whom I immediately bonded with over our mutual enjoyment of the class. Between the time it took us to dash through the crowded corridors of the Hunter East building, go down the escalators, and walk out to Lexington Avenue, I had learned about some of the other Hebrew ad hoc and formal groups she had attended, her extensive and rigorous study routines, and her excitement to speak with others in Hebrew. Outside of these venues, she had no family or friends with whom she could practice. Watching her face light up as she told me about her Hebrew interest, I realized I was hearing a story that was largely absent from the Hebrew education scholarship, which is widely focused on children and young adults.[17] When I told a colleague that I was thinking about starting a project exploring the motivations and experiences of American Jewish adults who were passionate about Modern Hebrew, her sardonic response that I would be done with data collection "in a week, maybe two at most" spoke volumes about the assumptive framework of American Jews and Hebrew. She was not the only one who thought the idea of the elective Hebrew learner was an oxymoron.

I was not dissuaded. Several weeks later I conducted my first open-ended interview with Sally, another student in the Hunter class, in which I asked her to tell me about her relationship to Hebrew. From the start she was thrilled to share her story, repeating several times that nobody had ever asked her about this before—a refrain I heard from many others as well over the course of the next two years. When Sally asked me whether I wanted to speak with others like her, my interest was piqued. My initial hope was that I would find fifteen or so people to interview during the winter and spring of 2020. Little did I know that my small sample would snowball the way it did. Much like the popular 1980s Faberge Organics Shampoo television commercial, each interviewee told two people, and soon enough people were contacting me to tell me their stories. By early February 2020 I had already surpassed my modest goals. When the COVID pandemic hit in mid-March 2020, I thought I would need to indefinitely pause the study. However, exactly the opposite occurred. Because people had extra time as they hunkered down at home, I was able to talk with a lot of people, many of whom were outside New York City. An added benefit of doing interviews over Zoom was that I had access to another dimension of these individuals' lives. I saw their artwork and family photos on the walls, as well as the books and tchotchkes on their bookshelves. I saw them sitting at their kitchen tables, making dinner, petting their dogs, and eating snacks. I don't know if it was because people were in the comfort of their own homes, needed an escape from the never-ending dire news coverage, or simply enjoyed talking about Hebrew, but many interviews lasted more than an hour.

Between April 2020 and the end of 2021, I conducted an additional one hundred interviews, which resulted in close to 115 interviews overall.[18] The depth of these interactions varied. While I spoke to some people multiple times, I met most only once. The interviews typically followed the same pattern. After I verified that the consent forms had been signed and returned, I asked interviewees about their prior Jewish learning experiences. At first I tried to slow down the interviewees so I could ask what I thought were the "important" demographic questions. Quickly I came to understand that I could not separate their present-day Hebrew-learning motivations from their histories and memories, as if the former were somehow a bounded activity in time and space. I complemented these interviews with discussions with Hebrew stakeholders, including instructors at Hebrew language schools, Hebrew educational scholars, creators and publishers of Hebrew language material, and producers of Hebrew teaching podcasts and YouTube videos. In addition, I was able to participate in several ongoing learning and meetup groups, which went online as a result of the pandemic lockdown. Taken together, the extensive outreach put me in conversation with a broad array of Hebrew enthusiasts and those who support their efforts.

Though I refer to people in this book as Hebrew enthusiasts, this category should not be taken as a description of a centralized, monolithic, or organized group. In truth, the more American Jews I interviewed, the more I realized how different many of them were—with the sole link being their interest in knowing and using Modern Hebrew. Outside of this shared passion, they were highly diffused and did not necessarily see themselves as belonging to a larger community of practice. While many of the Hebrew enthusiasts I spoke to certainly fit the mold of being Ashkenazi, middle and upper class, and well educated, not all were in this demographic. I also spoke with people who had Mizrahi and Sephardi heritage and some from working-class socioeconomic status. Among the Ashkenazi participants there was a great deal of diversity across other categories. They varied by Jewish upbringing and identification, geography, gender and sexual identification, health, and political affiliation. Seven identified as LGBTQ, three were Jews by choice, and two identified as Jews of color. They included recent university graduates, stay-at-home parents, home contractors, real estate agents, artists, attorneys, physicians, educators, scientists, and those who were unemployed. Some were retired, semi-retired, or at the stage of their lives when their own children were college students or no longer living with them. The youngest person was twenty-four and the oldest was eighty-three years old, with baby boomers and Gen Xers representing the majority. Those being at a later stage of life had fewer demands on their time and could indulge in elective leisure activities like language learning. In addition to having the precious resource of time, many of the older participants had the financial resources to pay for in-person or online Hebrew classes, hire private Hebrew tutors, purchase subscriptions to Hebrew learning printed material or online apps, and attend meetups at local cafes that offered space to the group in exchange for the purchase of a refreshment. Not surprisingly, given the career and familial demands of building careers and raising children, there were fewer Gen Z participants. Nonetheless, their presence among those I spoke with was critical to understanding the changing nature of knowing Hebrew across generations of American Jews.[19]

Finding Hebrew

Once a person decided to study Hebrew, it was not always clear how to start. Even those who lived in urban centers with robust Jewish communities spoke about the difficulty of finding opportunities to learn Hebrew. John, a self-described "very not practicing Jew" from New York City, wanted to learn Modern Hebrew despite learning only Biblical Hebrew as a young boy at his local synagogue in upstate New York in the late 1970s. His first inclination to purchase some books on Amazon proved foolhardy when he realized the books were not teaching colloquial Modern Hebrew but rather Biblical Hebrew. Jokingly, he told me he learned to say things like "My slave waits for me in front of the gate," but he did not know how to say "Where's the bathroom?" Thinking the best approach was asking a rabbi for some guidance, he turned to his local Chabad synagogue near his home in Brooklyn. There, he recalled, the rabbi was more interested in teaching him to don *tefillin* than to speak Hebrew. "Modern Hebrew is nice," he recalled the rabbi telling him, "but it's not important because it's not going to further the *moshiach* [Messiah] coming." Not discouraged, John spoke with a friend who did Jewish communal work; he explained to John the different contexts in which Hebrew is used and recommended finding an *ulpan* (intensive language course in Modern Hebrew), a suggestion that surprised John because he did not realize that the Hebrew he had learned for his bar mitzvah as a boy was not the spoken vernacular. Typing "*ulpan* and New York City" into the search engine on his laptop led him to a few sites for *ulpan* classes that "looked promising." John was extremely satisfied with the *ulpan* he ultimately landed on, but this happy ending highlights the layers of complexity he encountered. It also puts in sharp relief how a desire to learn vernacular Hebrew got religionized even when he sought it out nonreligiously. Crucially, John learned the difference between textual and modern forms of the language, and that each variety occupied a different place in Jewish life. Over several months he also interacted with a rabbi and a friend who was a Jewish professional. The persistence John described was not rare; it was a defining trait among many of the participants with whom I spoke. They did extensive research, reached out to others for help, and went through various trials before finding what worked for them. Too often terms like *hobby* or *leisure activity*—which

Hebrew learning certainly was for many—connote a lack of seriousness. These terms, however, when applied to Hebrew enthusiasts, obscure the effort many expended to become Hebrew literate.

Hebrew enthusiasts also grappled with the difficulty of learning a new language. One woman in her late forties who attended a synagogue-sponsored Hebrew-speaking class admitted that learning Hebrew was more mentally taxing than she had anticipated: "I literally get sweaty every time I have to do my homework, like the way I did when I was in high school." This reaction was not that surprising given that many Hebrew enthusiasts had not been in a formal classroom in many years and were trying to reactivate the muscle memory of learning new vocabulary and verb conjugations. As is well documented, language learning can be a cognitive challenge for adults. Studies consistently show that the earlier a person starts to learn an additional language, the easier it is to achieve mastery. In addition, adults contend with a host of noncognitive factors, including feelings of vulnerability over not being able to express oneself articulately in error-free language. On top of this insecurity, learning Hebrew has specific challenges for English speakers because of its right-to-left (RTL) directionality, consonant-based script, and unique orthography. One sixty-three-year-old woman compared learning to speak Hebrew to doing a handstand—two feats she perceived as equally difficult given her age. While many spoke about other leisure activities, such as playing bridge, gardening, and cooking, they put Hebrew learning in a different category from these pursuits. It was, in the words of one Hebrew enthusiast, his "great white whale" in his perception of its difficulty and his ability to learn it.

In addition to perceiving Hebrew as a challenging language to acquire, people associated the Hebrew-learning process with scrappiness and tenacity. Indeed, many who studied independently outside of a classroom context spoke about their doggedness in finding interesting Hebrew material, a search that included exploring local libraries and bookstores, as well poring over online sites. They marshalled a litany of methods, including translating Hebrew newspaper articles, using language-learning apps (e.g., Duolingo and Babbel), listening to Hebrew podcasts, connecting with other learners through apps like HelloTalk and Tandem, and recruiting Israeli friends or relatives to speak with them over FaceTime and WhatsApp. Others took more creative approaches. Barbara, from Los Angeles, told me about working with a private tutor and employing role play to acquire new vocabulary words. It must have been quite a sight to see two middle-aged women jumping up and down in the street in her neighborhood as she learned the word *likfotz* (to jump). In one of our Zoom talks, I saw a stack of popular Hebrew children's books on the kitchen table that she had received from an Israeli acquaintance whose children no longer wanted the books. Bob, a fifty-two-year-old living in New Jersey, shared how he had salvaged a collection of Hebrew nonfiction and fiction books that a synagogue library was throwing out and had pored over them despite their random topics. Someone in Los Angeles proudly shared that she approached Israeli neighbors to ask if they had any Hebrew books being thrown out. These examples underscored the significant efforts people made to locate learning material.

While some Hebrew enthusiasts studied Hebrew on their own, others saw it as part and parcel of a social gathering. In March 2021, I met over Zoom with four women of Chug Ivri, a Hebrew club in Wilmington, Delaware, which the members described as the oldest and longest-running Hebrew club in the United States. Over our hour of conversation, Sylvia Wagman, Faith Brown, Harriet Ainbinder, and Dorothy Flippen delighted me with stories about the club's history and their ongoing involvement over the years. Collectively, they recounted the creation of the club in 1964, when one person was assigned to present a piece in Hebrew at the monthly meetings.[20] The discussion of the text was followed by singing in Hebrew and Yiddish, and then some refreshments. When the group got too big to host at a home, it moved to the Jewish Community Center and continued to meet and grow continuously through the 1960s. Harriet recalled being a young child and listening to her mother, who was an original member, participate in the meetings. According to the women, at one point in the 1960s or early 1970s, the "group kind of disintegrated for a short time" but then was "rejuvenated in our synagogue," where it was open to anyone in the community, including nonmembers. With joy the woman spoke about the consistency of the group in their lives, including raising their children and working and still making time for the gatherings. It was, as one woman indicated, "a constant" in her life even though some members had moved or passed away. When we spoke in early 2021 during the pandemic lockdown, after the group had been forced to move to Zoom, they lamented that this new modality did not allow for refreshments, which was "definitely a downer." Nonetheless, the group, which included Jewish Federation of Delaware leaders and members, *shlichim* (Israeli emissaries), and others, continued to meet.

Café Ivrit, located at the Jewish Community Center in San Diego, was created in 2007. Defined by one member of the group as a "weekly or bi-monthly casual gathering, non-facilitated, just friends who speak some Hebrew gathering for lunch or a coffee," Café Ivrit was open to anyone who wanted to socialize in Hebrew. When we spoke in 2021, Glenda Sacks Jaffe shared with me that the group had occasionally expanded into other activities, such as going to Jewish films together, doing *shira b'tzibur* (public singing of Hebrew folksongs), and cooking Jewish traditional foods. Sacks Jaffe was equally effusive about the sociability the group provided. She was proud that, though most of the members had not been friends prior to joining the group, and had "very different politics about America and Israel," they had become "a really caring group" that over the years had gathered for "surprise parties and shivas," and had always "been there for each other." She was not the only one, she insisted, who planned vacations around the groups' meetings. While the exact number of Hebrew meetup clubs throughout the United States is unknown, these two long-running Hebrew meetup groups offer their participants an opportunity to build and sustain lifelong social networks and friendships around a shared love of Hebrew.[21] It was almost impossible for members to separate the draw of practicing Hebrew from the chance to socialize with old friends. Similar to other types of leisure-based activity clubs (e.g., book clubs and sports groups), these two Hebrew meetups provided community through ritualized get-togethers where members could read a story in Hebrew, catch up with others, and have a nosh. Seen in this way, Hebrew meetup groups offered a "third space" to engage Jewishly in a welcoming and judgment-free context—a topic that is further discussed in Chapter 4.[22] They offered unique spaces for Jews (and the occasional non-Jew) to do a Jewish-centered activity that connected them to each other and to their Jewish heritage.

While I was not surprised to see that Hebrew clubs were spaces of American Jewish conviviality and sociability, I was less prepared to see that these gatherings also attracted Israeli Americans. Elisha Blatt, an Israeli who had lived in the United States for more than twenty years and was an active member of Café Ivrit, rarely missed a meeting and voluntarily assumed the role of preparing comprehension questions and providing translation assistance when needed. Luckily, he took no offense at my asking him why he was involved. "You know," he told me, "it brings me joy. I enjoy the company. I enjoy the people, the camaraderie . . . and it's refreshing and it's fun and I feel that I'm providing them with some good help." If, as many claim, Israeli Americans are often seen as detached from other aspects of American Jewish life and American Jewish institutions, Elisha was a foil to this belief—a fact that he recognized when he noted that he was most likely an exception to the rule.[23] Elisha was not the only Israeli American I encountered in the Hebrew meetup groups. I also met Yoni, an Israeli who had been living in Florida for many years, who participated virtually in a New York City–based Hebrew meetup group during the pandemic lockdown by providing translation, pronunciation, and vocabulary assistance. Like Elisha, Yoni attributed his participation to his enjoyment in getting to know the other members, as well as the opportunity to think about Hebrew in a new way. He got a great deal of satisfaction thinking about "the derivation of words and what the right usage was under certain circumstances," which gave him a greater appreciation for his native tongue.

The Accidental Hebraist

People frequently describe their passion projects as something they were born to do. To be sure, some people I spoke to mentioned that knowing Hebrew was a lifelong dream. But for the most part, this was not the story I heard from Hebrew enthusiasts. Indeed, one of the most common themes was people's genuine surprise and disbelief over their own interest in pursuing this goal. I started to think of this phenomenon as "accidental Hebraists"—people who fortuitously, surprisingly, or unexpectedly found themselves learning Hebrew. Quickly I saw that these unlikely Hebrew enthusiasts' stories were important to tell because they show that a person's relationship to Hebrew is not static, predetermined, or guaranteed. Rather, this relationship takes on different forms over one's life based on experiences, interactions, circumstances—all of which shape and are shaped by notions of one's Jewishness. For this reason, understanding who the "accidental Hebraist" is and what meaning Hebrew holds for them is crucial for telling the broader story of the relationship of American Jews and Hebrew.

For many of the "accidental Hebraists" I met, their first experience learning Hebrew was as young children attending afterschool or weekend Hebrew programs at their local synagogues. Typically, they recalled learning to decode the letters (usually without comprehension) and participating in synagogue services and home rituals. Less common were those who attended yeshivas or day schools where they studied Jewish sacred texts or had some exposure to Modern Hebrew. With a few exceptions, the majority talked about these childhood Hebrew memories as unremarkable, uninspiring, unsatisfactory, or downright terrible. Marc, a student at a well-known New York City yeshiva in the 1980s, recalled that his Hebrew teacher was so "horrendous" that he was "still the butt of many a joke amongst my old high school classmates." Notwithstanding this experience, when Marc saw an announcement about a Hebrew-speaking class on the bulletin board of his local Conservative synagogue, he decided to sign up. Much to his surprise, the class "was really good." Thirty-five years after a negative Hebrew learning experience, Marc eagerly participated in his monthly Hebrew class. Lisa, a forty-eight-year-old woman, echoed that being a middle-aged Hebrew learner was not something she would have ever imagined, given "a not very positive experience with Hebrew education" as a child. Unlike Marc, Lisa did not blame the teacher of her childhood class for her dismal experience. The problem, she told me, was the other students' lack of discipline and motivation. As "someone who wanted to learn," Lisa was stymied by "all the kids disrupting the teacher." As a result, she "never really learned anything except for how to read Hebrew and about the same holidays year after year."

If Marc and Lisa recalled negative memories of childhood Hebrew learning experiences, there were also those who had little to no exposure to Hebrew in their youth—a reality that made their undertaking Hebrew classes as adults even more surprising to them. Brian, who grew up attending a Reform synagogue that did not teach Hebrew, became interested in the language after his marriage to an observant woman and their involvement in a Conservative synagogue that offered Hebrew classes as part of its adult education programming. For Liz, a twenty-eight-year-old woman, nothing in her childhood prepared her for becoming a Hebrew enthusiast. Despite her attending a synagogue-based program on Sunday mornings for more than eight years and participating in Birthright as a college student, it was only when she started working in social media operations at a Jewish organization that she became interested in Hebrew. Kevin, a seventy-year-old former government worker, told me that while his first introduction to Hebrew was as a study-abroad student at Hebrew University as an undergraduate, being in Israel at that time did not jumpstart an interest in the language. With "absolutely, or virtually no contact with Hebrew from the age of twenty," it was not until he watched an episode of *Fauda*—an Israeli series available on a popular streaming channel—that he found himself drawn to the language. Barry, a gay man living in New York City, recalled that his initial exposure to the language on a two-week trip to Israel in 1980 was disheartening: "It was hot and the people were not to my liking . . . I didn't understand what was Jewish about it . . . I just didn't like it." In 2014, however, a childhood friend convinced him to return and picked a tour that focused on gay life in Tel Aviv. Barry remembered thinking: "Oh, my god, I don't really want to take an LGBT tour to any place, and I don't really want to go back to Israel." However, he acquiesced and surprisingly met "a neat group of people." After returning to Israel the following year, he decided to learn the language, which led him to take a series of Hebrew classes in the States and in Israel.

Not everyone became an accidental Hebraist through an explicit interest in Hebrew. Maya, from a suburb of New York City, made her way to Hebrew when her non-Jewish roommate at Syracuse University in the early 1980s invited her to the Israeli folk-dancing club. Falling in love with the dance genre, Maya found herself frequently humming the Hebrew songs played during the dances. At the age of twenty-four, with no idea what to do with her life and seeing her friends go off to graduate school or start careers, Maya heard about "a place in Israel where you can pick fruit there and they'll give you a place to stay." She jumped on the opportunity. "Looking back on it I realize that if Romania had a program where you could pick fruit and it would give you a place to stay, I would have gone to Romania. But as it was, it was Israel." "Out of desperation for some sort of structure in my life," she found herself in Hebrew classes, studying "four hours a day, six days a week, for five and a half months." Maya quickly became "hooked on the language." Nothing about her adult ongoing interest in Hebrew was predetermined or expected. Rather it was a chance encounter with Israeli culture at an American college campus that resulted in Maya becoming a Hebrew enthusiast.

Like Maya, Barbara, a twenty-nine-year-old woman originally from the Panhandle area of rural Florida, found her way to Hebrew through other interests. Raised Christian and educated at Catholic schools, Barbara described her childhood religious education as "going through the motions" and not "ever really believing it [Christianity theology]." By the time she had reached her undergraduate studies at a university in Florida, she described herself as "probably more of an atheist agnostic." As a history major, she took a history course on Europe and learned about Jews in medieval Spain. Her budding interest in minority diasporas led her to write her undergraduate thesis on émigré literature and exiles in Berlin during the interwar period. "I was just fascinated about what that means to one's identity to not ever feel at home," she told me. On the advice of her history professor, she delved into the topic of Jewish diasporism, despite not being sure if she "had ever really even met someone who was Jewish." At school she befriended a woman, Sarah, from Miami, who became her "first Jewish friend." Barbara started to learn more about "this other monotheistic religion" and "this peculiar language" Jews used for religious rituals and conversations.

Wanting to pursue a graduate degree in modern European history and the Bauhaus movement, Barbara followed the suggestion of a professor and landed at a Jewish studies department that had faculty with expertise on both of these topics. "I ended up kind of essentially getting my master's in Jewish history," as she wrote her thesis on the development of Tel Aviv, Bauhaus, and the Zionist movement. Scholarly funding brought her to do archival research in Tel Aviv, where she toyed with the idea of writing about the city's first mayor, Meir Dizengoff. It was during this time that she was required to take an intensive one-month Hebrew course as part of her studies: "I just remember being like, I'm never going to be able to know this language. I don't know if I'll ever be able to figure it out. . . . I just remember it being so hard." Despite having learned other languages, Barbara felt that Hebrew was "a whole different ballgame." After finishing her graduate degree, she moved to New

York, and on her way to a work trip to Europe, she extended her travels to go to Israel to catch up with a university friend. What was originally planned as a short trip changed her life trajectory. At a dinner with her friend in Tel Aviv, she met an Israeli man living in New York who was "a friend of a friend of a friend." The rest of the story was much like a Hallmark Channel rom-com: "We hit it off and started dating immediately." Their relationship was "just like full circle, back to me having to learn Hebrew" at an intensive Hebrew program offered in New York City. She thought to herself: "I'm dating an Israeli . . . and it's non-negotiable. I need to know this language as soon as possible." Within the span of ten years, Barbara went from not being sure if she had ever met a Jewish person to converting to Judaism, marrying an Israeli, and becoming a Hebrew enthusiast.

Finally, John, a fifty-four-year-old man from the New York metro area, became an accidental Hebraist as a result of his interest in sacred texts. Having memorized his *haftorah* (a selection from the biblical book Prophets) as a teenager for his bar mitzvah, John did not have any interest in Hebrew or Judaism for almost forty years. "The last time I was in a synagogue was when I was in law school, and I found the whole thing so uninteresting that I never went back and I didn't miss it." However, about three years prior to our talk, he had undergone a transformative experience when, one day watching YouTube videos, he came across Jordan Peterson's Biblical Series videos. Peterson, a Canadian clinical psychologist, YouTube personality, and author, engrossed John, who had studied philosophy as an undergraduate student, through his appeals to understanding humanity through Bible study. After diving into stories in Genesis, John began attending lectures and reading the online material offered by Tikvah, an American philanthropic foundation whose mission is to explore and promote "the enduring riches of Jewish, Zionist, and American civilization." The more John read, the more he realized that "Hebrew was what ties it all together" and that "without the Hebrew, you don't really understand a lot of the stuff." From this John concluded that "if you want to be Jewish, if you want to think of yourselves as Jewish, you have to understand Hebrew, because it's what pulls it all together. It's the language of our people." A random video popping up in John's YouTube feed led to a sequence of events which resulted in his seeing the centrality of Hebrew in Jewish life. If the YouTube algorithm had presented different options, or if John had not clicked on the link, it is likely John would not have started studying Hebrew.

What do the stories of these accidental Hebraists reveal about the relationship between American Jews and the Hebrew language? First, they underscore the variability and fluidity of individual orientations toward Hebrew over the life course. These accounts challenge the prevailing assumption that early, often negative, experiences with Hebrew, particularly in childhood Jewish educational school settings, irrevocably shape one's disposition toward the language. Rather than being fixed, linguistic attachments are shown here to be malleable and subject to change, often shaped by a confluence of unpredictable and personal circumstances. Second, these language narratives also complicate the notion that language acquisition trajectories are primarily determined by formal instruction or long-term planning. In contrast, the individuals profiled here often came to Hebrew through idiosyncratic routes, marked by unexpected turns, serendipitous encounters, and contingent life events. While such developments might be dismissed as merely coincidental and therefore unimportant, a more productive reading interprets them as evidence of Hebrew's latent potential to resonate at various moments in an individual's life and to draw people in as a result of a variety of social, intellectual, or emotional factors. As these language biographies make clear, there is no single path to Hebrew engagement. The journeys are rarely linear; they are full of false starts, detours, and serendipity. And yet, at some point, each individual made a deliberate, agentive choice to embrace Hebrew as part of their identity. This messiness—the unpredictability and individuality of each story—is not a weakness in the data, but one of its most revealing aspects. In the zigs and zags, we see glimpses of the processes by which Hebrew becomes meaningful.

Had these individuals been asked earlier in life whether they envisioned themselves watching Hebrew-language YouTube content, listening to Hebrew podcasts, or attending midweek Hebrew meetups, they likely would have responded with skepticism, if not amusement. Yet, as their stories attest, they took on these practices because Hebrew fulfilled an intellectual, social, or affective need that prompted sustained engagement. In doing so, Hebrew became a vehicle for identity formation. Ultimately these narratives remind us that choosing to learn Hebrew is more than a hobby; it is a meaning-making project. But while these stories highlight the *how* of Hebrew learning, they leave open important questions about the *why*: What meaning does Hebrew hold for these individuals? What motivates their persistence? What do they hope to gain from it? The next section explores these questions by examining the goals and aspirations that animate Hebrew enthusiasts.

Ambiguous Objectives

"Why am I so into Hebrew and love it so much? I'm not really sure, to tell you the truth, because I know I will never really be great. But you know, that's completely okay because it's not about being a great speaker. It's about something else—something I cannot really explain." These thoughts were shared with me toward the end of a Zoom call one evening in May 2021. Ruth, a woman in her late fifties, lit up when she spoke about all the Hebrew "stuff" she did, including deciphering articles from an online Hebrew newspaper simplified for learners, watching Israeli television clips made for children on YouTube, and meeting with a fellow Hebrew-learning friend once a month for an hourlong Hebrew-only discussion. I had met many people who left me in awe of their efforts, but Ruth stood out because of the paradox she represented. Despite her passion for learning Hebrew, her goal was not communicative fluency. Ruth did not perceive linguistic mastery as a metric of her Hebrew success. To be honest, my talk with Ruth confused me: It was unclear why she spent so much energy learning a language if she did not have any desire to excel and be near or fully fluent. Listening to others talk about their Hebrew goals, I came to see that Ruth was not an anomaly. To be clear, they were not seeking to learn a few token words as a symbol of their Jewish identity—what linguist Lewis Glinert refers to as "smatteracy."[24] Indeed, they wanted to speak, read, and listen to Hebrew. The twist was they were not necessarily driven by the goal of linguistic mastery.

Foundational scholarship in the field of Second Language Acquisition (SLA) has long been concerned with defining and theorizing motivation.[25] Indeed, many researchers would argue that early SLA theorists, particularly during the late 1960s and early 1970s, were preoccupied with the question of what compels individuals to learn additional languages. This preoccupation is reflected in early motivational models, which typically posited two primary orientations: an integrative motivation, characterized by a desire to affiliate with speakers of the target language, and an instrumental motivation, oriented toward utilitarian goals such as employment or educational advancement. By the 1980s, SLA scholars began incorporating more nuanced contextual variables into their models. Yet the primacy of fluency in written and spoken language remained a persistent assumption across these frameworks. As a result, a central tenet of SLA remains that successful acquisition is marked by linear, incremental progress along a continuum from beginner to advanced levels of linguistic and pragmatic competence. Language learning is thus often conceptualized as a skill-based trajectory, akin to ascending a ziggurat in which discrete competencies are mastered progressively.

Against this backdrop, Ruth's account presents a notable incongruity. If she was not motivated by the aspiration to achieve linguistic mastery, what, then, sustained her engagement with Hebrew? Her story, along with those of others who expressed similar sentiments, points to motivational dynamics that elude conventional SLA paradigms. In particular they suggest that for some American Jews the relationship to Hebrew is driven by forces not adequately captured by prevailing models of motivation. This observation was echoed in my conversation with Glinert, who, despite his own lifelong "love affair" with Hebrew, acknowledged that this attachment resists easy classification. "This kind of stuff [Jews and their relationship to Hebrew] doesn't go down very well in the standard model of sociological interviews [that try to identify motivation]," he remarked. "If you were to give me a choice of, let's say, six factors that might have influenced me [in regard to Hebrew], I could maybe check them and give you a number. But ultimately, it's not a question I can really accurately answer."[26] In other words, the motivational schemas commonly used in SLA research, whether integrative, instrumental, or even more recent notions of investment, fall short of accounting for the complex, and often affectively charged, relationship that some American Jews have with Hebrew. Epiphenomenally, this relationship goes beyond the traditional integrative, instrumental, and investment measures commonly used to talk about language-acquisition goals and invites an expanded theoretical lens that accounts for motivations that are less about communicative competence and more about symbolic resonance, personal meaning, and affective attachment.

This framework begs the question: If the goal was not linguistic mastery, what was Hebrew doing for those most invested in its acquisition? Listening to people speak about their Hebrew-learning goals revealed a range of nuanced meanings. "My goal with Hebrew is not to become fluent," Ellen, a woman in her early fifties, told me in early February 2020 when we met in downtown Manhattan at Café Aroma, a popular coffee chain located throughout Israel, which at the time had a handful of franchises throughout the United States. Once we had ordered our coffee and found a seat, Ellen directed my attention to her large, overstuffed canvas bag full of Hebrew books and heavily marked-up articles from Hebrew newspapers written for beginner levels. Eager to show me what she was currently reading, Ellen pulled out *Ha'arye She'Ahav Toot* (The Lion Who Loved Strawberries), a popular children's board book in Israel. After I told her that I had enjoyed reading this book with my children when they were young, Ellen told me that she would always be at the level of children's storybooks. The ability to advance beyond early childhood literature was not what drove her to spend one to two hours a week studying Hebrew. That goal, she told me, "has never been what it is all about."

The ambiguity of the referent of "it" reverberated across interviews I conducted, and it became clear that individuals were driven by a range of "it" motivations. For some, the "it" was wrapped up in nonlinguistic factors, including the sociability and conviviality Hebrew classes or meetups offered. For those in this camp, their efforts were not focused on being able to do something with Hebrew in the future, when they had achieved a higher level of language competence. Rather, they were focused on present interactions in whatever Hebrew they knew. They were not "'on the way' to 'real' social interactions and contexts" in Hebrew; their interactions were already meeting their social needs.[27] Understanding Hebrew efforts helped to explain one woman's description of her participation in her meetup group, which she had attended for years: "My *dikduk* [grammar] is horrible. I really don't care if it's *pifall* or *poofall* [incorrectly identifying the names of two structures of the

Hebrew verb system]. I really don't care. I just open my mouth and speak, and in my writing, I constantly mix up *tet* and *taf* and *ayin* and *aleph* [different Hebrew letters with similar sounds]. That's my downfall. I read very poorly, but I truly don't care." This woman's motivation was not rooted in her achieving error-free Hebrew. Rather, her "realness" can be understood as a freedom to use the language in ways that made her feel good. For others, their "it" was being able to put their limited skills to use in a judgment-free context. Richard, a man in his mid-fifties, described his goals as "just being able to have a very basic, conversational level . . . at a fifth-grader level. No big vocabulary words . . . maybe a two-year-old level is the best I will reach."[28] Unlike his experiences playing golf, in which he strove to perfect his ball-hitting techniques, Hebrew worked differently. Being at a meetup group let him "play" and be around other Jews in a nonjudgmental context.

Though Richard was not perturbed by his inability to articulate a more sophisticated reason for choosing to pursue Hebrew, others expressed a sense of exasperation with their own inability to justify their choice. Interestingly, often the most enthusiastic learners were the least able to clearly express their rationales. Dana, a twenty-six-year-old woman in Brooklyn, took a long pause before talking about the reasons for and goals of attending a weekly online Hebrew class, despite a lack of free time due to her highly demanding job. Letting out a big sigh, she confessed: "It's a good question, because to be honest, I don't have a concrete answer. I kind of just have always wanted to learn Hebrew for the sake of learning Hebrew, because I kind of felt like, I'm Jewish, I should know Hebrew. Even though, obviously, it's not a requirement by any means, but I just always kind of felt drawn to it, so it's sort of an amplified Jewish on steroids." Clearly, Dana perceived Hebrew knowledge as a constitutive dimension of her Jewish identity. Yet her colorful "amplified Jewish on steroids" description also pointed to a broader set of considerations. At the time we spoke in 2021, antisemitism had already emerged as a central topic of conversation among American Jews. Though she had not experienced any personal verbal or physical attacks due to her Jewish identity, Dana was well aware of the trend happening across Jewish communities in the United States: "You could always say, I'm learning Hebrew in theory so I could go live in Israel whenever I want." It was her fear of Jews not being safe in the United States and needing to flee to Israel that led her to take Hebrew classes. Present-day fluency was not her main concern. It was her future safety: "I feel strange saying this, but if our history has taught us anything, Jews need to know when to leave." Seen in this way, Hebrew provided her with a lifeline—a means of survival if she ever felt endangered.

The narratives of Dana and others demonstrate that Hebrew learning carried a range of meanings and was shaped by diverse motivational forces. Learners were not always able to clearly articulate their goals. Nor did they converge around a singular or collective objective. Yet, in whatever way people spoke about their Hebrew-learning aspirations, the one evaluation that cannot be leveled against them is the charge of inconsequentiality. On the contrary, participants consistently ascribed personal meaning to their Hebrew learning, even when their measures of success did not align with conventional models of linguistic achievement. This insight brings us back to a central concern of this book: understanding the kinds of symbolic, affective, and identity-related work that Hebrew performs for American Jews. In contrast to a prevailing discourse that characterizes this group as largely disconnected from Hebrew, whether through lack of fluency, interest, or perceived relevance, the Hebrew enthusiasts featured in this chapter offer compelling counternarratives. Their experiences suggest that Hebrew occupies a significant, if often unconventional, place in their lives.

Notably, these stories also underscore the inseparability of Hebrew learning from broader Jewish contexts. Learners frequently engaged with Hebrew through explicitly Jewish spaces and networks. They enrolled in classes offered by synagogues and Jewish community centers, consulted rabbis and Jewish educators, accessed Jewish print and digital materials, observed Jewish holidays, and formed lasting friendships with fellow Jewish learners. Their motivations and learning trajectories were consistently informed by their lived experiences as Jews, as well as by their interpretations of Jewish history and identity. Attending closely to these trajectories helps clarify *why* individuals became and remained engaged with Hebrew. What is left to be explored more fully is *how* these learners understood the role Hebrew played in shaping their Jewishness. How did their attitudes toward and commitments to Hebrew intersect with their conceptions of American Jewishness? In what ways did Hebrew learning inform or transform their sense of being

Jewish in the American context? And how did it influence their relationship to Israel and to other dimensions of Jewish life, including its religious, spiritual, cultural, and communal components? These questions form the basis of the next chapter, which examines how Hebrew enthusiasts interpret the significance of Hebrew within the broader landscape of American Jewish identity.

4

EXPRESSING JEWISHNESS

"My Hebrew classes have become my Jewish thing. I feel part of something, but speaking Hebrew isn't automatically making me more interested in religious things like going to synagogue or lighting candles. And I am not thinking about moving to Israel. But it is still my Jewish thing." Before I could say anything, Sheila chuckled and sardonically asked: "Can you explain this to me?" This is how Sheila, a fifty-eight-year-old woman living in the suburbs of Boston, answered my question about her motivation to study Hebrew. A bona fide Hebrew enthusiast, Sheila invested considerable effort in improving her Hebrew and always looked for opportunities to be around other Hebrew speakers and learners. She read several online newspapers published for Hebrew learners, listened to Hebrew podcasts, and subscribed to services that streamed Israeli Hebrew television programming. Nonetheless, when she reached out to me in the spring of 2021 after hearing about my study, Sheila was hoping I could make sense of her choice. I understood her perplexity. While it is broadly accepted that Hebrew is a Jewish language, what this means for American Jews is less understood. What I heard in Sheila's question was a request to help her make sense of this "Jewish thing" in her life, especially because her sense of her own Jewishness was not rooted in traditional practices of religious Judaism. She knew that Hebrew filled a Jewish space in her life, but the boundaries and content of this space were unclear, as she was not observant or affiliated with a synagogue. While Hebrew ideologies often presuppose a connection between Hebrew and Jewishness, Sheila's case highlights that this connection is not always straightforward, nor does it follow the commonly held ideas of what religious identity is or the forms it takes in people's daily lives. This chapter takes Sheila's tongue-in-cheek question seriously and explores

Hebrew enthusiasts' beliefs about Hebrew in connection with their Jewish identities, which include their relationship to Jewish rituals, learning, spirituality, history, and Israel.

Building on the discussion in the previous chapter, this chapter turns to the Jewish meanings that Hebrew enthusiasts attribute to their language-learning practices. Simply put, it seeks to unpack the relationship between Hebrew and Jewishness by attending to how individuals articulate the significance of Hebrew in relation to their Jewish identities. Doing so requires some preliminary reflections about the terms *Jewish*, *Jewishness*, and *Jewish identity*. To be sure, I am not the first to note that these terms elide precise definitions. As many scholars have noted, these categories are especially difficult to delineate when not grounded in ascriptive criteria such as ancestry or matrilineal descent. Sociologist Samuel Heilman, for example, describes Jewishness as an "amorphous concept," referring to it as "the gigantic historical ambiguity involving God, ethnicity, and nation."[1] At a minimum, Jewishness encompasses a wide range of religious, spiritual, moral, political, and cultural orientations, each shaped by intellectual, philosophical, and affective considerations. Given the indeterminate nature of Jewish identity, this chapter focuses on the specific facets of Jewishness that emerged most consistently in interviews with Hebrew learners. It explores how participants framed their engagement with Hebrew in relation to Jewish textual traditions, spirituality, attachments to Israel, and broader forms of Jewish expression and belonging. Attending to these areas, this chapter sheds light on how Hebrew functions not simply as a language but as a meaningful conduit for expressing, shaping, and negotiating American Jewish identity. Taken together, these perspectives reveal what Hebrew offers to some of its most devoted American Jewish learners as a religious and identity-inflected endeavor.

Hebrew Enthusiasts and Their Jewish Diversity

Early on in this study, I decided to limit this project to American Jews, knowing full well that it would omit non-Jews' experience with Hebrew. I made this decision to give some coherence to the project, though I knew that it could also belie the spectrum of Jewish diversity that existed among the participants. Though everyone in the study self-identified as Jewish, there was variation among their Jewish practices, beliefs, and orientations. For some being Jewish was the central frame through which they lived their lives, while for others their Jewishness intersected with other identities. While some used denominational identifiers (e.g., Reform, Conservative, Reconstructionist, Modern Orthodox), most used a colorful array of terms to describe themselves, including *culturally Jewish*, *observant*, *secular*, *lover of Judaism*, *member of the tribe*, *seeker of the truth*, *Jew-ish*, *atheist*, *spiritual seeker*, *nonpracticing*, and *Jewishly inclined*. The plethora of terms reminds us that Jewish definitions are full of uncertainty, equivocation, fragmentation, and habituation. As one woman quipped after telling me about her relationship to Judaism, "I come in and out of doing Jewish things. That's the story of my life." Janet, a woman in her late fifties told me, "I don't consider myself Conservative. I don't consider myself anything." Nonetheless, she talked about being active in her synagogue and raising her two children as Jews and being married to a Christian man and having "technically Catholic" stepchildren. "I get mad when people think that [having non-Jewish family members] changes who I am as if I don't have a Jewish house." While she lit candles every Friday night, she did not have a kosher home because her stepchildren ate nonkosher meat in the kitchen. Throughout our conversation, Janet struggled with describing her Jewishness, expressing at one point that "I think of being Jewish as an important purpose of my life, but I don't consider myself religious"—a comment she reconsidered after a short pause. "I don't know. Maybe I am religious because synagogue is very central to my life." Exemplifying the tension between traditional markers of Jewish religious life (e.g., adherence to Jewish rituals, endogamy, and synagogue participation) and her own experiences in a mixed-faith family, Janet navigated her Jewish identity with a mix of certainty and ambiguity.

I did not hear a lot of strict definitions of what was or was not in the fold. Rather, my interviewees talked about their Jewish embodied, sensual, educational, leisure, and formative experiences. They told me about speaking or hearing Yiddish or other Jewish languages at home, sitting in a certain row at their synagogue during services, crying during the final scenes of *Fiddler on the Roof* when they saw it the first time, being bullied and experiencing antisemitism at school when they were children, tasting bacon or brisket for the first time, being involved in Jewish advocacy and social justice projects, and memories of shopping for the clothing they wore for their bar or bat mitzvah celebrations. I heard about their varying levels of engagement with Jewish communal institutions, including synagogues (where some held leadership positions), Jewish Community Centers (JCCs), and Jewish organizations such as Hadassah, Jewish National Fund, J-Street, AIPAC, YIVO, Holocaust museums, and Jewish federations, among others. As engaged as some were in religious and cultural Jewish life, others had no connection to any formal Jewish organizations, rarely participated in Jewish cultural events, and had little to no formal Jewish education. If some talked to me about their frequent trips to Israel to visit family and friends, others had not been to Israel in decades, while still others had never been. While some spoke about their ongoing interactions with Israeli Americans and exposure to Israeli culture in the United States, others had no direct contact with Israelis.

Talk about Jewishness intersected with individuals' interest in Hebrew, though not in always predictable ways. Mark, a fifty-six-year-old investment banker, grappled with what he saw as the paradox of being averse to religious Judaism but having a desire to know Modern Hebrew. As he told me, "I'm non-religious, and I've always pretty much been except for having a bar mitzvah. I've been pretty much synagogue unaffiliated during my life, and I have really no intentions of affiliating." He added, "I don't talk to God or anything." For these reasons he called himself an "odd duck, interested in Hebrew, not interested in Judaism at all." Judaism, for Mark, was understood as a set of halachic commitments and synagogue worship. As for a cultural connection to Jewish life, he went to his friend's Passover seder and had a few Jewish friends, "but that's about it." Yet Mark still identified as a proud Jew, even if he rejected institutional and theological Judaism. Standard models of Jewish social-scientific inquiry would likely dismiss Mark as unaffiliated or unengaged—a "none" in religious studies scholarly parlance.[2] Yet this term obscures the role that Hebrew learning played in Mark's Jewish identity. Speaking Hebrew afforded him a way to connect to his Jewishness in ways that other forms of Jewish traditions and rituals did not sustain.

Modern Hebrew as an Entry to Jewish Sacred Textual Tradition

An ongoing debate among Hebrew linguists revolves around the relationship between Biblical Hebrew and Modern Hebrew. On one side are claims that, though many elements of Biblical Hebrew have been incorporated into Modern Hebrew, the grammatical and syntactic distance between the varieties remains substantial, akin to "Shakespeare's and today's English."[3] On the other side are arguments that Modern Hebrew is closer to the older forms of Hebrew "than Modern English is to the English of Caedmon or *Beowulf*."[4] However this debate plays out in academia, Hebrew enthusiasts widely understood Hebrew varieties as intertwined and mutually reinforcing. Barbara, a regular synagogue service participant, decided to learn Modern Hebrew as an adult because she loved to attend High Holiday services and listen to the melody of the Torah chanting. Being a child of the 1950s, she had not been able to acquire Hebrew literacy because her synagogue excluded girls from formal Jewish education, which is where her brothers acquired Hebrew literacy. "I always had it in mind, I was going to learn how to chant. I was going to get my bar [sic] mitzvah." With a great deal of pride, Barbara told me that learning to read the Hebrew letters deepened her understanding of the meaning of words in the liturgy, and enabled her to chant a Torah portion at her synagogue. "Every year," she said, "I look at the portion and I say 'Oh, I get that grammar or meaning and I didn't get it the year before and that's very fulfilling.'" Learning Modern Hebrew allowed her to fulfill one of her lifelong dreams of participating in a religious ritual.

Barbara was not the only person for whom Modern Hebrew learning transformed a prior relationship with liturgical Hebrew. Marc, who as a child had attended an Orthodox yeshiva in New York City, recalled learning only the technical skills of reading Hebrew sacred texts. Decades later, as a participant in a monthly Hebrew meetup group, he found himself having "a lot of aha moments." A discussion about a grammar point in an article the group was reading led him to think: "Oh, that's what Rabbi Goldberg [the name of Marc's teacher at yeshiva] was after." Similarly, Irene, a member of a long-running Hebrew group, recounted her wonderment when she learned a Modern Hebrew word and realized she could relate it to a text she had read in synagogue. "When you understand what you're saying, 'and God said to Moses,' and understand *'lech lecha'* [Go forth], I got a new sense of what the text is saying and how meaningful it is."[5] She noted, "For me, these words make me more connected to Judaism." Like an archaeologist whose excavations reveal the depth of human activity over time, Irene discovered that Hebrew's temporal varieties exposed layers of meaning, allowing her to engage with Jewish sacred texts on a deeper level than before.

Ruth, a sixty-year-old woman who had grown up in a family in which both the girls and boys received a comprehensive Hebrew education, spoke proudly about understanding the commonalities across the temporal varieties of Hebrew and her sense of Jewishness. Conversing one evening in the spring of 2021, she told me about the time she and her husband had lived in Israel when he was a visiting professor at an Israeli university. Taking advantage of the circumstances, she had decided to audit a class on ancient Hebrew and Canaanite literature. "I sat there and the professor was amazed that I was the only one who knew the word *hoshieni*" (Biblical Hebrew: rescue me).[6] Even though everyone in the class was a Hebrew-speaking Israeli enrolled in "a senior class of Hebrew literature majors no less," her religious background and knowledge of Biblical Hebrew provided insight that was unavailable to the secular Israelis in the class. John, who had found his way to Hebrew after seeing psychologist and author Jordan Peterson's YouTube videos on the book of Genesis (see Chapter 3), got emotional when speaking about suddenly grasping the significance of Jewish religious ritual as a result of learning spoken Hebrew. Receiving a short email from a local Jewish organization in 2020 about the death of Rabbi Lord Jonathan Sacks, the chief rabbi of the United Kingdom and an influential international religious leader and intellectual figure, John read about the completion of the *shloshim* (the thirtieth day from burial), a period of mourning in which mourners refrain from attending parties or festive events, wearing new clothing, or getting a haircut or shaving. Though he had previously heard of this tradition, John was transformed by being able to understand the meaning of the word. "Look," he said, "you could learn the word *shloshim* [the number 30] and have no idea what it means religiously, or you could learn what it means in Judaism without knowing what the Hebrew word means in daily life." Being able to bridge the distinction between the religious and the secular uses of this Hebrew word provided him with new insight into the Jewish perspective on loss and grief. Understanding the religious and secular meaning of this word allowed him to think about Jewish tenets in a new and powerful way.

Hebrew teachers I interviewed spoke about these eureka moments when students uncovered new ways of thinking about Jewish traditions and ideas as a result of learning Hebrew vocabulary words. Abby, a longtime teacher at one of the well-established *ulpans* in New York City, referred to this phenomenon as "the turn"—the moment when Hebrew learning became meaningful. "I can't tell you how many times it happens that students are in class, and we learn a certain verb or something, and they ask if it's like that word in this prayer." She never tired of seeing her students' reactions when she revealed how a Biblical and Modern Hebrew word shared the same root: "That's when I see the connection and reconnect them to what they used to think of as Hebrew and their experiences [as children learning Hebrew], except this one is more fun." Being able to make the connection between liturgical and Modern Hebrew was, as she saw it, a key element that was too often missing from the Hebrew classes children attend, and what made Hebrew come alive as a Jewish language.

Hebrew enthusiasts likewise noted that learning Modern Hebrew led them to a new appreciation of the study of Jewish sacred texts and their interactions with Hebrew liturgy. Ben, a longtime member of a New York City meetup group and active member at his Conservative synagogue, noted that learning Modern Hebrew had changed the way he related to synagogue services: "When I'm reading through the prayerbook now, I got to tell you, I look at words . . . I look at the translation, and then it sort of hits me in the head. If you look at the middle letters [the roots], you see its [the word's] meaning in there." With this new insight, Ben described feeling much more connected to and interested in the liturgy. Kara had a similar reaction, delighting in knowing she could "understand many of the *tefilot* [prayers] and get the gist of what they're trying to say." If in the past she had read the Torah portion in English during Saturday morning services, now, with "a little Hebrew practice," she understood more of what she was reading, which helped to decrease her feelings of being an outsider to Jewish religious life. Having a new, unmediated experience opened her eyes to the beauty of the words and the synagogue service. It was "like I had crossed into a new world and rediscovered something I thought I had already known."

If a sense of discovery between Biblical and Modern Hebrew emerged in many conversations, it took on different forms when speaking to those who did not grow up in Jewish homes or had little or no prior Jewish education or exposure to Hebrew. Kristin, a woman who had converted to Judaism from Christianity after meeting an Israeli American man, was eager to tell me about her experiences learning Hebrew "from scratch." As her now-husband had grown up in a religiously traditional (*masorti*) family in Israel, Kristin had chosen to undergo a stringent Orthodox conversion, which required her learning Modern and Biblical Hebrew. Surprisingly, she found Modern Hebrew more difficult than learning about liturgy and *halacha*. "It's the spontaneity and your ability to generate your ideas and put your ideas into meaningful terms that's been really hard for me," she noted. In contrast, having the prayers "right in front of you" did not require creating new sentences or expressing new thoughts. Liturgical Hebrew, in other words, was easier because it was rote—"you're just reading the same things over and over again." Kristin also discovered that learning Modern Hebrew afforded her access to Jewish sensibilities in ways that liturgical Hebrew did not. As a Jew and Hebrew learner by choice, Kristen was attuned to how "the language itself communicates something about the [Jewish] culture." Without knowing it, Kristen channeled a central tenet of the Sapir-Whorf hypothesis, an influential albeit controversial idea developed around the mid-1900s positing that the structure of the language shapes its speakers' worldview or cognition. She believed Hebrew speakers understand their worlds differently from English speakers. As she saw it, the "order of the [English] words matters very much," so the syntactic rules impact English speakers' ability to express themselves. In contrast, she observed that Hebrew's less restricted syntax allowed its speakers "a certain flexibility and creativity," which represented "a mobility that expresses the heart of an idea and a people."

Kathy, another convert to Judaism, expressed that learning Hebrew anchored her religious transformation and helped her gain acceptance into the Jewish community. Being a Black woman born and raised Roman Catholic, Kathy started to learn Hebrew in the early 1990s, when she began her conversion program at the age of twenty-two. At the time, she felt that if she was going to be a Jew, "Hebrew was part of the whole package," and she seriously undertook her Hebrew studies. Her dedication to acquiring the language did not stop after conversion. She wanted to know "everything I could get my hands on" and started taking additional Hebrew classes at a university in New York City. Paradoxically, she noted that her Hebrew passion, which she saw as a key to Jewish insiderness, made her an oddball among other undergraduate students whose interest in the language did not match her zeal. While Jewish-born Americans could be "Jewish without Hebrew," "know how to read their letters," and not feel "any kind of need to go beyond that," Kathy felt "there would have been something missing" if she did not know how to communicate in Hebrew. As a convert to Judaism, she felt Hebrew ambivalence was not an option for her: "There are people who grew up being Jewish, and they were never questioned about their Judaism. They are like, 'I don't need to know Hebrew. It's not a big deal.' I think for me, coming into the picture as a newbie, it felt like I had to have all the tools in my toolkit." As a Jew of choice and color, Kathy believed that Hebrew gave her legitimacy, especially when navigating the tacit racism she experienced when people commented to her: "You don't look Jewish." If non-Black Jews did not have to prove their Jewishness through Hebrew language knowledge, Kathy understood that being able to speak Hebrew was her way to "sound Jewish" even if her race marked her as a non-Jew in the eyes of others.

Converts were not the only ones who saw Hebrew acquisition as a path toward Jewish acceptance. Meredith, a woman in her late twenties living in New York City, spoke about her desire to learn Modern Hebrew as a way of blazing her way into Jewish textual study—a space she felt excluded from as a person who identified as LGBTQ. At the time of our conversation, Meredith had been an active participant for a year and a half at SVARA, an organization that marketed itself as "a traditionally radical yeshiva dedicated to the serious study of Talmud through the lens of queer experiences."[7] Committed to reading the sacred texts in their original form (and not in translation), SVARA's mission is to open up Jewish textual study to everyone: "queer, straight, trans, alef-bet beginners, experienced Talmudists, secular, religious, Jews, non-Jews." For Meredith, SVARA provided inclusion for those "left out of the *beit midrash* [the traditionally male-centered place of textual study], for anyone whose perspective has been written out." While she acknowledged that Talmud study did not require knowledge of Modern Hebrew (as it was written in older forms of Hebrew and Aramaic), she perceived Modern Hebrew as central to moving from the margin to the center of Jewish life.

Hebrew enthusiasts already possessing deep knowledge of the sacred textual corpus believed Modern Hebrew study offered alternative Jewish ways of living. Jacob and David, two brothers raised in a Haredi (ultra-Orthodox) family in Brooklyn, spoke directly to this phenomenon. Educated in Haredi yeshivas, the siblings had strong foundations in reading Talmud and other sacred texts but almost no knowledge of spoken Hebrew, which their teachers discouraged. Both brothers opted to leave the Haredi community in their twenties. Jacob recounted a trip to Israel after high school when he started to think about Modern Hebrew: "It [the trip] was an opportunity to let loose a little bit. I was doing yeshiva, but I was still going out and partying. So one night, I had too much Carlsberg [beer], and I went up to a couple of women. I think I tried speaking old Hebrew, and I said to them, '*Yofat panim yofat to'ar*' [a biblical term used for a beautiful captive woman or prisoner of war]."[8] Even as a sheltered young man at the time, Jacob realized that this Hebrew expression was counterproductive as an effective pickup line. Once he went off the *derech* (literal translation: off the path; left the Haredi community), Jacob was drawn to understanding different forms of Hebrew and their uses in order to be part of the non-Haredi New York City Jewish community.[9] While Jacob wanted to experience secular life in a new register, his older brother, David, pursued spoken Hebrew to "salvage some of the learning" of his Orthodox upbringing as a part of his non-Haredi Jewish life. Using his knowledge of "old Hebrew and Aramaic," David "parlayed that into Modern Hebrew study," hoping to find "something of value" in his new life. Desiring to learn spoken Hebrew as a step toward (re)discovering a new form of Jewishness, David did not reject the knowledge he had acquired as a Haredi man. Rather, he sought to repurpose this knowledge: "Funny that I do feel that I'm reverse engineering my learning," he told me about his experiences using spoken Hebrew. "I know the *tefilot* [prayers] by heart, and I could say them by heart in my mind." Rather than rejecting his prior knowledge, he looked to "the stuff in the old Hebrew, to see what I can glean from it" as part of his new lifestyle. From his perspective, learning Modern Hebrew opened up a new way of being Jewish.

While scholars may debate the linguistic distinctions among Biblical, Rabbinic, and Modern Hebrew, Hebrew enthusiasts saw these boundaries as far less rigid or clearly defined. Rather than viewing these varieties as discrete forms of Hebrew, they often perceived their convergence as a meaningful resource for articulating Jewish identity and practice. The ability to move fluidly between the sacred language of liturgy and scripture and the vernacular of Israeli society enabled them to draw on Hebrew in multifaceted ways that reflected their own complex relationships to Jewish tradition, culture, and community. For instance, Meredith's motivation to study Modern Hebrew stemmed from her desire as a queer woman to access the traditionally male-dominated domain of Jewish textual learning. In contrast, Jacob and David sought knowledge of Modern Hebrew as a means of distancing themselves from the insular, text-centered world of Haredi Judaism while finding alternative paths of Jewish expression. Though seemingly moving in opposite directions, Meredith's, Jacob's, and David's experiences point to the symbolic and practical work Hebrew does for American Jews as they navigate their relationships with spaces, traditions, and texts. Importantly, the Hebrew enthusiasts discussed here did not adhere to a binary framework that casts Textual Hebrew as inherently religious and Modern Hebrew as secular or cultural. Instead, they engaged both registers as interrelated and mutually constitutive modes of Jewish expression. In doing so, they reimagined the boundaries of Jewish identity, crafting expressions of Jewishness that could be at once secular and religious as well as traditional and innovative.

Hebrew Letters and Jewish Spirituality

One of my favorite experiences of attending synagogue services is locating "sitings" of Hebrew in the sanctuary or other rooms in the building. The aesthetic force of these Hebrew letters and words—in the bronze or plexiglass memorial plaques, in the stained-glass windows, adorning the ark where the Torah is held, or in other artistic renderings of biblical expressions on the interior and exterior walls—always moves me emotionally. Speaking with Hebrew enthusiasts, I learned that I was not the only one drawn to the materiality of Hebrew letters. In many interviews they spoke about visual renderings of Hebrew letters as a source of Jewish spirituality. Despite many of my interviewees not identifying as religious, they talked about the ephemeral and mystic dimensions they found in written Hebrew letters. In this way material renderings of Hebrew letters acted as a speech act; the encounters with letters created a change in people's experiences beyond merely communicating information.

The connection between Hebrew letters and spirituality that some Hebrew enthusiasts expressed follows millennia of Jewish tradition, which is full of reverence for the forms and shapes of the Hebrew letters. Jewish mystics and sages believed that God imbued each of the twenty-two Hebrew letters of the alphabet with hidden significance, including its name, pictorial form, numerical equivalent, and respective position in the alphabet. Midrash teaches that when Moses ascended to receive the Torah, he saw God designing crowns for each individual letter, endowing each form with transcendency. The Talmud speaks to the power of Hebrew letters and their permutations in emulating the divine's creation of heaven and earth. The Hasidic sage the Baal Shem Tov extolled the Hebrew letters as vessels of the divine, believing that all things were created through combinations of the twenty-two Hebrew letters. As many Jewish children learn in preparation for reading from the Torah and becoming *b'nai mitzvah*, a scroll with a single letter omitted, distorted, or compromised by contact with other letters must be invalidated.

Hebrew enthusiasts had their own beliefs about the power of Hebrew letters, which they acquired when learning Modern Hebrew. As she learned Hebrew during her conversion process, Kathy saw "beauty in the letters" and spoke about the "excitability of seeing the letters" as well as "looking at the letters and feeling uplifted or moved." The letters on the pages were "magical," even if the texts in which they appeared in textbooks or newspapers were about quotidian topics such as music or television shows. Another woman spoke about the metaphysical properties of the letters when she studied children's literature written in Modern Hebrew: "I could see that the *lamed* stood up, and sometimes I saw two *lameds* near each other, and I heard this *L* sound, and suddenly it felt spiritual." Much like the medieval Jewish mystic Rabbi Isaac Luria, who constructed complex methods of visualizations for each Hebrew letter as a form of strengthening an individual's *kavannah* (intentionality) while praying, Kathy saw learning Modern Hebrew as "finding the magic key to spirituality" and "discovering myself and the bigger questions in life." Seeing Hebrew letters carved out a space for thinking about her understanding of herself and her place in the world. Her discovery reminded me of literary scholar Ilan Stavans, who wrote in his language memoir about recovering his atrophied Hebrew as a form of self-resurrection. "I realized that my search for Hebrew was far more multifarious than a language," Stavans concluded. "The Hebrew of my dreams wasn't only a system of sounds; it was an existential condition, a way of being, of establishing contact with others, with God, and with myself."[10]

Hebrew letters held spiritual meaning even when they appeared in everyday objects. Marc, who was educated in an Orthodox yeshiva but had left behind adherence to Jewish law and synagogue affiliation, remained enamored by Hebrew letters. When we spoke in 2021, he recounted that he had recently discovered a store receipt in the pocket of a jacket he had last worn during a trip to Israel in 2018. Typically, he would have thrown out the detritus without thinking twice, but something held him back. He contemplated, "Should I save this damn receipt . . . or should I just throw it out?" and tried to wrestle with his indecision. "What does this piece of paper represent to me? Why don't I just throw it out?" Similar to the religious tradition of disposing old, used, or damaged sacred manuscripts into a *geniza*—a repository built in a basement or attic to honor the sacrosanct nature of God's name—Marc had endowed this receipt with a form of spiritual meaning that made him unable to throw it into the trash. Holding the crinkled piece of paper in his hand, Marc realized that the barely visible inked Hebrew letters represented more than proof of a purchase of a bottle of water; these words held a spiritual and sacred significance because of the form in which the words were written.

If Marc grappled with the boundaries between the sacred and the mundane in his Hebrew receipt, others spoke about interactions with Hebrew letters as a negotiation between part and whole. Once he understood that the Hebrew root system fit into morphological templates that could be used to form new words, Alex, a forty-year-old accountant, noted that the letters became "almost like a mystical puzzle that's been revealed." Alex believed that, like a cryptic map encompassing different layers of meaning, each Hebrew letter contained a distinct purpose that, when combined with other letters, had the capacity to create an infinite universe of words. Alex was not the only person to discuss Hebrew as a mystical puzzle or riddle. Many spoke about each letter holding a special place and the joy they experienced by discovering how the letters worked together to create words. Another woman shared with me that seeing Hebrew letters and understanding how they created new words gave her "this absolute chemical rush" as if she were opening "a present." And another spoke about Hebrew's transcendental and afferent aspects. Rather than simply translating words from Hebrew to English, she had developed a metaphysical methodology: "I would stare at a table until it became a *shulchan* [table]. I would just look at it and will it to become a *shulchan*, and I would just sit there until I looked at it until I saw a *shulchan*. And I did that with everything, nouns, colors, moods." Each letter helped to build this image in her mind. Another person commented that seeing Hebrew letters was similar to experiencing a strange but familiar phenomenon: "It's like when I go outside and a butterfly flies right over my head, and I'm like, wow. That's how I am with when the letters connect, and something suddenly makes sense that I've been singing or hearing forever." In her Israeli dancing club, Miriam described interacting with Hebrew letters as an aesthetic force: "It was like a code that I was motivated to break that made the dancing richer and meaningful." For her, the letters that made up the words of the songs she danced to offered her a new way of moving through space.

I acknowledge that some of the accounts presented here that describe individuals' metaphysical, embodied, or sensory responses to Hebrew letters may appear far removed from conventional understandings of language learning. In presenting these narratives, I am mindful of the risk of exoticizing either Hebrew or its learners. Yet overlooking these experiences would be to disregard a meaningful dimension of how Hebrew functions for a particular subset of Hebrew enthusiasts, especially in relation to their Jewish identities. For these individuals, interactions with Hebrew letters opened pathways to forms of Jewish spirituality and mysticism. The letters were not merely linguistic units. They became vessels through which individuals could find personal insight, spiritual growth, and existential meaning. Participants described the shapes of the letters as possessing an ineffable power that was capable of permeating the skin, moving the body, and expanding the mind. Their descriptions often drew on a religious idiom, even if not explicitly framed in terms of creed, dogma, or formal theology. Rather, the letters operated as symbolic tokens of mystery and transcendence. For these individuals, the aesthetic and affective dimensions of Hebrew were central for deeper levels of thinking about the self.

Hebrew, Jewishness, and Israel

Connection with Israel constitutes an important component of Jewish identity for many American Jews.[11] This connection reflects a complex constellation of meanings—spiritual homeland, safe haven, cultural center, and political project. For many of the Hebrew enthusiasts discussed in this book, Israel was a touchstone of their Jewish identity.[12] Their experiences visiting Israel shaped their interest and attachment to Hebrew. At the same time, their interactions in Hebrew learning contexts in the United States shaped how they talked about Israel. To begin to unpack the relationship between their experiences in Israel and the form that talk about Israel took in their classes, I consider two overlapping phenomena. First, as most of the Hebrew enthusiasts involved in this study were baby boomers and Generation Xers, many had visited Israel at some point in their lives. For those who had visited the country during their early adult years, Hebrew connected them to meaningful and formative experiences in their past. The second phenomenon recognizes that the Hebrew learning classroom is a space in which American Jews talk about Israel. This should not be unexpected, given that modern language pedagogy has long emphasized integrating authentic "cultural realia"—songs, movies, stories, news articles, and other cultural products—into lessons. In the case of Hebrew, this content material is about Israeli history, culture, and society—given that Israel is the only country in the world where Hebrew is used as the vernacular. These two framings are central to the current analysis and help to explain the complex ways Hebrew learning—as a dimension of Jewish identity—forms different forms of Israel engagement.

The rise of Israel homeland tourism fundamentally shaped how a generation of American Jews experienced and connected to Hebrew. For many Hebrew enthusiasts, their relationship with the language began during these transformative youth trips to Israel. Such trips became popular when Israel homeland tourism took hold in the 1950s and 1960s, when American Jews began to embrace Israel as a key dimension of their Jewish identity, and grew throughout the final decades of the century.[13] As a result, many Hebrew enthusiasts took advantage of a variety of volunteer or study programs in Israel when they were young adults in the 1960s–1980s. It was common in the interviews to hear those over the age of fifty recount their experiences participating in kibbutz programs, volunteering in underserved cities, or studying in a semester- or year-long program at an Israel university. As many of these programs sought to introduce and strengthen the connection of diasporan Jews to Israeli culture and history, it was common for those who traveled to Israel to participate in an *ulpan*—a typical component of the different homeland tourism programs.

Hebrew enthusiasts' descriptions of their *ulpan* and other Hebrew learning experiences in Israel linked Israel's history in parallel with their own shift into adulthood. Ann, a member of a Hebrew meetup group in New York City, noted that her ongoing involvement in Hebrew groups in New York were directly tied to her positive memories of being a university student in Israel in the 1970s: "Hebrew reminds me of a period of my life that was really special and formative. It was the language of a time that was special, so it is just cool to bring that back, even in a distant way." Hebrew classes served as a mnemonic through which Ann recalled pleasurable memories. Clearly, there was some nostalgia at work in her reflection. Yet chalking up Ann's participation in her Hebrew group as simple yearning for bygone days of youth obscures the foundational presence these experiences constituted in her life. Cultural theorist Svetlana Boym identifies two types of nostalgia. Restorative nostalgia "puts emphasis on *nostos* (returning home)" and patching up "memory gaps," while reflective nostalgia "dwells in *algia* (aching), in longing and loss."[14] Neither of these forms of nostalgia adequately describes Ann's impulse to seek out Hebrew experiences as an older adult. She had no desire to dwell in her memories. Nor did she have any desire to relive those experiences. She was not looking to recapture the feeling of a place or time in her life. Rather, her Hebrew-learning memories in Israel were an integral part of how she understood the past in her present-day life. As she related, "So much of what my life has been is an outgrowth of those years and has given me new ways to think about being Jewish in so many aspects of my life." Similarly, Janet, who had lived in Israel for almost half a year in the late 1970s, regularly attended her monthly Hebrew group but had no desire to return to Israel: "I'm probably never going to go back. I'm sixty-nine years old, and there's a lot of other places I want to go." Janet did not live in the past. Nor did she view Hebrew as bounded to a particular time or place. Instead, her Hebrew engagement in the early 2020s derived from her prior experiences in Israel, but had shifted to an American Jewish experience. Hebrew was "everything" she "loved about being Jewish distilled into words and sounds." Hebrew thus functioned for them neither as nostalgia nor as escape, but as an ongoing thread connecting past experiences to present meaning-making.

Where nostalgia was most evident was in expressions of personal triumph and achievement. First visiting Israel in 1969 as a participant on Sherut La'am (translation: service to the nation—a work-study program), Barbara vividly recalled her strict daily Hebrew-learning regimen, which included being in class for four hours each morning, taking a siesta, and then starting "the real work"—walking to the local town every day so she could see and hear how the locals used Hebrew and copy down the words in her notebook: "I was determined to learn, and somehow, after about six months, I opened up my mouth and out came Hebrew." Looking back at this experience, Barbara described her achievement as a direct result of her determination and desire to succeed. "I worked at it like a demon. . . . I wanted it desperately from day one. I worked very hard. For other people, there were other reasons for them to be in Israel. . . . For me, language acquisition was one of my main motivators, because I wanted to be able to maintain these relationships with my friends and to the land and to the people." Barbara made clear that the experience was fundamental to her sense of self: "That year was just revelatory. . . . I look back at this as one of the highlights of my life that forms who I am today." Others expressed similar feelings of their Hebrew learning experiences being instrumental to their understanding of themselves. With a huge smile on his face, seventy-two-year-old John told me about his experience studying Hebrew on a kibbutz for several months in 1968: "I was on a high. I was mastering Hebrew and living in the best place in the world. . . . I was becoming myself." Maya, who told me about doing Israeli folk-dancing in Beer Sheva in the early 1970s (which she humorously referred to as the "Yonkers of Israel"), saw her ongoing interest in Hebrew as directly related to crossing gender and class boundaries: "I think this love affair with Hebrew is my way of staying connected to that feeling of freedom." She added, "That it is a part of being in Israel that I loved—the excitement of being twenty-three years old in this new country . . . traveling, living on my own, doing all these adventurous things that were very out of my wheelhouse of how I grew up as a middle-class American Jewish woman in the suburbs of Pittsburgh." Others discursively framed formative Hebrew learning opportunities in Israel as an odyssey, often invoking religiously infused language to describe their experiences. One man, for example, recounted that he "was on a holy grail of sorts," while another spoke of it as "his Hebrew pilgrimage." Whether described as odyssey, pilgrimage, or personal triumph, these nostalgic narratives situate Hebrew learning as a transformative experience through which individuals had discovered freedom, mastered challenges, and forged the Jewish identities they carried into the present.

These memories reflect not just personal experiences but the particular sociohistorical moment of postwar American Jewish engagement with Israel. The 1967 Arab-Israeli War marked a turning point in American Jewish identity, igniting an unprecedented surge of solidarity with Israel and reshaping communal life in the United States.[15] As the Holocaust had already become a touchstone of American Jewish memory in the postwar period, the perceived existential threat to Israel elicited collective fears of a second destruction.[16] This context explains why so many American Jews experienced Israel's swift military victory as a symbol of pride, security, and even redemption.[17] Not only celebrated as a geopolitical and military triumph, Israel's survival in this war was understood as a moral vindication and affirmation for Jews worldwide that they could defend themselves against those who sought their demise. In the war's aftermath, philanthropic donations, organizational support, and religious attachments to Israel expanded dramatically.[18] Whether this new phenomenon was Israelolatry (a portmanteau fusing "Israel" and "idolatry" used to criticize an excessive, uncritical devotion to the State of Israel that borders on idol worship) or a new form of civic religion—or both—the post-1967 period ushered in an Israel infusion into American communal, educational, and political life.[19]

Hebrew enthusiasts' memories of learning Hebrew in Israel during this period reveal a combination of postwar euphoria and the apogee of youth. For many, Hebrew learning was experienced and remembered as a moment of pride and joy. Barbara, who participated in a three-hours-a-day, five-days-a-week *ulpan* in 1968, shared with me that it was "the most phenomenal time to have been in Israel. . . . I couldn't have planned it better. I mean it was euphoric, riding high. . . . They opened up the Banias [river in the Golan Heights], you could go to the *Kotel* [Hebrew: Western Wall], and you could go into *har habayit* [the Temple Mount][20] and into the mosques. And it was just a magical, magical, magical time to be young and in Israel." Rita, a woman in her seventies from New York City, also recounted how the mise-en-scène of Israeli exuberance and her introduction to learning Modern Hebrew overlapped. Interested in learning about socialism, Rita had arrived at a kibbutz in the north of Israel in 1969. Recalling that "it was a very happy time in Israel" and a "really special time in life," she described the experience as "literally a life-changing event" in which Hebrew learning played a significant part. She arrived with very few practical skills, and the kibbutz "couldn't find a job that I could do, and I failed at every job they gave me." Eventually, she ended up working in the *gan* (preschool) with young children. Not having attended Hebrew school, Rita found that the three-year-old children became her Hebrew teachers. With a little notebook in her pocket, she sounded out words phonetically and wrote down each one along with its English translation: "I didn't even know how to read or write, but I could speak Hebrew by the end." More than fifty years later, Rita saw her Hebrew acquisition on the kibbutz as "one of my proudest Jewish moments and overall proudest moment in my life."

Rita's experience learning Modern Hebrew mirrors and encapsulates the transition of Israel from a fledgling state to a burgeoning nation. When seen as such, her personal language development becomes a metonym for the collective growth and Jewish renewal. Her recollections offer an interesting twist on the muscular imaginary that underlies early Zionist thinking about building the state. Instead of the brawn of her body, Rita used pen and paper to build herself into a new type of Jew—who could take on any task, even the extremely difficult one of interacting in Hebrew with unforgiving preschool children. This parallelism among individual growth, the maturation of the State of Israel, and language-learning success went beyond a nostalgia rooted in individual memories. Rather, it is a nostalgia that mediates "the relationship between individual biography and the biography of groups or nations, between personal and collective memory."[21] Rita's memories of her Hebrew acquisition resulting from her experience as a young adult were not stuck in the past. Recognizing that much has changed in her personal life and in the trajectory of the state since her formative experience in the late 1960s, Rita neither idealized the past nor reduced it to a wistful sentimental yearning. Rather, she understood her enduring commitment to practicing and improving her Hebrew as a project of ongoing Jewish identity formation: "When so much is going on in the world, I speak Hebrew. It sounds silly, but it grounds me. I know I am Jewish [and] how I can think about what that means for today and tomorrow."

Baby boomers were not the only ones whose Hebrew-learning experiences as young adults on Israel visits shaped their sense of being Jewish. Sociologist Shaul Kelner shared with me his story of being a twenty-three-year-old volunteer working in the pomelo and date fields on Kibbutz Elifaz in 1992–93, when he participated in Otzma—a yearlong leadership development and volunteering program in Israel.[22] His interest in acquiring Hebrew led him to "do something crazy": He decided he would speak only in Hebrew and convinced his Otzma coparticipants to do the same. Starting a few years after the program ended, twenty-five to thirty people of the original group annually have tried to gather to recreate their Hebrew-only kibbutz experience, wedding Jewish symbolism and traditions, language practices, and reunion rituals.[23] In addition to inventing a *Chag Elifaz* (Kibbutz Elifaz holiday), the alumni meetups have mobilized Jewish traditions, including producing a Hebrew *Haggadah* they read together (in the tradition of a Passover seder) and creating a ceremony that mirrored the dipping rituals of the Passover seder—though their invented tradition had them dipping dates in *schug*, a fiery hot sauce, to symbolize the debilitating pain they suffered during their kibbutz labor when the thorns of the harvested dates stabbed their arms. Looking back, Shaul understood this ritual as a literal embodiment of "*al hadavash v al haoketz*" (the honey and the sting).[24] On a metaphorical level, the dipping ritual taking place at an annual gathering reflects something more: the fruits of one's language-learning labor. Not lost on Shaul was the profound meaningfulness of becoming a speaker of a language that was revived after not being spoken for millennia, and which allowed him to "articulate an identity around

Hebrew . . . that became part of my own [Jewish] story." Like the baby boomers before them, this younger cohort experienced Hebrew learning in Israel as transformative identity work. However, these Otzma alumni went further, institutionalizing their experience through invented rituals that ensured their formative encounter with Hebrew would continue shaping their Jewish lives decades later.

What can Hebrew enthusiasts' Hebrew learning in Israel stories tell us about their current Jewish selves? Seeing these personal Hebrew acquisition stories as nothing more than nostalgia runs the risk of ignoring how these experiences shaped their ongoing sense of Jewishness. Take, for example, Nancy, a woman who noted that "Hebrew has given me a way to be an American Jew." What she meant by this was that her Hebrew learning experience in Israel was an inflection point in her Jewish trajectory: "Many times I've thought that if I had not gone to Israel and gone into that program [WUJS: World Union of Jewish Students], I would have become an assimilated, kind of nominally Jewish person here in the States." Nancy did not live in the past or look to recreate it in the present; however, she did recognize the profound effect learning Hebrew had on her life.

> I have not been back now forty years, but I've never fit back into the States the way I did before I left and had this experience. . . . I mean, a year and a half [of being in Israel], it's not so terribly large . . . but for me, it was very significant . . . and it wasn't about being Jewish, like keeping kosher, or going to synagogue or the more religious stuff that people think of. . . . This was a much different way of thinking [about being Jewish] and speaking as a Jewish woman. . . . It has stayed with me as I go through my life.

Nancy understood herself as a particular kind of Jew in the early 2020s when we spoke, and because of her eighteen-month visit to Israel as a young adult, an experience she recalls through her lens of learning and using Hebrew. Without this pivotal experience, she believed she would be "nominally Jewish," with no meaningful cultural or religious Jewish attachment. It is then worth considering how she recognized that her ongoing interest in Hebrew made her an outcast of sorts among the majority of American Jewish adults who had no meaningful relationship to Hebrew. On this score Nancy was cognizant that her experiences with Hebrew and Israel were no longer the norm, particularly among younger generations. "Everything is different today," she remarked. If fifty years ago American Jews were "proud to speak Hebrew with one another" and "wear Israel on their sleeve," she knew this was no longer the case. Bob, who had spent a semester at an Israeli university in the early 1970s, touched on this same point when he reminisced that "those days were beautiful," because "we could learn Hebrew and love Israel without any caveats. It was so simple and fun, but clearly those days are gone." What they mourned, then, was not simply their youth but the loss of a shared cultural script in which learning Hebrew and loving Israel were uncontroversial expressions of American Jewish identity.

Others spoke directly to the connection between the American Jews' relationship to Hebrew and broader political and cultural shifts in American Jewry. Betty, a New Yorker who had spent some time in Israel throughout the 1970s and 1980s, noted that the shift away from Hebrew was an irredeemable outcome of these changes.

> If you don't have a favorable view of Israel, if you don't have Israeli friends, if you don't know people there, what's the point [of knowing Hebrew]? And unfortunately, the politics destroyed a lot of people's desire to learn [the language]. You have to know people there and you have to have connections, whether they're religious or liberal. But the whole idea of the Zionist fever that most of us grew up with our generation is gone. The politics has absolutely destroyed any real desire to maintain that connection [to the language].

Betty's continued interest in improving her Hebrew was not driven by a desire to recapture a prelapsarian period when Israel was a unifying cause among American Jews. Yet at the same time, Betty astutely understood that talk *in* Hebrew can never be fully removed from talk *about* Israel. Individuals' memories of Hebrew learning served as a touchstone of a particular time in their lives and in Jewish history. Interestingly, conversations about Israel in Hebrew meetup groups and classes in the 2020s assumed their own navigational dynamics that also worked to unify Hebrew learners. The following section turns to the specific interactional practices through which Hebrew learners talked about Israel while sustaining the group solidarity that made language learning possible.

Avoiding the "Third Rail" in the Hebrew Classroom

While many of my interviewees who had learned Hebrew in Israel as young adults in the late 1960s and early 1970s told me stories replete with pride, excitement, and hope about the country and their own learning experiences, Jonathan's confessional comment to me at the end of our Zoom call in February 2021 presented a new set of considerations. "You know," he lowered his voice an octave and leaned into his computer screen as if to reveal a secret, "sometimes in my Hebrew class it is so much easier to just avoid talking about Israel altogether." Jonathan's revelation took me by surprise because it ran in contradiction to one of the leading beliefs about Hebrew: that it can create an irrevocable bond between American Jews and Israel. If adult Hebrew learners eschewed speaking about Israel when they met, what did this mean for the validity of this bond? Given the positive attachments Jonathan and many Hebrew enthusiasts had with Israel, I wondered what Jonathan meant by "easier" and "avoid." What made talking about Israel "hard"? I wondered if a Hebrew class could avoid talking about Israel altogether, and if not, what topics were avoided. More broadly, his comment led me to think about the types of discussions about Israel that were taking place in the Hebrew classroom and how talk in Hebrew revolved around talk about Israel.

Scholars, journalists, and communal figures have long noted that American Jews do not speak with one voice about Israel, its political leadership, its connection with the United States, or much else for that matter. If Israel unified American Jewish communal life throughout much of the twentieth century, this was no longer the case for much of the early twenty-first century, when we consider how Israel has become a divisive topic for American Jewry. The 2020 Pew Research Center survey showed that American Jews were increasingly politically and religiously polarized in terms of their level of connectedness with Israel, with much variation about feelings toward Israel across denominational identity, political party affiliation, and age.[25] Another study from 2019 looked closely at the topic's impact on communal interaction and found that some synagogue leadership considered Israel a wedge topic because it flared up tensions among congregants, especially between older and younger congregants.[26]

It was against this backdrop of polarization that Hebrew learning groups developed strategies to talk about Israel without replicating the fractures fraying other American Jewish communal spaces. As one Jewish educator put it, "Increasingly conflicted feelings about the connections with the modern state of Israel, with people being opposed to positions of the Israeli government" had gotten "mixed into the question of learning Hebrew." Specifically, the discord raises a series of challenges for Hebrew educators and learners regarding the pedagogical material they choose for their classes. Modern language pedagogy has long emphasized integrating authentic realia—songs, movies, recipes, news articles—into lessons. Indeed, a foundational premise of language acquisition in educational settings promotes language classes as a way to learn about another culture, its traditions, people, and history. As much of the Hebrew learning material comes from Israeli media or educational publications, decisions about which Hebrew songs to play, which articles to read, which words to emphasize became politically fraught. As one *ulpan* instructor noted: "How do you teach about Hebrew without talking about the only country in which the language is used?" A second challenge for deciding on the content of adult Hebrew language classes derived from another core principle of formal language acquisition. To learn to speak an additional language, learners must feel comfortable taking chances, pronouncing new words and trying out a new grammatical structure. Language learning, in this sense, requires vulnerability to make errors, because it is through this process that progress is made. For Hebrew enthusiasts gathering in meetups or in classes, this reality presented an additional question about how to talk about Israel among learners with diverging political and religious perspectives. Were there topics that needed to be avoided to create a convivial and supportive classroom environment? Assuming divergent opinions exist, how can learners navigate them to not derail the social dynamics of the group? Taken together, these layers of complexity offer some perspective to Jonathan's comment that it was often "easier" to avoid talking about Israel.

More succinctly, they underscore the need to address what happens when Israel becomes the "third rail" of American Jewish life and what this means for those invested in learning Modern Hebrew.

The unresolved dynamics of discussing Israel when learning Hebrew emerged in many conversations. Stephanie, who defined herself as "a passionate Hebrew user," grew visibly agitated when the topic of Israel arose in our conversation in early 2021. "I hate to use too strong of a word," she admitted, "but I despise the government of Israel right now, and it is very difficult for me. Years ago my husband and I were very active in AIPAC, and I don't want to have a thing to do with AIPAC anymore. I don't like the fact that I can't support the government." Her ire with Israeli's political leaders had negatively impacted how she discussed her Hebrew passion with her adult-aged children who were "very cynical about Israel." As she admitted, it was "a major problem with trying to get young American Jews to feel that there should be any relationship with Israel, because all they're seeing is the government and what the government does. . . . They don't know the history and they don't understand the people that are living there." Despite her best efforts, Stephanie was unsuccessful in getting her family to understand her love of the language. For them the language was reduced to being a signifier of specific political leaders and their policies. "In that regard," she lamented, "trying to even speak about Hebrew becomes almost a nonstarter."

Elinor, a fifty-eight-year-old from New York City and a self-identified "Hebrew geek," similarly spoke about grappling with her own complicated relationship with Israel. "I love the idea of a Jewish homeland," she declared proudly. However, she acknowledged some ambivalence: "I struggle with what the Israeli government is doing today, which has made me think, am I being complicit learning Hebrew?" Though feelings of complicity did not ultimately prevent her from Hebrew engagement, she could understand why others held back. Alternatively, some Hebrew enthusiasts argued that, as American Jews, learning Hebrew was a marker of their support for Israel and what it represented as a Jewish nation. Karen, a fifty-three-year-old woman, remarked that she had intentionally chosen to study Hebrew because of the growing antisemitism in the United States in the early 2020s—acknowledging that she had "even started talking to AIPAC," which was "a little more right-wing" than her typical political affiliations. Listening to her congressional representative, Alexandria Ocasio-Cortez, inject antisemitic tropes into her speeches and call to limit American military and financial support for Israel, Karen felt "nervous." Her intentional choice to study Hebrew was a political act that allowed her to make a statement about American politics. The political meanings mapped onto Hebrew varied dramatically—from marker of complicity to act of resistance—yet what these stories revealed was the impossibility of pursuing Hebrew study in the 2020s without confronting one's relationship to the contemporary Israeli state. These unresolved tensions set the stage for how learning communities themselves would navigate Israel as an unavoidable yet potentially divisive topic.

Shalom Bayit: Peace in the Hebrew Classroom

To navigate divergent opinions about Israel, instructors and adult learners employed classroom strategies that created and sustained a welcoming and politically neutral Hebrew learning space. As part of this strategic choreography, Hebrew class participants engaged with reading material that focused on broadly defined cultural topics, such as food, science and technology, movies, art exhibitions, and other nonpolitical topics. These noncontroversial topics were often found in popular Hebrew-learning publications such as *Jerusalem Post Ivrit*, *Bereshit*, and *Yanshuf*, which offered simplified Hebrew short pieces along with English–Hebrew (and in the case of *Jerusalem Post Ivrit*, French) glossaries. The February 2020 edition of *Jerusalem Post Ivrit*, used in a class I attended, included a short biography written by a hearing-impaired woman which described her experiences learning Hebrew, an abbreviated news article about the president of Guatemala's visit to Jerusalem, an article about animals being added to the protected species list in Israel, a short article about reducing air pollution in Israel, and a text about reducing fats and sugar in one's diet. Though this issue did have a short blurb about the dissolution of the Knesset (the Israeli parliament) and the need for an election in March 2020, by and large this issue avoided controversial or political topics, allowing adult Hebrew learners to read and talk about politically neutered topics that were still connected to Israeli culture.

This is not to say that politics were entirely absent from Hebrew learning material. Interestingly, the most fraught topics were introduced when learners studied song lyrics—a common language-learning methodology.[27] I participated in one class in which we read the lyrics to Israeli singer Ehud Manor's well-known "Ein Li Eretz Acheret" (I Have No Other Land), written in 1982 in response to the war in Lebanon, and "Ma Avarech" (With What Shall I Bless Him), another famous song written about the death of an Israeli soldier during the 1967 War.[28] In two other classes in which I participated, the group read and listened to "Hayeladim Shel Choref 1973" (Children of Winter 1973), a song whose lyrics explore the anxiety surrounding ongoing wars in Israel and their effects on future generations.[29] Arguably, these three songs about wars in Israel can be grouped together as a canon of anthems—one might even say a secular Kaddish—given that they are often played on the radio during Israel's Memorial Day and other days of mourning.[30] Others spoke about learning Hebrew in their classes while listening to Israeli hip-hop, Israeli song entries in the Eurovision contest, contemporary Israeli Top 10 pop songs, and dance songs.

Not surprisingly, song lyrics shaped the tone of the lessons in which they were used. Notably, I found that when classes studied the lyrics of solemn songs written about events in Israel's history, they did not engage in any extended extemporaneous discussion about the 1967, 1973, or Lebanon wars. More typically, teachers (if there was one, which was not the case in most Hebrew meetup groups) and participants focused on the denotational meaning of the lyrics' words. That is to say, they translated each word to reach a coherent understanding of the lyrics. Observing groups prioritize vocabulary learning or grammatical structures over the broader context of these lyrics reminded me of what linguists call indexical bleaching—the process by which the indexical (or associative) link between a linguistic form and its social meaning is downplayed, while its dictionary meaning is prioritized.[31] Linguistic bleaching, as scholars have pointed out, confers on words a degree of neutrality. Focusing on the definitions of Hebrew words in songs about Israel avoided potential dissension and kept the Hebrew class a nonthreatening learning space. Taken together, choosing neutral and nonpolitical texts about cooking and animals and focusing on the translation of Hebrew words sidestepped potentially controversial discussions about Israel. Rarely did I hear any classroom discussions about specific Israeli (or for that matter, American) political topics, despite major events happening on the ground during my fieldwork between 2019 and early 2023.[32] And when political comments did emerge, students (or teachers) were quick to change the topic to something less contentious.

Curated generic readings, a focus on learning words' referential meanings, and strategic circumvention allowed the Hebrew classroom to take on a *pareve* quality. By this I mean that just as *pareve* food is neither meat nor milk and therefore acceptable at any meal according to rules of *kashrut* (kosher dietary laws), Hebrew functioned as a politically neutral agent that made talking about Israel palatable. While some might argue that this type of Hebrew diet is bland or inedible and lacking a spicy sensory kick, this choice came with other benefits. Most important, it worked to accentuate group cohesiveness by mitigating differences around highly controversial and political issues. To understand this process, we might look to the work of peace education theorist Roger Mac Ginty.[33] Noting that "everyday peace" is a form of agency enacted at the local level, Mac Ginty shows that processes of politeness and avoidance work to prioritize sociality and solidarity. I want to be clear that my drawing from this framework should not be taken as equating the Hebrew classroom with the conflict- and violence-ridden societies Mac Ginty writes about. Rather, I apply his ideas here to instantiate how adult Hebrew learners navigated divisiveness around Israel and negotiated "a way through a complex range of social norms, practices and aspirations that shape their inter- and intra-communal experience."[34] *Pareve* Hebrew practices ensured a form of everyday peace in the Hebrew learning context. Translated into a Jewish idiom, it facilitated *shalom bayit* (peace in the house)—a religious value originally applied to spousal relationships but now used to refer to efforts to build peaceful and supportive atmospheres through acts of mutual respect.

Notably, creating a *pareve* Hebrew-learning space counters a dogmatic tenet that sits at the nexus of many Hebrew educational initiatives: that Hebrew is one of the surest and most direct ways to acquire a deep knowledge about Israel and Israelis. However, the impulse to have an inclusive *pareve* Hebrew learning space muddles the ideological waters that Hebrew can function as the linguistic glue among Jews and create a peoplehood despite differences. In other words, if Hebrew must be deliberately stripped of its political valences in order to bring diverse learners together, then the language cannot bear the weight that Hebrew ideologues place upon it—that it is robust enough, on its own, to bridge deep divisions of belief, politics, and identity and forge a shared Jewish collective. While there are surely many who would have qualms with Hebrew *pareveness* in philosophical terms, in practice the choice of prioritizing "everyday peace" may reveal itself to be a wise one. As a member of a New York City Hebrew meetup group told me, the monthly gatherings had lasted for so many years because "*davka* [precisely], they were not a place where they had to do any political heavy lifting." Instead, he valued being able to engage with other Jews in Hebrew in a "nonpolitical, low-stakes setting." Talking in Hebrew about the weather, movies, and other general happenings in Israel (and in New York) allowed his Hebrew group to function, endure, and succeed.

The *pareve* Hebrew learning setting also challenges Hebrew's reputation as a language of "straight talk" or what Israelis call *dugri*—a cultural style of speaking characterized by its directness, bluntness, and truth telling. Linguist Tamar Katriel has shown in her careful analysis of this distinctive speech style that *dugri* signifies the ethos of Israeli toughness and candor, which is often interpreted by non-Israelis as rude or insensitive. *Dugri* works, as Katriel claims, because it is taken as a sign of the interlocutors' integrity and strength.[35] Thus being able to talk *dugri* is a sign of respect; there is no need to beat around the bush. If *pareve* signals deliberate neutrality, *dugri*—as a defining feature of Israeli communicative culture—is its opposite, prizing directness and candor over the careful management of difference. Importantly, *pareve* American Hebrew learning spaces invert *dugri-ness*. Instead of accentuating straightforwardness and sincerity, Hebrew learners deploy the language in ways that skirt direct confrontation and disagreements, and thereby follow features of politeness that characterize American English interactions.[36] Paradoxically, Hebrew *pareve-ness* makes the Hebrew class less Israeli in character—and perhaps more American.

Given that some of the Hebrew groups did not have a teacher organizing interactions, it is interesting to analyze how this *dugri-less* process looked in practice. Mac Ginty is again helpful here. He writes that the desire for sociality, reciprocity, and solidarity in everyday peace interactions among friends and colleagues is rarely explicitly discussed or planned.[37] Rather, he argues, they are co-constructed in real time through implicit interactional agreements about what should or should not be said. When applied to the Hebrew class, the rules of engagement about what could be said were rarely (if ever) explicitly discussed. Janet, a veteran member of a meetup group in New York City, helped me to understand the parameters of these unstated rules, noting that the only way the group could function was if members prioritized the chance to talk in Hebrew over the desire to change opinions or win a political argument. If this meant "checking their politics at the Hebrew door," this was the price everyone was willing to pay, even without explicitly being asked to do so. "These are people [in Hebrew meetup groups] who have nothing really in common, absolutely nothing except Hebrew, so in the restaurant, we talk about food," she told me. "It is a really nice group, but it is very diverse, and we stay away from controversial topics. No Israel. No American politics. That's the only way this works."

Implicitly agreed-upon interactional rules facilitated groups' longevity. Jay, the volunteer organizer of a Hebrew meetup group in New York City, underscored the importance of the group sticking to neutral topics, such as "a movie or a show, or just some event going on [in Manhattan] or something like that" and not getting "too politically involved." Ben, the organizer of another Hebrew meetup group, recalled that when the group originally formed in early 2010s as one of the synagogue's adult education offerings, the Israeli teacher at the time was a big supporter of Prime Minister Benjamin Netanyahu and would encourage the class to discuss politics. After she retired and the group decided to continue without a teacher, they ceased having political discussions. Though membership enrollment ebbed and flowed, the core group of members remained, he ventured, largely because of the group's apolitical stance. This apolitical approach appealed not only to long-standing members but also to newcomers from different generations. Dana, a woman in her early twenties, who during the pandemic joined an online *ulpan* made up of mostly Generation X'ers who she assumed held an array of perspectives on Israeli and American politics, appreciated the complete absence of any political talk in the lessons: "I think most of my classmates vote Democrat, but to be honest, I don't know." She remarked that the only time they had discussed politics explicitly was during the class on the evening of January 6, 2021, several hours after the insurrection at the Capitol in Washington, DC. As Dana recalled, the class could not avoid discussing what had happened that day, though as far as she could remember, that was "the only time we've talked about and learned some of the vocab words for politics." At no time did the class discuss Israeli politics or policies: "We haven't really talked about the party system in Israel or anything like that. I know about that more from my own, just browsing the internet, than from this class." Putting it directly, she noted, "This class has been very much like: We're here to learn Hebrew, and this is where we are. It's almost like a little utopia in that way."

Anyone familiar with Thomas More's work *Utopia* may read Dana's description of her Hebrew class with great interest. Writing in 1516, More coined the word *utopia* from the Greek words *ou-topos*, meaning "nowhere," and the similar-sounding word *eu-topos*, meaning "a good place." As scholars have pointed out, by joining these meanings More created an unresolved tension: Utopia is simultaneously a nonplace and a paradisiacal place; in essence, a place that is as much aspirational as it is rare, comprised of affirmation and denial.[38] Dana was most likely unaware of More's philosophical treatise when she used the term *utopia* to describe her *pareve* Hebrew class, but nonetheless it raises an important point about the duality present in the Hebrew classroom. While for many Hebrew enthusiasts Israel is an important component of their Jewishness ("a good place"), the Hebrew class is also a space in which controversial topics about Israel are absent ("nowhere"). Yet there is an irony in this juxtaposition. The utopic Hebrew space succeeds because it prioritizes speaking *in* Hebrew over speaking *about* Israel. By functioning as a space where Jews with different opinions can form an inclusive Jewish community of practice, the adult Hebrew gathering manifests the Hebrew ideology of peoplehood—albeit at the cost of narrowing the terms on which Israel could be discussed.

Dueling Jewish Languages

If the adult Hebrew classroom reveals how carefully American Jews navigate what can be said about Israel, it also surfaces another set of tensions—those between Hebrew and Yiddish—that are equally revealing about how Hebrew and Jewishness are understood and experienced.

Any analysis of Hebrew enthusiasts' connection between Hebrew and their Jewishness must account for the role of Yiddish. Talking about another Jewish language might seem tangential here, since this book does not focus on Haredi Jews—the only community that uses Yiddish as its vernacular in both Israel and the United States. Yet the dueling relationship between Yiddish and Hebrew is too revealing to set aside. It serves as a potent lens through which to examine the ongoing debates about Jewish religious and cultural vitality in the United States, and it adds an important dimension to understanding how Hebrew language ideologies and Jewishness are interconnected.

It is not an understatement to claim that the clash between Hebrew and Yiddish was one of the most charged cultural battlegrounds in the Zionist project. Zionist leaders at the turn of the twentieth century positioned the revitalization of Hebrew not only as a means of communication but as a symbol of Jewish nationalism, sovereignty, and renewal. As such, Hebrew revitalization was cast as a linguistic and moral imperative. Though spoken by millions of diasporic Ashkenazi Jews across Eastern Europe, Yiddish, by contrast, was portrayed as atavistic. The same forces that prioritized Hebrew revival efforts denigrated and delegitimized Yiddish by associating the language with the enfeebled, degenerated, and asthenic Jewish condition of exile and victimhood.[39] Yiddishists, by contrast, repudiated the idea that diaspora Jewish life was inferior and championed the Bund's slogan "*doikayt*" (hereness), affirming the right and value of Jews to live "here"—in whatever country they inhabited—as full citizens and as Jews.[40] The "language wars" of the British Mandatory era—most dramatically seen through the 1913 Technion controversy over Hebrew versus German as the language of instruction—were fought in the streets, in newspapers, in families, and in classrooms through consolidated language policy and planning. Even prior to the establishment of the State of Israel in 1948, Hebrew had effectively "won" the linguistic battle—not through natural adoption alone, but through ideological pressure, propagandistic campaigns, and policy mandates that transformed Hebrew-speaking from a cultural choice into a national obligation.[41]

However, Yiddish never completely disappeared. Rather, it has endured as a cultural and political linguistic force in Israel, as well in the United States.[42] While Yiddish-speaking immigrants arriving in the

United States in the late 1880s eventually shifted to English to attenuate their religious alterity and gain acceptance into American society, Yiddish continued to be used in cultural domains throughout the turn of the twentieth century, especially as a language of Jewish theater, literature, and radio. Its presence among non-Haredi Jews is still felt to varying degrees.[43] If we were to ask contemporary Jewish Americans to name two Jewish languages, it is likely that Hebrew (as an umbrella term encapsulating all the temporal varieties) and Yiddish would top their list of responses.[44] Digging further would reveal that these languages are perceived as Jewish in distinct ways and provide access to different forms of Jewish expression and practice.[45]

What do Yiddish-Hebrew dynamics reveal about American Jews' relationship to Hebrew and their Jewish identity? The answer to this somewhat convoluted question can be found in present-day American Jews' understandings and uses of Yiddish. Cultural theorist Jeffrey Shandler describes contemporary Yiddish cultural practices as "postvernacular" in nature.[46] By this he means that Americans' relationship with Yiddish is defined more by ideological and affective engagement to the language than by linguistic mastery. Postvernacularity, in other words, privileges a language's symbolic meaning over its everyday communicative function. As Shandler's extensive scholarship on Yiddish shows, this postvernacular relationship explains American Jews' participation in klezmer music festivals, Yiddish cultural festivals and retreats, and Yiddish theater—cultural spaces that do not require Yiddish literacy or communicative fluency. Importantly, Shandler argues these metapragmatic practices should not be dismissed as trivial but rather be seen as defining characteristics of American Jewish life.

The entangled relationship between Yiddish and Hebrew continues to pit one language against the other, but in a modern idiom. Part of what makes Yiddish postvernacularity function as a diasporic Jewish practice is that it is not the vernacular of a particular territory or nation. A "national language of nowhere," Yiddish instead conjures up images of an idealized Jewish past, champions diasporism—the state of living outside a Jewish homeland—and evokes Jewish nostalgia, humor, and pathos in ways that Modern Hebrew, tied to contemporary statehood, cannot.[47] With a nod to Max Weinreich's famous dictum, not having an army and a navy means that Yiddish can signify the countercultural, raunchy, fun, and folksy dimension of Jewish life. Textual Hebrew (the language of sacred texts and rituals) and Modern Hebrew (the vernacular of a nation-state) cannot be postvernacular in the same way. Thus the language war is no longer about what language should be the language of the Jewish state in Israel. It has evolved into a debate about different ways of being Jewish in the United States. Just as Hebrew is ascribed with a set of language ideologies about what it can do for American Jews, Yiddish similarly accrues its own set of social meanings and ideological investments—different in content but parallel in function. On one hand, American Yiddish enthusiasts situate Yiddish as outside the parameters of religious Judaism by construing the language synecdochically as the Jewish underdog for the "politically progressive, culturally avant-garde, feminist, or queer."[48] In this way, Yiddish gives voice to alternative forms of Jewishness that are removed from synagogal Judaism. On the other hand, it has become the anti-Hebrew. As one scholar of Jewish studies pointed out in an interview, "[Hebrew] is a language of a living society that makes a lot of demands on American Jews. . . . Yiddish is free of all those obligations that you have to politically support Israel. . . . Yiddish emerges as a counter Hebrew, as free of all that baggage of the Israel-Palestinian conflict."[49] Scholar of Jewish literature Ilan Stavans underscores the "baggage" that Hebrew carries, arguing that "for some, the language [Hebrew] symbolizes far-right Israeli militarism." Yiddish, Stavans argues, perseveres because of its soft power—the combination of its "stubbornness" as well as its "nimble, clearheaded and improvisational nature."[50]

Other scholars and activists have imbued Yiddish learning and use with an ethical diasporic imperative. As their argument goes, the deliberate suppression of Yiddish was a political act that yoked Jewish identity to the Zionist nationalistic efforts, and thereby foreclosed on other possibilities of Jewish modernity. As a corrective to this injustice, they understand Yiddish reclamation as a diasporic, antihegemonic language that can offer an alternative Jewish political possibility untethered from Jewish nationalism.[51] Thus a new element of postvernacular Yiddish usage underwrites a political urgency to reassert diasporism as a viable and alternative form of Jewishness. When American Jews chant protest songs in Yiddish, make pilgrimages to the Yiddish Book Center to "rediscover the real Jewish language" (as one interviewee told me), and use Yiddish instead of Hebrew in ritual spaces, their embrace of Yiddish is not simply about linguistic preference but about political alignment. In this way, Yiddish becomes more than recuperative or nostalgic. It is a generative vehicle for imagining and enacting a form of Jewishness that is diasporic, politically oppositional, and unbeholden to the nation-state.

Not all Hebrew enthusiasts, however, accepted the stark binary between Hebrew and Yiddish as dueling forms of Jewish expression. Nor did they accede to being typecast as advancing a particular political agenda. Allison, a New Yorker in her early thirties, perceived her Hebrew "activism" as an act of Jewishness because it afforded her the means to express her connection to Israel in her own way. Hers was not an anti-zionist endeavor. Rather, she saw her interest in learning Hebrew as a way to show her commitment to the country, but "talk back" to the Israeli leadership and policies she deplored and "stick it to the AIPACs of the world." Meredith, a Brooklynite in her late twenties who self-identified as a progressive leftwing liberal "with all the stereotypes that comes with these adjectives," likewise did not buy the argument that Yiddish had a monopoly on liberal forms of Jewish culture and practice. When asked if she had ever considered learning Yiddish rather than Hebrew, her face registered clear annoyance, matched only by the critical tone of her response: "Don't get me started," she responded curtly. "Listen, I have my criticisms of the Israeli government like many American Jews. I am not a fan of Netanyahu's Likud policies and Gaza and the West Bank, et cetera. But you're not liberating anybody by not engaging with Hebrew and learning Yiddish instead." Later in our conversation she added, "It's not Hebrew's fault Israel has bad leaders." As others pointed out when the topic of Yiddish versus Hebrew came up, the most committed leftwing activists in Israel, as well as most of the Palestinian-Israeli organizations seeking coexistence, conduct their activism in Hebrew and not in Yiddish. Additionally, others pointed out that the only Jews using Yiddish as a daily vernacular were the *haredim*, whom many considered illiberal fundamentalists and not representative of their Jewish beliefs and values. For this reason, Samantha, a woman in her thirties living in Brooklyn, rejected the ideological premise that "Yiddish was countercultural and progressive" in ways that Hebrew could not be. Hearing Yiddish spoken by the *haredim* in her neighborhood caused her to associate the language with a "repressive lifestyle" in which women were subjected "to constant control of their bodies and minds."

To be sure, there was a generational dynamic to the beliefs regarding the types of Jewishness that Yiddish and Hebrew offered. I found that younger Hebrew enthusiasts made more explicit comments about language as a political tool. All the same, Meredith provided an interesting twist in her decision to pursue Hebrew despite her misgivings over the policies and practices of the Israeli government. With an implicit understanding that languages are not inherently political objects, and that it is people who endow languages with particular social, cultural, and political associations, she remarked that "Yiddish is not inherently more or less apolitical [than Hebrew]." From her perspective, both languages had the capacity to eschew or advance social change. Indeed, Meredith had little patience for rallying cries to reclaim Yiddish as a diasporic rallying call: "You don't see Jews doing the same thing with Ladino or Judeo Arabic, where they're like, 'Screw Hebrew.'" Put differently, Meredith saw how Yiddish was being mobilized to delegitimize or critique Israel in ways that other Jewish diasporic languages were not. Moreover, she questioned why Yiddish learners committed to social justice were not studying "Arabic instead to show Palestinian solidarity." For Meredith, learning Hebrew was not an ethical compromise; rather it enabled her to express her Jewishness and her political stances—which she saw as mutually constitutive. Yet she understood the powerful force of language ideologies. "I get so much criticism about learning Hebrew," she lamented. "People have given me a hard time [for learning Hebrew], but this is such an oversimplification [of how language works]."

Meredith's trenchant critique of people who believe that Yiddish is the only language that can serve as the language of Jewish liberalism, activism, and diasporic vitality underscores an interesting point about language usage and Jewish expression more broadly. Telling me in 2021 about an online webinar she had recently heard on the topic of language and American Jews, Meredith noted that the speaker had talked about American Jews integrating Yiddish and Hebrew words to create a distinctive American Jewish English. Hearing this, Meredith found the idea of linguistic syncretism appealing: "I don't see it as either/or. I'd like to learn Yiddish too maybe one day. It gives me more options to be Jewish."

Rather than pitting one language against the other, Meredith embraced Jewish multilingualism, and in doing so challenged the beliefs that Hebrew and Yiddish are foils for expressing Jewish beliefs and values. In this sense, navigating the contested terrain between Yiddish and Hebrew is not merely a linguistic choice. It is a Jewish act in itself—another way of expressing, debating, and inhabiting Jewishness.

Connecting Hebrew and Jewishness

This chapter explores how Hebrew enthusiasts' Hebrew engagement shapes their understanding of Jewish life by demonstrating that their Hebrew beliefs and practices are deeply tied to how they construct their identities as American Jews. For some, studying Modern Hebrew opened new interpretive possibilities for religious practice, deepening their relationship to synagogue liturgy and sacred texts. For others, seeing Hebrew letters on the page carried a spiritual or mystical charge. Still others connected Hebrew to formative memories of young adulthood visits to Israel, connecting their personal growth to the development they witnessed in Israeli society. For others, Hebrew learning became an expression of social and political activism.

Given Hebrew enthusiasts' divergent political and cultural perspectives about Israel, the adult Hebrew classroom emerges as a microcosm of American Jewish diversity. Participants in Hebrew classes and meetups followed implicitly agreed-upon rules of engagement that regulated what could be said or read about Israel, redirecting attention to grammar and vocabulary rather than polarizing political debates. This strategic narrowing created an inclusive space, where what was said *in* Hebrew took precedence over what could be said *about* Israel. In this way Hebrew learning becomes a vehicle for Jewish coexistence, though not necessarily in ways this term is used traditionally as a marker of interreligious conditions. While certainly there are those who would find the *pareveness* disturbing, there is another way to look at it. Rather than flattening or restricting Jewish identity, Hebrew learning in this way expanded the range of what Jewishness could offer for its learners of diverse backgrounds and aspirations. This variability is worth pointing out, if for no other reason than to remind us that while not all Hebrew learning means the same thing to all its learners, it can lead to multiple ways of thinking about Jewishness.

It is important to note that Hebrew enthusiasts' expressions of Jewishness did not mirror the tone or priorities of Hebrew ideologies advanced by scholars, communal leaders, or journalists—ideologies that often foreground collective concerns such as peoplehood, Jewish literacy, and continuity. While these themes were not entirely absent, Hebrew enthusiasts typically spoke about their relationship to Hebrew in intimate, experiential terms rather than as part of a grand narrative about American Jewish life. They used Hebrew to forge personal meaning that involved liturgy, spirituality, and memory. However, these personal engagements with Hebrew did not occur in a vacuum; they were constantly shaped by, and sometimes in conflict with, dominant language ideologies about what constitutes good or legitimate Hebrew. The next chapter thus turns to Hebrew enthusiasts' reflections on Israel and Israeli Hebrew, focusing on how they negotiate prescriptive and descriptive ideologies of "authentic" Hebrew usage outside of Israel. By analyzing how learners talk about their American Hebrew accent, this chapter reveals how pronunciation becomes a key site for performing and contesting American Jewish identity. Understanding how American Jews confer on the American Hebrew accent symbolic capital and authenticity offers fresh insight into how American Jews position themselves within homeland–diaspora dynamics, and how they construct a sense of Jewishness that is both relational to and distinct from their Israeli counterparts.

5

ACCENTUATING THE AMERICAN JEWISH HEBREW SPEAKER

On February 22, 2021, at the height of the COVID pandemic lockdown, I woke up and found my email and Facebook feed full of links to the clip of Rafi Reshef, a veteran broadcaster on Israeli TV, speaking with Effie Hertzke, an eighty-one-year-old great-grandmother and volunteer nurse living in Ramat Gan, Israel. Hertzke, who had just received her COVID vaccination, was seen working out at her local gym for the first time since the pandemic had started. A celebration of the return of normalcy and the success of Israel's vaccination efforts, the three-minute clip went viral among American Jews, but not solely because of its hopeful public health message. Rather, what captivated American Jews about this clip was Hertzke's personality, and specifically her subversive take on the Jewish grandmother—the *bubbe* figure. Hertzke may have been an octogenarian, but here she was, walking on the treadmill with large dangling earrings, wearing a shirt with "BADGIRLS" emblazoned across the front, appearing with a full face of makeup, and flirting with Reshef about her biceps and her interest in meeting a young man at the gym.

Two aspects of this cultural moment immediately struck me. The first was her seamless way of integrating English and Hebrew. When Reshef asks, "*Ve'ech hakosher*?" (meaning: Are you in good shape?), Hertzke responded without missing a beat: "Oh, my god! *Ata rotze lirot et ha* muscles *sheli*?" (Do you want to see my muscles?). The second focused on the responses her American-accented Hebrew elicited. One poster on Facebook commented: "I've never heard anyone that fluent and [with] that strong of an American accent before," while another wrote, "OMG. Is that what I sound like to others when I speak Hebrew? But you have to give her credit. At least she isn't putting on that fake accent so many Americans do when they speak."

In response to this feel-good news clip, I wrote a short piece for the online news site *Jewish Telegraphic Agency*. My aim was to underscore a larger sociolinguistic point of this newsworthy item: Accents matter because we make judgments about speakers' worth and place in society based on how they sound. I ended the piece with the following:

> The strong responses to Hertzke's iconic accent strike me as evidence that there are nevertheless common perceptions that Hebrew should "really" sound a certain way, and that American-accented Hebrew isn't it. My hope, however, is that Hertzke is in on the joke, and knows intuitively that her way of speaking Hebrew *is* Hebrew, without the need for any modifier. Hertzke owns her multilingualism, and her translanguaging celebrates the idiosyncratic beauty of both of her languages, as well as her national identities. Ownership of who we are and how we put it out into the world—now that is a linguistic achievement we should all be proud of.[1]

I had assumed my take on the Hertzke story would attract a small, linguistically minded audience, and was therefore unprepared for the range of responses the article received. Hertzke's sister, Susan Morgenstern, posted in the comment section on the *JTA* site about her own language usage as an American living in France, and a member of Hertzke's family reached out to me by email to tell me more about her aunt's personal history. Another American living in Israel emailed me to share her Hebrew-accent experiences:

> I made *aliyah* 45 years ago from Chicago at the age of 20. I studied at Hebrew U [University] and have been working as an OT [occupational therapist] for 40 years in Jerusalem. Your article was excellent. I have felt on so many occasions that I am being tagged and stereotyped because of my American accent although I speak Hebrew like a Sabra [native Israeli]. When I ask something as simple as "Eifo hasherutim?" [Where is the bathroom?] I find people break their teeth to answer me in English and sometimes treat me

as though I am less intelligent. I have given up completely trying to speak with an Israeli accent but I wish I could.

Other American Hebrew speakers emailed me to express gratitude that I had taken up the subject of American-accented Hebrew—a topic that was near and dear to their hearts but that was not discussed enough, in their opinion.

Pushing the limits of Warhol's fifteen minutes of fame dictum, Hertzke became a local celebrity and cultural phenomenon. The initial interview on Israeli television led to various writeups in the American Jewish media, and the story even had legs in the Israeli mediasphere. Reshef granted her a follow-up interview, where he continued his playful banter while maintaining his straight-man persona. Additionally, a popular American Israeli comedian, Benji Lovitt, did a follow-up interview for the blog *Life in Israel*, in which he and Effie spoke about their experiences immigrating to Israel, as well as Hertzke's philosophy about dealing with life's adversities and challenges.[2] Not to miss out on an opportunity to cash in on this minor media sensation, *Bagels*, an online site of curated Jewish videos and Jewish items, got in on the action. The site not only produced a four-minute video entitled "Effie's Firsts and Favorites in Israel" under the category "Inspiring People," but also began selling "Muscles Sheli" (my muscles) red T-shirts with the transliterated Hebrew "ata rotze lirot et ha muscles sheli?" written underneath an outlined image of a bicep muscle "in honor of Israel's favorite *Olah* [immigrant to Israel], 81-year old Effie Hercky [sic]."[3] United with Israel (UWI), a pro-Israel advocacy group that advertised itself as the world's largest pro-Israel community, with nearly ten million followers in more than 170 countries, also got in on the fun by featuring an almost nine-minute English interview with Effie.[4]

Beyond the diasporic Jewish community, Hertzke also had crossover appeal to the Hebrew-speaking Israeli audience. *Eretz Nehederet*, a popular satirical comedy hour in Israel, performed a piece in which Roy Bar-Natan, an Israeli male actor, parodied Hertzke's appearance and sass to great comic effect.[5] However, not everyone saw Hertzke's popularity as merely a source of humor. Eylon Levy, a news anchor on the English-speaking program *i24News* in Israel, started a petition on Change.org directed to the Israeli Ministry of Culture,[6] which as of summer 2021 had one hundred supporters:

> Effie Herzky [sic] captured Israelis' hearts with her adorable interview on the treadmill for Rafi Reshef on Channel 12, thanks to her bubbly, eccentric, and adorable character. But for hundreds of thousands of "Anglo" immigrants in Israel, Effie Hercky [sic] is a symbol. The 81-year-old great grandmother's heavy American accent made her an instant icon of the struggle to integrate into Israeli society, despite the language and accent barrier. Jews from Britain, the United States, Australia, Canada, South Africa, and New Zealand instantly identified with her powerful question to Israeli society, as they seek to prove their mettle: "Ata rotze lirot et ha muscles sheli?"
>
> We Anglo olim [English-speaking immigrants], along with friends, allies, and the rest of the Anglophone Diaspora, POLITELY REQUEST that the Israeli Ministry of Culture honor/honour Effie Hercky [sic] by inviting her to light an Independence Day torch on behalf of all English-speaking immigrants in Israel. (capital letters in the original)

Clearly, Hertzke had struck an emotional chord among English-speaking Jews in and outside of Israel, becoming a figurative (and potential literal) torchbearer for the epitome Israeli experience. Her wry humor, inscrutable candor, and raffish fashion choices endeared her to many and turned her into an immigrant icon. Yet to focus solely on her distinctive look and her sassy personality obfuscates the reason she reached meme-worthy status in the American Jewish media. For this, we need to look at the cultural work involved in her uninhibited and unabashed American-accented Hebrew. To her American Jewish fans, Hertzke epitomized the construct of "Muscular Judaism."[7] Zionist thinkers at the turn of the twentieth century envisioned strong, intrepid, and healthy Jews replacing the portrait of the enfeebled diasporic Jew. Effie, an American Jew living in Israel, showing off her muscles and proudly speaking Hebrew on her own terms, embodied this construct, but with a twist.[8] Not by force or valor, Hertzke proved her patriotic mettle through her Americanized pronunciation of the Hebrew letter *resh*.

Putting aside the commercialism of this phenomenon, we can see the responses to Effie as a tacit call for reimagining the title of the "real" Hebrew speaker. This framing takes us to Pierre Bourdieu, the social theorist, who argued that definitions of language legitimacy can be understood only with respect to how language is used within a specific social context (in his word, "field"), which is embedded in unequal struggles over meaning, access, and power.[9] Seeing Hertzke's story in this framework raises a host of consequential questions about the field of American Hebrew speaking, including what types of Hebrew uses are considered authentic, how non-native Hebrew accents are perceived, and how differing Hebrew accents take on social meaning. As a case study of language ideologies about the Hebrew accent, the Effie phenomenon reveals how these ideas shape and are shaped by broader debates about notions of authenticity. Focusing on the American Hebrew accent, this chapter sets out to probe what this accent signifies to its speakers and how this accent constructs and challenges American Jewish authenticity. What Hebrew enthusiasts say and think about their accents offers a unique perspective for considering how they understand themselves in relation and in contrast to Hebrew speakers in Israel. Accent, in this way, becomes a symbolic site of Jewish identification and difference. In defending, explaining, or celebrating their American accents, Hebrew enthusiasts actively forge distinctly diasporic forms of Hebrew authenticity.

Authenticity

More than half a century ago, literary critic Lionel Trilling anticipated the rise of authenticity—invariably defined as that which is sincere, essential, natural, organic, and real—in response to modernization and its effects on contemporary society.[10] Concerned with the question of why the idea of authenticity arose as a social virtue in modern society, anthropologist Charles Lindholm writes that centering the collective takes us in a different direction, "away from the self, and toward history, tradition, and ancestry, all of which are associated with collective identities of nation, tribe, and race."[11] Taking this as a point of departure, we can understand why ruminations about collective authenticity most often surface at crucial moments when "communal consensus is under attack and when borders between acceptable and un-acceptable practices have become unbearably fuzzy."[12]

This fuzziness is particularly relevant to notions of Jewish authenticity—a term that often gets caught up in the unresolved debates over what constitutes Jewish identity. Religious studies scholar Stuart Charmé notes that authenticity has been wielded as a formidable weapon in defining, controlling, and disciplining who has access to claims of Jewish insiderness.[13] On one hand, Jewish authenticity is constructed in relation to difference with non-Jews. At the same time, Charmé shows that Jews evoke authenticity to differentiate among themselves. These internal debates operate according to a set of principles that pit Orthodoxy against non-Orthodoxy (e.g., "halakhic Judaism is more authentically Jewish than liberal [non-halakhic] Judaism") and demarcate types of Jews (e.g., "religiously observant Jews have more authenticity than assimilated, ethnic Jews").[14] Crucially, Charmé points to the high stakes involved in claims of authenticity in Israel–diaspora dynamics (e.g., "Jewish life in Israel is more Jewishly authentic than Jewish life in the Diaspora"), and the tenet that prioritizes Jewish life in Israel over Jewish life in the diaspora.[15]

Claims to Jewish authenticity also emerge in debates about language use. Language authenticity, as most sociolinguists would agree, is a chameleon of a notion, used to camouflage culturally constructed beliefs about the moral, intellectual, or aesthetic qualities of a language and its speakers. Thus beliefs about language authenticity are central to how societies determine who the real speaker of a language is. Literary scholar Tamas Dobozy shows how this applies to Hebrew, arguing that the claim of Hebrew authenticity "is dangerous precisely because it is used not to enable Jewish identities, but to maintain an authenticity by designating the inauthenticity of 'other kinds' by all who do not speak in the language of legitimacy."[16] This phenomenon has the potential to leave some Hebrew speakers at the mercy of others in their quest to be recognized as legitimate speakers, regardless of the value of their thoughts or contributions. This is why ideologies of language authenticity are so powerful; they prioritize "who one is, rather than what one has to say."[17] While claims of language authenticity can hinge on any feature of language use, I focus the remainder of this chapter on the Hebrew accent.

What We Mean by Accent

Etymologically, the word *accent* dates back to the thirteenth century to the French *acent*, which derived from the Latin *accentus*, or "song added to speech." The *Merriam-Webster Dictionary* defines *accent* as "a distinctive manner of expression" that can refer to "a way of speaking typical of a particular group of people and especially of the natives or residents of a region" as well as "an individual's distinctive or characteristic inflection, tone, or choice of words." Whereas the first part of this definition points to the community of language users, the latter speaks to the individualistic features, which linguists have shown comprise a combination of factors, including one's social class, education, geography, ethnicity, and language exposure.[18] As a "dustbin category," the construct of accent includes "all the technical meanings" as well as the "general and subjective" ones.[19] Crucially, it is in the subjective realm that we can better understand the social meaning of accents, and how they shape how individuals and groups of speakers are perceived and treated. Serving as audible proxies of belonging or exclusion, some accents are endowed with symbolic power and associated with prestige and authority, while others are stigmatized and linked to cultural inferiority. A New York City accent stereotyped as abrasive or aggressive, or a foreign accent that triggers assumptions about a speaker's intelligence or loyalty, are familiar examples of how this dynamic plays out in everyday life.

It is not surprising therefore that linguistic scholarship is replete with studies demonstrating people deploying or manipulating their pronunciation and prosodic patterns to present themselves in beneficial ways.[20] I can personally relate to playing around with my Hebrew accent to achieve favorable outcomes. Every time I introduce myself to Hebrew speakers, my decision to use the American or Israeli pronunciation of my first name (SHA-ron/ Sha-RON, respectively) is wrapped up in impression management about the kind of persona I want to project. While there are times when I want my Israeli bona fides to come through, there are times I want to lean into my Americanness. Accent is irrevocably tied to conceptions of nativeness. Linguists note that nativeness is a combination of features including phonetics (the production and articulation of sound), phonology (the relationship of sound patterns), and prosodic features that include stress, intonation, and rhythm (which are known as suprasegmentals). Yet they also recognize that nativeness is perceived as a marker of authenticity because it signifies a group's primordial essence and its territorial associations.[21] Like an individual's eye color or gait, accent nativeness is widely understood as a hereditary acquisition that requires little to no exertion to achieve. Learning a non-native language and particularly the "right" accent, on the other hand, requires an investment of time and effort.[22] If the non-native accent represents the "labored artifice of a secondarily learned language," the native accent, in contrast, is heard as accentless and a signifier of one's mother tongue.[23] It simply is.

Admittedly, many language learners would likely agree that getting the accent of a target language right is a significant component of the language-learning process. If you have had the experience of having to repeat a word in another language several times because a native speaker does not understand what you are saying, you know the importance of accent. Indeed, to the language learner there is no greater compliment than being told one sounds native or local. This feeling is beautifully captured in Alice Kaplan's language memoir *French Lessons*, in which she describes her efforts to rid her pronunciation of its American vestiges and sound like a French native speaker. When she finally acquires the French /r/, she recognizes the extent of this achievement. "It felt normal! I had it. With this 'r' I could speak French. I wouldn't be screaming my Americanness every time I spoke. 'R' was my passport."[24]

Passing as a native French speaker afforded Kaplan a form of anonymity that became a source of both linguistic and cultural capital—what Pierre Bourdieu terms *habitus*. It is precisely this allure of the native accent that makes the Effie Hertzke phenomenon, which opens this chapter, so compelling. Hertzke's distinctly Americanized Hebrew disrupted the expectation that legitimacy as a Hebrew speaker required sounding Israeli "native." Listening to Hertzke and seeing the public reaction she engendered prompted me to listen more closely to how Hebrew enthusiasts themselves talk about their accents and the meanings they ascribe to them. In the interviews, accent frequently emerged as a focal point, linking participants' reflections on nativeness, authenticity, and American Jewish identity. At once a source of pride and an object of critique, the American Hebrew accent provides a valuable lens for exploring how enthusiasts negotiated their identities as American Jews and positioned themselves in relation to Israeli Hebrew speakers.

The Sound of Jewish Nationalism

Before examining contemporary Hebrew enthusiasts' views on the American Hebrew accent, it is essential to understand the historical language ideologies that connected Hebrew pronunciation debates to Jewish nationalism. A useful point of departure is the understanding of how Jewish nationalists saw the revival of Hebrew as a modern, spoken, and secular language as an endeavor that symbolically linked the Jewish people to their ancestral tongue and the Land of Israel. Debates about the Hebrew accent thus became central to Zionist efforts to reject what they perceived as the emptiness of diasporic Judaism and to reaffirm an ontological connection with the Land of Israel. Hebrew revivalists—a group that came to comprise linguists, educators, and language policymakers—devoted themselves not only to constructing syntactic structures and the vocabulary necessary for modern life but also to defining the very sound of Hebrew speech. As Harshav noted, pronunciation was "not just a phonetic issue, it gives specific character to Israeli speech and its speakers."[25] The establishment of a standardized Land of Israel accent became a cultural, aesthetic, and political imperative—an attempt to unify Jews from diverse diasporic backgrounds and forge a shared national identity. In this sense, accent emerged as a crucial component of Zionist nation-building, transforming phonetic differences into ideological battlegrounds over authenticity, belonging, and the character of the emerging nation.[26]

Standardizing Hebrew pronunciation, however, was a deeply contested process. At its center lay the question of which Hebrew phonological model should serve as the national standard. Eastern European Ashkenazi Jews—many of them nationalists, socialists, secularists, and revolutionaries—arrived in Palestine with a range of Ashkenazi Hebrew accents that were influenced by Yiddish, German, Russian, and other Central and Eastern European languages. They encountered long-established, religious Sephardi and Mizrahi communities in Jerusalem, Safed, Tiberias, and Hebron who adhered to pronunciation traditions rooted in Iberian and Middle Eastern Hebrew.[27] The linguistic differences were significant, involving the articulation of pharyngeal consonants (such as *chet*, *tet*, *ayin*, and *kaf*), stress patterns, and vowel quality. The Ashkenazi Hebrew used for Torah reading in the diaspora—marked by Yiddish phonetic features—was derided by revivalists as evidence of "perverse, sloppy, irrational behavior" born of exile, further underscoring how pronunciation became entwined with ideological projects of renewal and self-definition.[28]

Historian Miryam Segal's work examining the genealogy of the proto-Israeli accent in Hebrew literature in the early days of the Yishuv (the Jewish community in Mandatory Palestine) helps us understand the stakes of these language fights. Segal argues that, by the late 1920s, accent functioned as "a nationometer" that gauged the success of Jewish nationalism.[29] For Hebrew revivalists, this meant addressing existing accent variance and determining their authenticity claims. For Mizrahi and Sephardi intellectuals, debates about the Hebrew accent were a "matter of not only aesthetics; they were also a matter of gaining material access to Zionist circles and shaping the national project."[30] In the end, the revivalists (who were mostly Ashkenazi and Yiddish speaking) opted for the Sephardic variation (that of Syrian Jews), believing that this pronunciation was pure and aesthetically pleasing, best preserved the phonetic characteristics of Biblical Hebrew, and represented the prestige of the Iberian literary and scholarly traditions of the Sephardic Golden Age.[31] This accent, they believed, could promote nation building among a disparate Jewish population; it "provided a linguistic garb to the animosities, mutual contempt, and even hatred between Jewish ethnic groups that had lived for centuries in different territories."[32]

If the Yiddish of the Ashkenazi immigrant was dismissed as the degraded tongue of irredeemably diasporic Jews, the massive influx of Sephardic and Mizrachi immigrants from the Middle East and North Africa arriving with their own varieties of Hebrew pronunciations carried their own set of concerns. As the Sephardi accent was similar to the pronunciation system of Arabic, it represented a competing source of regional and historical concerns, with revivalists fearing that if Jews sounded too much like Arab speakers it would endanger their distinctive claims to the land.[33] "Jews could run afoul in two ways," writes scholar

Marco Di Giulio. They risked being either "too Arabic in their pronunciation or not being Arabic enough."[34] They would be perceived either as overtly Arab and raise doubts about their distinctive Jewish ethnic identity or as not sounding Arabic enough and thus jeopardize claims of Jewish indigeneity to the region. Put plainly, Jews had to sound native to the territory, but not too much.

Debates over the proper sound of Hebrew mobilized a wide range of stakeholders, each advancing arguments about the "right" degree of Arabic influence on Hebrew diction. Some framed their objections aesthetically, claiming that the articulation of the pharyngeal phonemes *chet* and *ayin*—shared with Arabic—was harsh or unpleasant to the ear. Medical professionals and public health advocates went further, warning that incorrect production of certain Sephardic sounds could damage the "soft tissue" of the vocal apparatus of Yiddish-speaking immigrants, leading to hoarseness, throat pain, or even worsening asthmatic symptoms.[35] Others, drawing on racialized and pseudoscientific claims, argued that Ashkenazi Jews were physically incapable of producing these sounds because their speech organs had undergone evolutionary transformation as a result of living in shtetls that were rife with parasites, germs, and infirmity. On that score, moderating or eliminating some of the overly Arabic demands of the Sephardic accent was framed as a therapeutic intervention required to treat the debilitated, subjugated diasporic Jewish body and remake it as strong and healthy in the Land of Israel. Taken together, these arguments reveal that the codification of Israeli Hebrew pronunciation was not a purely linguistic matter but part of a broader ideological project linking language, nationhood, and Jewish authenticity. While these debates are central to understanding Zionist historiographies, their legacy also continues to shape contemporary discussions about the Hebrew accent in Israel.[36] They also raise new questions about the Hebrew accents of diaspora Jews. Against this historical backdrop, the next section turns to Hebrew enthusiasts' own reflections on their Hebrew accents and how such talk negotiates what it means to be an American Jew.

The American Hebrew Accent

Hebrew enthusiasts consistently described the American Hebrew accent as unmistakable.[37] They reported being able to identify it immediately upon hearing it, even if they struggled to articulate its precise linguistic features or to specify all the ways it diverged from Israeli Hebrew pronunciation.[38] Though a full analysis of the linguistic differences between these two accents is beyond the scope of this book, the main differences are due to phonetic substitution and phonological transfer. Phonetic substitution refers to replacing consonants that are not part of the American English phonetic inventory with ones that are. Because the Hebrew letter *resh*—the uvular fricative /ʁ/ (think of the r-sound in the French *rendez-vous*)—is a challenging phoneme for American English speakers to pronounce, they often replace this sound with one of the /r/ phonemes (e.g., the alveolar flap, retroflex rhotic) more commonly used in American English, or with an [l] phoneme depending on the phonological environment. The second category, phonological transfer, refers to applying the rules of American English phonology to Hebrew. Common examples of this are when voiceless velar fricatives are glottalized, such that /x/ becomes [h], as in the case of *Chanukah* being pronounced as *Hanukkah*. Another example is when the voiceless alveolar sibilant affricate /ts/ becomes [s], as in the case of *tsabar* (an Israeli-born person) being pronounced *sabar*. Other examples of phonological changes include the use of epenthesis—the process of adding a schwa—in certain consonant clusters, such as when American Hebrew speakers say *kesat* and not *ktsat* (a little). Differences are also found in prosodic features, including stress patterns. Israeli Hebrew speakers stress the last syllable, or the second to last syllable, whereas American English speakers typically stress the first syllable. The easiest example of this is again to refer to my own name: Sha-RON versus SHA-ron. As a prosodic phenomenon in spoken language, word-level stress is what allows listeners to distinguish between words with the same segmental sequence (i.e., the individual phonemes of a sound). Word stress makes it difficult for American Hebrew speakers to discern between two nouns, as in the case of *BO-ker* (morning) and *bo-KER* (cowboy).

Many of these features are taught to American Hebrew learners in synagogue services and supplemental religious classes, where the vast majority of American Jews are first exposed to Hebrew sounds in prayer and ceremonial rituals. This is best captured in the difference between American and Israeli Hebrew speakers' pronunciation of the words *tallis* (American) and *tallit* (Israeli)—a fringed garment Jews wear as a prayer shawl. Hebrew enthusiasts rarely described the distinctions between these words or others in technical linguistic terms. Yet when prompted, they readily generated numerous examples. Equally important, conversations about the American Hebrew accent elicited a wide spectrum of affective responses—ranging from shame to pride, and everything in between. Their reflections about their own pronunciation and that of other American Jews and Israeli Hebrew speakers showed how accent carried meaning far beyond its acoustic properties. These differences were not merely matters of sound; they were imbued with cultural and symbolic weight and functioned as markers of American Jewish identity.

Self-Deprecation, Insecurity, and Defeatism

Hebrew enthusiasts readily supplied comments about their Hebrew accents. Most strikingly, these sentiments included feelings of embarrassment, shame, and insecurity. As one woman remarked, she wished she sounded "more real." Participants characterized the American Hebrew way of speaking using descriptors such as:

> It is not using the correct letters because we don't say the *chet* or *ayin* strong enough. We don't roll the *reshes*.
>
> American Hebrew sounds like someone speaking in the rhythm of English but with Hebrew words. The stress is all wrong.
>
> It sounds like a Hebrew speaker has a bad cold or something. Very nasal. As soon as I hear "Ani rotze" [I want], I know [it is an American speaking]. Everyone knows [it is an American speaking], sadly.

With a nod to Theodor Herzl's famous dictum, "If you will it, it is no dream," George, a former teacher from New York, quipped: "I can will it all I want, but the reality is that my desire to sound native will always be that—a dream." For others, the emotional toll of sounding too American when they spoke in Hebrew was even more pronounced. Bob, a corporate lawyer, shared his frustration: "I sound terrible and feel like others are pitying me, which makes me want to stop talking." His frustration was amplified by the knowledge that his Hebrew was largely error-free. What mattered, he understood, was not *what* he said but *how* he said it. For Bob, his accent determined how others perceived him.

Jennifer, a woman with advanced Hebrew skills, recounted listening to a short audio clip she had recorded for an Israeli friend and feeling a visceral sense of dismay: "I knew I did not sound great, but I had no idea I sounded like *that*." Richard, an accountant from New Jersey, expressed similar resignation: "The way we speak Hebrew is something that many American Jews share," he observed, "but never take pride in." For him the American Hebrew accent was a "stain" on what was otherwise a robust commitment to Jewish culture. Others described a sense of personal defeat when commenting on their Hebrew pronunciation. Barbara, a polyglot in her early sixties, contrasted her Hebrew accent with her experience speaking French: "I think I did have a pretty good French accent," she said. She noticed that native French speakers rarely switched to English when she spoke to them. However, this was not the case in Israel. "But when I listen to my Hebrew," she admitted, "I know that I'm not making the sounds right, so yes, it does bother me." Betty, an avid Hebrew learner, was strikingly critical of her classmates' speech: "The accents in that class, by the way, are horrendous. I couldn't understand people for weeks because of their accents." Though she did not claim to sound like a native Israeli, she took pride in avoiding what she called "the worst American attributes" of Hebrew pronunciation: "Even if I'm only speaking with other Americans, I work hard to use an Israeli accent." Another woman mentioned that she tried to compensate for her American accent by physically changing her body's positioning when she spoke Hebrew. To demonstrate this transformation, she sat up straight and spoke louder. Returning to her regular posture and volume, she admitted that this projection of confidence had a downside. "Sometimes," she worried that she looked like "some high-strung looney causing everyone else to ask, what is wrong with this woman?"

Feelings of insecurity were not limited to amateur Hebrew users.[39] Literary scholar Alan Mintz wrote candidly about being heard as a

Hebrew-speaking imposter. Once he had decided to go from "a Hebrew-loving doctoral student studying Victorian literature to being a scholar of Modern Hebrew literature," he experienced a change in his relationship to the language, which "left him plagued with self-doubt." Being a professional scholar of Hebrew literature raised the stakes of sounding authentic. "As long as I did not aspire to be regarded as a Jewish studies scholar, my facility with Hebrew, the accoutrement of an amateur, was regarded as impressive and noble. But once I decided to profess Hebrew, the rules of the game changed demonstrably. The glass that had been half full, or at least filled up part of the way, seemed, in my eyes, proportionally empty." Even after an impressive scholarly career, he admitted that speaking Hebrew was never fully natural but rather a "self-conscious performance."[40] For Mintz, as for other Hebrew enthusiasts, accent was an indelible marker of outsider status, a reminder that no depth of knowledge or love of Hebrew could completely dispel feelings of linguistic imposture. These metalinguistic commentaries about accent convey an American Jewish Hebrew inferiority complex, defined by feelings of inadequacy or insecurity. For some, accent inferiority was a *fait accompli*, perceived as an irredeemable aspect of being an American Hebrew speaker. When perceived as such, Hebrew enthusiasts begrudgingly accepted their fate. Others were unwilling to accept a defeatist attitude and looked to approximate Israeli Hebrew accent patterns. In both cases, language ideologies about the American Hebrew accent were rarely solely about the actual phonetic or prosodic features. Rather, when Hebrew enthusiasts spoke about their Hebrew accents they engaged in a discourse of comparison, judging themselves in relation to their Hebrew-speaking counterparts in Israel. Even when they had a high degree of Hebrew competence in grammar and vocabulary usage, the American Hebrew accent signified inferiority. Reflections on their own pronunciation and that of other American Hebrew speakers revealed that accent mattered in ways that exceeded the purely phonetic. While Hebrew language ideologies of peoplehood position Hebrew as a unifying force among Jews, commentaries about accent suggest how sound can function as a marker of difference.

One might assume that Israeli Hebrew speakers would welcome American Jews' efforts to learn and use Hebrew. However, the opposite was more common. Hebrew enthusiasts often remarked that it was difficult to get Israelis to speak to them in Hebrew at all, a phenomenon many attributed to Israelis' knowledge of conversational English and their lack of patience. Yet many also faulted Israeli Hebrew speakers' disdain for the American Hebrew accent. Whether this blame was real or imagined, many believed that once they started speaking and their "accent came out," Israelis made a series of judgments about them. Sarah, a New Yorker, shared with me her Israeli son-in-law's request that she refrain from using Hebrew when she interacted with her young grandson being raised in Tel Aviv. It was not her grammatical errors that bothered her son-in-law. Rather, her son-in-law was afraid his son would pick up the American Hebrew accent, which could cause the preschool children to ridicule the young boy. Yet this request was not without some irony. Sarah was also acutely aware that one of her roles as grandmother was serving as the English educator, as her daughter and son-in-law wanted their child to speak fluent English with an American accent because of the professional benefits it offered in Israeli society. Immersed in Israeli culture, Sarah understood that the American Hebrew accent lacked linguistic and social capital, and was often used in popular media as shorthand to depict characters that were dimwitted, lazy, weak, and cultural outsiders.[41] In other words, the American Hebrew accent underwent enregisterment—a linguistic process in which a form of the language is "linked to stereotypic pragmatic effects" and shapes how people come to understand themselves in relation to others.[42]

Barbara, the aforementioned woman who felt that her Hebrew accent was never as good as her French accent, noted that her Israeli Hebrew-speaking interlocutors in New York City did nothing to refute this stereotype or boast her confidence. Indeed, it was her close Israeli friend, she recounted to me, who told her, "Give it up, Barbara. You don't sound any worse than everyone else [who speaks with an American Hebrew accent]. It isn't going to happen." Josh, an avid learner with "really good Hebrew," had decided speaking Hebrew with Israelis he interacted with was no longer worth the effort. Nonetheless, he did note the irony that he was expected to endure Israelis' English mistakes or bad English accent. Andy, from Westchester, echoed this point, expressing that he did not understand why he had to be the one to "give in" and listen to error-filled English instead of having an error-free conversation in Hebrew. Yet like Josh he did not take Israeli Hebrew speakers' obstinacy personally. "They have absolutely no interest in speaking Hebrew to me," he acquiesced. "They'll speak Hebrew to their friends and their family, but they're not going to speak Hebrew to an American." Others noted a paradox. Hebrew is frequently celebrated for its ability to link ancient and modern forms, evolving to meet the needs of its modern speakers. Yet, as Frances remarked with biting sarcasm, this supposed flexibility seemed not to "have any room for my bad *resh*" or to "accept me putting the stress on the wrong part of the word."

Despite their disappointment, many Hebrew enthusiasts recognized that accent differences reflected broader divergences in how American and Israeli Jews construct Jewish identity. As scholars of language ideology remind us, linguistic forms such as accents are not neutral but index or signify particular social groups' experiences. David, an active member of his Reform synagogue, considered his Hebrew pronunciation reasonable, explaining that American Jews "spend a lot of their Jewish lives in synagogues or doing rituals at home in which they are using the pronunciation of *siddur* Hebrew." By contrast he acknowledged that, for many Israelis, "Hebrew is a cultural and national identity." In this sense differences in accent indexed more than divergent ways of sounding; they articulated divergent forms of Jewish experiences. While participants could rationalize these differences, accepting their social implications was not always easy. Rachel, an American-born daughter of an Israeli father who did not speak Hebrew at home, recalled being mocked on a kibbutz where her cousins lived for speaking what they called "old Ashkenazi Hebrew." "They thought it was the funniest thing in the world," she remembered, and described her Hebrew as "American archaic Hebrew" that did not match what Israelis spoke.

These moments heightened her sense of being positioned outside the Hebrew-speaking community, underscoring how linguistic features can constitute symbolic boundaries of belonging. Laura, another participant, recounted a similar experience of linguistic estrangement. Growing up in the early 1980s, she struggled to reconcile the Ashkenazi-inflected Hebrew of her synagogue where congregants said *SHA-bbes* and *Rosh Ha-SHA-na*—with the Ashkenazi Hebrew pronunciation. At the same time, her Sunday-school Israeli teachers said *Sha-BBAT* and *Rosh Ha-sha-NA*. It was only during her undergraduate studies in Modern Hebrew that she realized the distinction between what she called "synagogue Hebrew" and "street Hebrew"—the everyday spoken form used in Israel. This awareness prompted her to change her pronunciation, shifting from the Americanized *MA-zal tov* ("a Hebrew that Israelis don't recognize as their own") to the Israeli pronunciation of *ma-ZAL tov*. Doing so made her feel "in the know" and that she was no longer an "ignorant American." Importantly, Laura framed this shift not as an attempt to pass as Israeli or reject her religious upbringing. Rather, it was a choice to take on a different form of Jewish authenticity. In this way, choice of accent helped her navigate American and Israeli forms of Jewish identity.

Dayenu: Judgments of Enoughness

Claims of American Jewish authenticity were often entangled with implicit judgments about what kind of Hebrew accent was "enough" for a speaker to be recognized as a legitimate user of the language. In coding and analyzing interview transcripts, I was struck by how frequently participants used the word *enough* when linking their pronunciation to their sense of Jewish and American identity. Sociolinguists Jan Blommaert and Piia Varis's concept of "judgments of enoughness" provides a useful framework for understanding this dynamic.[43] As they explain, the benchmark for inclusion in an identity category—being accepted as a "real" or "authentic" member—depends on whether one displays *enough* of the expected features, even if not all of them. The precise threshold, however, is rarely explicit. Authenticity, in this sense, is not an absolute state but a negotiated assessment of sufficiency within a particular social and cultural context. Applying this concept to Hebrew learners' self-perceptions invites questions about which criteria of "enoughness" they invoked and what these reveal about their imagined place within American Jewish life.

While many participants described their Hebrew accents from a deficit perspective—lamenting what they lacked compared to native Israelis—others articulated their own standards of "enoughness," expressing satisfaction with their distinctly American accents as reflections of who they were. Some, like Richard, a longtime Hebrew student in New York City, criticized peers who tried "to sound more Israeli than the Israelis." When describing this tendency, he exaggeratedly mimicked fellow learners who overemphasized the glottal consonants *resh*, *ayin*, and *chet*, remarking that "you can almost feel the spit land on your face from the effort." For Richard, adopting a "fake Israeli accent" meant trying "to be something they weren't." His critique echoes William Labov's notion of *hypercorrection*—when speakers, aiming for prestige, overuse linguistic forms associated with higher-status varieties and thereby reveal their insecurity about linguistic legitimacy.[44] In Richard's view, American Hebrew speakers' exaggerated pronunciations represented precisely this kind of hypercorrection. For Richard, these attempts at authenticity overshot the mark and violated the subtle boundary of "enoughness," paradoxically signaling inauthenticity instead.

Gloria, a member of a Hebrew meetup group on the West Coast, connected her sense of Hebrew "enoughness" to her American Jewish identity, though with a twist. Recalling her experience as a student in a small *ulpan* in the early 2010s, she vividly remembered her teacher once pulling her aside and saying it was "harder to teach me than somebody who knew nothing, because I talked so fast in Hebrew, I made mistakes all the time, and my accent was terrible." Rather than feeling demoralized, Gloria embraced her Americanized Hebrew with pride: "I couldn't care less," she told me, grinning. Rejecting the option of hypercorrection, she described her style of Hebrew as "present-day male Hebrew," which for her meant, "I don't do past [tense], I don't do future [tense], I don't do female [conjugations], and I don't make any distinction between *ayin* and *aleph*. But if you understand Hebrew, you know what I am talking about—which is good enough for me. I'm having fun, and it's making me happy."[45]

Although her teacher commented that Gloria's Hebrew contained so many grammatical and phonological errors that she did not know where to begin to correct them, Gloria refused to define her success by native-speaker standards. Instead, she set her own criteria for what counted as "good enough," prioritizing the joy and empowerment she felt when using the language over linguistic exactness: "I couldn't care less because I know I am understood." From an ideological perspective, Gloria's position offers an instructive counterpoint to the notion that there is only one "real" way of speaking Hebrew that serves as a unifying agent for world Jewry. For her, what brought Jews together was not conformity to Israeli Hebrew standards. It was a shared commitment to using Hebrew at all. Seen in this way, her proudly American accent was not a marker of failure or inferiority. Rather, it was an articulation of an ideology that Hebrew's strength as a Jewish symbol lies in its ability to accommodate diverse forms of expression.

Gloria interpreted "enoughness" within a broader understanding of Jewish community, emphasizing shared commitments rather than precise linguistic practices. Allison, by contrast, framed "enoughness" in terms of her positionality as an American Jew. Reflecting on specific Hebrew phonemes, she noted, "I've learned that *chet* [a voiceless pharyngeal fricative] and *chaf* [a voiceless uvular fricative] are really different when an Israeli says them." However, from her perspective, this was a difference without a distinction: "My ear isn't going to hear the difference between the two." While sounding more nativelike was "definitely doable," Allison did not feel compelled to acquire "their [Israelis'] language." She was comfortable that her accent was "good enough," even if she did not distinguish between phonemes or if she put the stress on the wrong part of a word. In her calculations, mastery of these distinctions was meaningful to Israeli speakers. As an American Jew, she was exempt from such expectations: "We are all Jews, but we are different in a whole bunch of ways. My experience as an American Jew is different, and so it makes sense that my relationship—and whatever connection I have—to Hebrew is going to be different." Allison's perspective highlights how judgments of "enoughness" are relational and perspectival and reflect broader social and cultural conditions rather than purely linguistic norms. As she saw it, these differences extend beyond one's accent: "It is more than how I pronounce my *resh* or my inability to say *ayin* correctly. It is how I see the world, my experiences, and everything that makes up how I live my life as a Jew in the United States." In Allison's perspective, her way of speaking Hebrew was a marker of American Jewish identity that gave voice to her lived experience.

For a handful of Hebrew enthusiasts, the Americanized Hebrew accent was even a source of pride. One woman who had long been uneasy about her pronunciation considered hiring an Israeli news broadcaster to help with accent reduction but eventually embraced her accent: "I've decided to just embrace mine. Getting to this point has been a lot of work, and I have nothing to be ashamed of." Similarly, Sally, from Long Island, who had worked with an accent coach for several years, reached a turning point in 2019 while watching news coverage of Israel's *Beresheet* spacecraft's failed attempt to make a soft landing on the moon. Noticing that the head of the space agency "was clearly American, because he spoke with an American accent," she realized, "If you can get to that level and it's okay to have an American accent, I'm okay with mine." This realization—that an American accent was not an obstacle to professional achievement in Israeli society—led her to discontinue her accent coaching and reframe her accent as a sign of accomplishment. Judy from New York experienced a similar understanding of "enoughness" through social acceptance. Having considered a $350 Hebrew accent reduction class, she recounted a "sea change" after speaking with a close Israeli friend: "I always thought that my accent sounds bad to Israelis," she explained. However, her friend reassured her that "the American accent sounds adorable . . . and we [Israelis] love it." This validation allowed Judy to assert her legitimacy as an American Hebrew speaker and prioritize the joy of speaking Hebrew: "I don't know if it [this opinion about the American accent] is right or wrong, but it changed my whole thinking. I'm not embarrassed anymore at all and ready to say to anyone who says anything about it: 'Yeah, I'm an American Jew and I've got an accent in Hebrew. You got a problem with it, it is your problem. Who cares?'"

Taken together, these accounts reveal how American Hebrew speakers negotiated judgments of "enoughness" by balancing broader ideological understandings of what Hebrew signified with their own lived experiences and linguistic needs. For Gloria, Jenny, Sally, and Judy, the American Hebrew accent did not signal linguistic deficiency but rather embodied a meaningful expression of identity. Although none claimed full mastery of the language, they viewed their proficiency as more than sufficient. It was, in other words, more than enough for what they needed. Their Hebrew, with its distinctly American inflections, represented Jewish diversity, personal commitment to the language, and pride in a localized expression of American Jewish identity.

Being an American Hebrew Speaker

When Hebrew enthusiasts discuss their American Hebrew accents, they are doing more than commenting on pronunciation—they are engaging with the broader terrain of Israel–American Jewish relations, competing visions of Jewish life, and the ongoing question of who defines Jewish authenticity. Many participants joked about or even mocked their own accents, sometimes viewing them as inferior to the "real" Hebrew of native Israeli speakers or expressing frustration when Israelis failed to respond to their Hebrew attempts. Yet these reactions rarely discouraged them from speaking, nor did they diminish their sense of American Jewish identity. While some expressed regret over their inability to perceive or produce particular Hebrew phonemes, many reframed these so-called errors as markers of authenticity in their own right. By embracing their distinctive pronunciation, they claimed ownership of Hebrew as part of their diasporic identity, rather than as a linguistic domain exclusively tied to Israeli norms. Much like Effie Hertzke, whose story opened this chapter, these American Hebrew enthusiasts metaphorically rolled up their sleeves, flexed their diasporic muscles, and asserted agency through their Hebrew usage.

Notably, several speakers explicitly rejected the notion that authenticity in Hebrew could be determined by a single accent or by a group of speakers. "No one can claim ownership of any language," one woman declared during our interview. "Hebrew belongs to anyone who wants it to be theirs." Acknowledging the multilingual reality of Israeli society, she added, "I'm not sure there is one Hebrew sound anymore."[46] While such reflections illustrate Hebrew enthusiasts resignifying diasporic belonging through talk about accent, they also highlight the complex forms of agency involved in negotiating homeland–diaspora linguistic relations. Literary scholar Nancy Berg has described this dynamic as an incommensurable tension, one she herself has experienced as a non-native Hebrew-speaking American scholar of Hebrew literature.[47] In a 2019 Zoom conversation, Berg emphasized that even as Israeli society has become increasingly multilingual, debates over Hebrew authenticity continue to reinforce symbolic boundaries between Israeli and American Jews. "You have Israelis who think they're the only ones who know anything," she remarked, describing a "possessiveness of knowledge" that marginalizes even highly proficient American Hebrew speakers. When Israeli Jewish life is understood as impervious to American Jews, it not only potentially silences American Jews but "leaves the American who is serious about learning and speaking Hebrew in an anomalous position."[48]

Education scholar Sam Wineburg similarly reflected on this sense of anomaly. When he requested that we conduct our Zoom interview in Hebrew, his fluency and ease in the language were striking.[49] Yet, as he explained, this hard-earned linguistic mastery placed him in an unusual social position: "I'm not Israeli," he said. "I'm a Jew who knows the language." In Israel, his expertise rendered him "a strange bird," someone who defied expectations of what an American Jew could sound like. Such experiences underscore the broader homeland–diaspora tension that Hebrew proficiency exposes. Wineburg's Hebrew, in other words, is not merely a linguistic achievement. It is a provocation that exposes the fragility of the categories themselves and reveals that the boundary between Israeli and American Jew is maintained not only by geography or citizenship but by who is and is not supposed to sound like they belong. This provocation is similarly noted by historian James Loeffler, who observes that "too much Hebrew [among non-Israelis] raises a red flag," because it disrupts the conceptual binary separating Israeli and American Jews. "If one has taken the trouble to learn Hebrew," Loeffler writes, "then the logical step is to become a citizen of the State of Israel. There is no other conceptual place to situate American Jews inside the Israeli political imaginary except as foreign visitors or fellow citizens. An American who speaks Hebrew risks destabilizing that neat binary division."[50] The premise that Hebrew can bring Jews together, it turns out, may rest on an unspoken condition that each group speaks it on its own terms, from its own side of the divide.

Loeffler's insight underscores the ideological weight that ways of speaking Hebrew continue to carry as markers of authenticity and belonging. His argument also points to the challenges facing Hebrew educators in the United States, who, while aware of these ideological debates, must engage in the pragmatic work of teaching the language. As scholars of education have long noted, language policy and pedagogy are never ideologically or politically neutral. Hebrew classrooms are no exception. The next chapter turns to the formal educational domain and explores how Hebrew educators in the United States since the early 2000s have designed programs that reflect distinct ideological visions of what Hebrew can *do* for American Jews. By examining these educational initiatives and the language ideologies that underlie them, we gain deeper insight into how Hebrew remains central to ongoing debates about educating the next generation of American Jews.

6

HEBREW EDUCATION AND THE EDUCATED JEW

Marsha, the Hebrew language teacher at Golda Meir Jewish Day School (GMJDS), a pluralistic Jewish school located in the New York metro area, organized the books needed for her fifth grade Hebrew class.[1] This lesson was the culmination of a unit on Honi HaMe'agel ("the circle drawer"), a pious figure from the first century BCE, written about in the Talmud, who was committed to Jewish theological tenets and environmental conservation. The connection between Honi and nature is why tales of his miracles are often taught around Tu B'Shevat, a biblical holiday that has come to represent Jewish Earth Day. The lesson in Marsha's class, which took place at the start of the holiday, entailed the students collectively reading a story from a unit called *Yomano Shel Choni* (Honi's Journal).

As it was already halfway into the academic year, the students were well versed in the participatory structure of the Hebrew class. Marsha picked a student to read several lines of the story out loud, students translated the text into English, and Marsha assisted with unknown vocabulary words. Occasionally, other students would collaborate on the translation, with this pattern repeating itself until the end of the story. Except for the Hebrew text being read out loud, Marsha's short instructions (e.g., "Ben, *ata rotze leekro bevakasha*?"—Ben do you want to read, please?), and the frequent use of words such as *yofi* (great) and *tov me'od* (very good) affirming the students' efforts, the class was conducted in English. After finishing the story, the students completed reading-comprehension exercises, whose instructions were written in Hebrew. Students were asked to respond to a variety of question types, including fill-ins, inference making, identifying main ideas and supporting details, and sharing thoughts—which the students did in a mixture of Hebrew and English.

This lesson echoed many I observed during my four-month ethnographic study of Marsha's fifth grade Hebrew class.[2] Once the class period ended and the students ran off to eat their lunches in the cafeteria, I helped Marsha reorganize the classroom. Usually at this point, I talked about the lesson with Marsha, who was incredibly generous in answering my incessant questions. Born and raised in the United States, Marsha had moved to Israel as a young adult to teach English and had studied Hebrew in an *ulpan*. Years later, she had married an Israeli living in the States and had become an active member in her local Jewish community and synagogue. She had a sardonic sense of humor and a warm personality, and it was clear her students adored her. During our debriefings, I listened to Marsha talk about the goal of her lessons and her pedagogical choices. With almost twelve years of Hebrew teaching experience under her belt, Marsha still had many questions about the goal of Hebrew education in Jewish day school education. Well trained in the components of the school's selected curricular program, Tal Am, Marsha enjoyed teaching it and made ample use of the abundant program material. Nonetheless, that afternoon after the Honi lesson, our post-lesson debriefing quickly shifted to a discussion about the challenges of teaching Talmudic stories and Jewish values, while also teaching Hebrew language.

Truth be told, this balancing act had been a recurring theme in many of our conversations. Though not responsible for Judaic studies at GMJDS, since there was also a Bible and rabbinics teacher, it often fell on Marsha to "cover" the Jewish topics, which included teaching about Jewish holidays, celebrations, commemorations (e.g., Holocaust Memorial Day, Israel Independence Day), Shabbat and synagogue rituals, and prayers—all of which integrated temporal varieties of Hebrew to various degrees. While teaching Jewish content and Hebrew skills often overlapped, they were not always aligned. GMJDS chose to use Tal Am—a curriculum that combined Hebrew language education and Jewish studies education for day school elementary-aged students—because the school perceived Hebrew learning as part and parcel of religious praxis. In practice, this juxtaposition was challenging. For the Hebrew lesson on Honi, Marsha had to decide between prioritizing the importance of the

Jewish values of humility, responsibility, and prayer, which the story of Honi exemplifies, and teaching discrete Hebrew language topics, including vocabulary acquisition and grammatical features, which were part of the school's official Hebrew curriculum. On top of this challenge, Marsha grappled with the school's classroom language policy regarding how much to speak in English or Hebrew during the lesson. Though Marsha knew that school administration wanted her to speak in Hebrew, she was not always sure what to do in real time, given what she knew about her students' receptive Hebrew skills as well as her desire to limit confusion among students with varying behavioral and cognitive needs. What was clear to Marsha was that she had to make a choice because "unlike Honi," she quipped, "I have no magical powers."

Part of this deliberation involved deep reflection about the purpose of Hebrew education at GMJDS. When pressed to articulate the school's vision, she responded:

> One of our primary goals is to introduce our children to Hebrew as a second language, as the language of the Jewish people, as a vehicle to connecting with the Jewish people, with the State of Israel, with their heritage when it comes to everything from prayer to text to Torah. Another goal, or complementary goal to that end, is to be able to speak. It [Hebrew] is a living language, and so [the goal is] to master it as students are comfortable conversing, writing, and reading as they build their identity as young Jews and hopefully the future generation of American Jews.

Quite clearly, this statement reveals an ambitious set of goals for teaching Hebrew. It covers acquiring Textual Hebrew to read sacred texts and participate in synagogue and home religious rituals, as well as learning Modern Hebrew for cultural and communicative goals. In principle, Marsha agreed with these dual goals, but also admitted that at times she felt like a "schizophrenic Hebrew teacher"—answering to the diverse voices involved in rationalizing and determining the goals of Hebrew education as a core component of Jewish education. One can accept the supposition that both forms of Hebrew—Textual and Modern—are critical to Jewish education in that they afford access to different forms of Jewish practice and still feel that trying to do both in the Hebrew language classroom defies reality, particularly given the constraints of time devoted to Hebrew education within the broader school-day schedule. Seeing Marsha juggling these overlapping demands put into stark relief the multitasking that Hebrew educators are asked to do.

Marsha's description of the school's dual-pronged Hebrew-learning outcomes is not unique among Jewish institutions educating American Jewish youth. Indeed, as education scholars Alex Pomson and Jack Wertheimer attest, teaching Textual and Modern Hebrew "remains a defining feature of day schools" and is "also perhaps the most prominent feature shared by a highly diverse, and frequently fragmented, collection of such schools."[3] The tacit assumption is that Hebrew education is not solely focused on language acquisition. Rather, it is wrapped up in the ethical urgency of shaping students' Jewish identities, comprised of religious, spiritual, cultural, and identity dimensions. Hebrew education is, in other words, a moral enterprise oriented toward two aims. The first is presentist in nature, concerned with equipping students with the necessary literacy and spoken Hebrew competencies for their immediate studies. The second aim, while connected to the first, is prospective and grounded in the premise that education enables particular forms of beliefs and behaviors in the future. Intertwined, these two goals position Hebrew education as an agent of participatory Jewishness. As such, the Jewish-educator-cum-Hebrew-language-instructor is tasked with shaping and cultivating students' orientations and beliefs so they can take up their role as Jewish adults who will ensure Jewish continuity.

What are we to make of Hebrew teachers like Marsha, who must grapple with the overlapping aspirations and expectations of teaching students to adopt positive feelings about Hebrew, see the language as a core component of Judaism and Jewish life, acquire the literacy know-how to participate in ceremonial rituals and textual study, develop communicative competence—all within the broader goal of ensuring that students will become the next generation of educated Jewish adults? Education scholar Tali Zelkowicz is not far off when she sardonically refers to multilayered efforts like this in Jewish education as the "misery of making Jews." As Zelkowicz notes, the obsessive focus on cultural reproduction and the belief that Jewish educators "make Jews" powers a learning culture in which "what matters most is what students will do with the learning one, five, or 25 years in the future, and not necessarily what it means in the present, this week, this day, and this class."[4] To prove her point, she writes that math teachers are not "responsible for cultivating math identities that will be strong enough to motivate them to date other math students, join math clubs in college, marry a mathematician, and ultimately raise good little mathematicians."[5] Yet Jewish educators are held to a different standard. When considered in light of Marsha's experience, we can see that Hebrew teachers are held to an even higher level of expectation, as their work is inescapably tied to efforts to cultivate a Jewish present and future through language educational praxis. Confronting this formidable task requires defining who counts as an "educated Jew," determining what forms of knowledge constitute that category, and articulating the desired outcomes of a successful Jewish education.[6]

Though philosophical in nature, these questions also have a pragmatic dimension. If the study of curriculum has taught us anything, it is that schools, with their limited time and resources, must prioritize what knowledge and values they want to pass on to the next generations. Sites of religious schooling are no different. Educational scholar Alan Peshkin astutely observed that "about every school it can be asked, 'what kind of person does it strive to develop?'"[7] It is a good question, meant to remind us that pedagogy and curriculum are never neutral but are to varying degrees part of the transmission of particular kinds of knowledge that schools, and by extension, society wants to (re)produce. Marsha's balancing act in her classroom, in this light, is understood as a high-stakes endeavor. The response to why teach Hebrew invariably shapes a broader discussion about different visions of Jewish life and, in some respects, what kind of Jewish community will exist in the future.[8]

While the previous three chapters examined Hebrew language ideologies as they emerged in the lived experiences of adult Hebrew enthusiasts, this chapter shifts the focus to a broader institutional level. It considers how Hebrew education functions as a vehicle for producing particular forms of Jewish knowledge and identity. Specifically, the chapter explores how beliefs about Hebrew learning intersect with wider educational aims, most notably, cultivating the "educated Jew" and ensuring Jewish continuity. By tracing the language ideologies embedded in Hebrew curricular initiatives over the past two decades, I show how Hebrew education has been positioned within larger debates about the purposes of Jewish education in day schools, supplementary programs, and public school contexts. As scholars of language ideology remind us, metalinguistic discourse is never confined to technical questions of grammar or usage; talk about language education always reflects the moral and political interests that shape schooling itself. Attending to this dynamic, I examine how specific beliefs about Hebrew instruction underwrite particular visions of Jewish knowledge and community. Educational theorist William Pinar's question, "What knowledge is of most worth?" offers a useful frame here.[9] In this light we can examine how responses to this question within the context of Hebrew education illuminate underlying assumptions about what kinds of Hebrew knowledge are considered most valuable for Jewish learners and Jewish life today.

How Hebrew Education Became Part of Jewish Identity Initiatives

This chapter is not a history of Hebrew education in the United States.[10] More modest in scope, it highlights some of the most significant central events, pioneering key figures, and groundbreaking Hebrew initiatives in day school, supplementary schools, and public schools over the past two decades—work that represents the creativity and commitment of Hebrew policy makers and educators navigating an evolving educational and American Jewish landscape. Nonetheless, taking on the topic of the state of Hebrew education does require some historical context, if at least to show that mobilizing Hebrew for Jewish desired outcomes is not new, but it has evolved over the years to adjust to the changing needs of the community. Historian Jonathan Krasner's extensive scholarship reminds us that, until the early 1900s, much of Hebrew education in the United States consisted of a "hodgepodge" of Jewish schools and institutions often taught by women volunteers who themselves had limited opportunities to learn the language but were charged with educating the (mostly male) children of poor immigrant families.[11] These conditions meant that Jewish children learned most of the prayers and Torah readings in English, along with some basic Hebrew literacy skills.[12] This all changed in the early decades of the 1900s, when Samson Benderly transformed Jewish education in the United States by promoting a modern, progressive vision that placed Hebrew language at the center of Jewish cultural and national renewal (see Chapter 1). As the founding director of the Bureau of Jewish Education in New York (established in 1910), Benderly and his team of progressive educators—who came to be known as the "Benderly Boys"—trained a generation of instructors to teach Hebrew as a living, spoken language rather than as a purely liturgical or textual one. By rejecting rote, synagogue-based instruction, he popularized *Ivrit b'Ivrit* (teaching Hebrew in Hebrew) and promoted Hebrew as a vehicle for cultivating modern Jewish identity for a new generation of American Jews. Importantly, the Benderly Hebrew revolution not only transformed the shape of Hebrew education in the United States; it also elevated the importance of talking *about* Hebrew, which became part of broader discussions about ensuring a robust Jewish future in the United States.

Benderly's revolution was driven by his admiration for and concerns about Protestant America. While he respected its emphasis on moral education and civic virtue, he also understood that American public culture was influenced by Protestant assumptions that cast Judaism as premodern and parochial.[13] For this reason, he appropriated the tools and rhetoric of Protestant schooling, yet he couched them in distinctly Jewish language, content, and purpose. Doing so, Benderly sought to secure Jewish belonging within the American civic project without yielding to the full assimilatory pressures of modern life. Less than half a century later, Jewish communal leaders and educators were worried that American Jews had become victims of their own acculturative success. By the early 1980s, communal leaders feared that American Jews were integrating too well and distancing themselves from traditional forms of Jewish practice and identification. The 1990 National Jewish Population Survey (NJPS), which revealed a surge in rates of intermarriage, Jewish apathy, disaffiliation, and below replacement-level birthrates, galvanized a collection of rabbis, scholars, educators, professional leaders, philanthropists, and national Jewish organizations across the religious and ideological spectrum to coalesce around an agenda to thwart these discouraging trends.[14] Rather than flounder on the shoals of paralysis, these stakeholders took action and focused on Jewish identity construction and reinforcement.[15] An influential report in 1990, aptly entitled *A Time to Act*, unequivocally stated that "the responsibility for developing Jewish identity and instilling a commitment to Judaism for this population now rests primarily with education."[16] With large investments in hand, philanthropists and communal thought leaders were convinced that a shift in communal priorities, along with an infusion of educational "innovation, experimentation, and growth," would galvanize efforts to ensure Jewish continuity.[17]

Institutional support and an influx of targeted funding resulted in two significant developments. First, it put renewed attention on Jewish education, an area of Jewish life that had struggled through "perfunctory treatment and neglect by the organized Jewish community."[18] Moving forward, Jewish educators and other sectors of the Jewish community saw each other as mutual soldiers in the battle for Jewish continuity. Second, the focus on pedagogical, curricular, and policy change spawned a "veritable identity industrial complex" whose reach extended into almost all aspects of American Jewish life.[19] Significant philanthropic investments, often in partnership with Jewish Federations, led to national initiatives, including Birthright Israel, the Foundation for Jewish Camping, Synagogue 2000, Partnership for Excellence in Jewish Education, and the Wexner Heritage Foundation. If assimilation and attenuating Jewish identification were identified as the causes of weakened Jewish identity, Jewish organizations' response was strengthening an affective connection to Jewishness through Israel-heritage tourism, summer camping, congregational schooling, day schools, and lay and professional leadership. Hebrew education was part of this massive effort, as communal leaders considered what aspects of the language could best buttress children's Jewish identity.

AVI CHAI and Hebrew Education

The role of Hebrew education in battling waning Jewish identity was a common topic at conferences and symposia at the turn of the twenty-first century.[20] Literature scholar Ruth Wisse recalled attending Alan Mintz's retreat focused on the role of Hebrew in America at the University of Maryland in 1990. Engaging in difficult conversations about the decline of Hebrew in the United States since the heydays of the Benderly revolution, participants reflected on potential strategies to "reverse this process."[21] The growing consensus at this event and others taking place in Jewish communal organizations was the need to focus on Jewish day schools, which were at the time undergoing a period of expansion and were seen as a solution to the limited hours supplementary afterschool or weekend Jewish schooling could offer. Day school growth required an urgent need for Hebrew curricula and age-appropriate materials.[22]

The AVI CHAI Foundation became a key player in responding to the need for Hebrew educational resources. A successful financial investor, Zalman Bernstein, created the AVI CHAI Foundation in 1984, with the goal of encouraging Jews "toward greater commitment to Jewish observance and lifestyle" and toward "mutual understanding and sensitivity."[23] After selling his investment firm in 2000, Bernstein used his liquidated share to provide "an enormous cash infusion to AVI CHAI's endowment," which grew to nearly half a billion dollars.[24] For close to two decades, AVI CHAI was seen as the "dominant force in the field of day school education and significantly impacted day school Hebrew education."[25] With the largest share of AVI CHAI's annual budget dedicated to its programs in North America, the foundation viewed day schools as a safeguard against assimilatory pressures and as the energizing nucleus to produce the next generation of committed American Jews. Susan Kardos, senior director of strategy and education planning at AVI CHAI between 2008 and 2019, recounted that as the organization embraced day schools, its mission evolved into a three-pronged focus on Jewish literacy, religious purposefulness, and commitment to Jewish peoplehood centered on Israel—a formula abbreviated as LRP. In Kardos's words, "Hebrew fit into all three," especially because there were not a lot of other curricular topics that could seamlessly work across these focal areas.[26] Joel Einleger, who served as senior officer and director of strategy at the foundation between 1998 and 2019, recalled that the AVI CHAI board never hesitated in their decision to embrace Hebrew as core to the organization's mission. As he noted, officers at the foundation believed that Hebrew programming for day schools was "the sweet spot" and offered a common purpose that could strategically advance the priorities of the organization.[27]

With a preliminary budget allocation, AVI CHAI funded the development of two comprehensive Hebrew curricular programs.[28] The first, Tal Am (an acronym for *Tochnit Limudim Ivrit U'moreshet*—Teaching Hebrew and Heritage Program), was an integrated Jewish studies–Hebrew education program. Aware of the work being done in Montreal with Tal Sela, which was already in use in first grade classrooms at 175 Jewish days schools by 2001, Lauren Merkin, a trustee at AVI CHAI, spearheaded the collaboration between AVI CHAI and Tal Am, with the plan to expand the program to into second and third grade. The second program, NETA (an acronym for *Noar LeTovat Halvrit*—Youth for the Good of Hebrew), was a day school Hebrew curriculum for middle and high school grades developed by Hila Kobliner and colleagues in partnership with Hebrew College. In 2001–22, the initial units of the NETA curriculum were piloted in thirteen schools. Within a decade, it was being used in eighty-eight schools in North America and more than twenty-five schools internationally.[29] AVI CHAI's commitment to Tal Am and NETA reflected its conviction that Hebrew education was a Jewish educational multiplier. According to Einleger, the organization was "interested in Hebrew as part of its mission to reinforce Judaism for Jews in America" and saw these curricular programs as an urgent corrective to the field of Hebrew education, which many believed had been neglected for years.[30] From the start, AVI CHAI was fully committed to revitalizing Hebrew education.[31] The foundation's "big bet" on Hebrew education was not merely ideological or rhetorical. According to Einleger, by the time AVI CHAI sunset its grantmaking in 2019, the foundation had invested close to $25,000,000 in these two Hebrew education programs, more than was spent on any other curricular initiatives.

Much of the foundation's fervency can be attributed to the individuals who spearheaded the programs. AVI CHAI had a great deal of faith in Tal Am's founder, Tova Shimon. Prior to leading the Tal Am team, Shimon had worked extensively as an educator.[32] Before meeting Yossi Prager, executive director for North America of the AVI CHAI Foundation (1994–2019), Shimon had created Tal Sela in Canada, and had a clear vision of the type of Hebrew curricular program she wanted to develop.[33] According to Shimon, Prager was hesitant about getting into the textbook-writing business, but was ultimately convinced of the program's importance. Perhaps what convinced Prager was the potential of Tal Am to distinguish itself from other curricular material being used at the time, which primarily focused on teaching decoding skills or presented decontextualized word lists with little Jewish content. As Shimon described it, Tal Am was conceptualized not merely as a Hebrew curriculum but as a "gestalt program" that rested on several core principles derived from brain-based research on how individuals learn languages, use their memory for retrieval functions, and process new information. Drawing on this scholarship, Tal Am articulated a pedagogical approach grounded in two key assumptions: that comprehension of every lexical item is not required for meaningful engagement with texts, and that language teaching should have far-reaching goals and not solely focus on what a learner needs in the short term to perform a particular task. In Shimon's words, the blueprint for a successful language-teaching program moved along a trajectory from "*tifkudi*" (functional) to "*inyani*" (pragmatic) to "*yetzirati*" (creative).[34]

Put together, these pedagogical assumptions underwrote Tal Am's epistemological pillars. In practice, they informed its curricular and programmatic design in three primary ways. The first was the espousal that Hebrew learners needed to "settle in" and process information through different cognitive tasks. The second prioritized learners' exposure to rich texts written at levels beyond their comprehension, utilizing the various temporal forms of Hebrew (e.g., Biblical, Mishnaic, and Modern) on the same page. The third advocated the connection between Hebrew learning and learning the *musagim va'arachim* (concepts and values) of Judaism (e.g., Shabbat, Jewish holidays, prayer, and Torah). These principles also dovetailed with AVI CHAI's belief in the integration of Hebrew and Jewish studies as a cornerstone of Jewish day school education. As Prager noted, "It wasn't, now close your religious books and we're going to take out your Hebrew language text." Instead, it was, "We are going to teach Hebrew as you're learning *Tanach* [Bible] and as you're learning *siddur* [prayerbook] and as you're learning about the *chagim* [Jewish holidays] and life in Israel."[35]

AVI CHAI committed to a long-term relationship with Tal Am, independently funding the full cost of its expansion to additional grades. Tal Am was not required to bring in investments from other philanthropic organizations.[36] The enormous extent of this commitment can be understood only in light of the massive scope of the project, which included creating and publishing books, workbooks, posters, games, and original music, as well as the logistical undertaking of shipping the created materials, much of which was stored in a warehouse in Canada, to schools across North America. At its height of production, the Tal Am team consisted of close to seventy full- and part-time workers and consultants (in both Montreal and Israel). AVI CHAI also invested heavily in professional pre-service and in-service training for Tal Am Hebrew teachers and principals at day schools.

The second Hebrew learning program, NETA, was created by Israeli Hila Kobliner, a teacher and curriculum writer for the Rothberg International School at the Hebrew University in Jerusalem. Kobliner's involvement in Hebrew education can be traced back to a sabbatical she took in 2000, when she taught a summer Hebrew class at Harvard and met Ruth Wisse, a Harvard professor and AVI CHAI trustee, who sat in on a Hebrew class.[37] Wisse recalled being drawn to Kobliner's "intelligent" and "energetic" teaching methods. Kobliner remembered the immediate connection between the two women.[38] As Kobliner recounted, as she and Wisse discussed the creation of a Hebrew program that could nurture and grow the future of Jewish leadership, they came to the conclusion that the university classroom was not the right venue, because it served students of various faiths and was too late for Jewish students who needed this intervention before they reached university age. Identifying high schoolers at Jewish day schools as the target learners, they created a survey that was distributed to Hebrew educators and organized a convening for day school principals and Hebrew coordinators to understand the barriers facing high school Hebrew educators. For Kobliner, it was clear that the biggest hurdle was the lack of professionalization among the Hebrew teachers, many of whom were native Hebrew-speaking Israelis who lacked training in language pedagogy and experienced high turnover rates due to low pay and lack of opportunities for professional growth. With an understanding of these challenges, Kobliner and her team of writers saw their mission as creating high-quality material so teachers could be trained to see "what was possible to do in the Hebrew class." This emphasis underscored their belief in the connection between learning material and Hebrew teachers' success. As Kobliner summarized, the "classroom materials were the stage on which the choreographers and dancers could dance."

Unlike Tal Am, NETA was not conceived as a program to teach Jewish studies through Hebrew. Rather, as Kobliner indicated, it was conceived as an "intellectual, academic, emotional, creative, and aesthetic" endeavor. This meant focusing on thematic content and not on grammar or on topics about historical Judaism or Israel. NETA intentionally did not focus on "the Galil, the Negev or the Western Wall [Kotel]," because Kobliner's belief was that "children need to understand that Hebrew isn't just about the righteous . . . or Abraham and Sarah, the angel and the *Akedah* [the biblical narrative describing God's commandment that Abraham sacrifice his son Isaac]." NETA also avoided producing childish texts. Instead Kobliner wanted to appeal to a broad range of cultural and historical interests, including "Salvador Dali, [Nachum] Gutman [an Israeli artist], Tel Aviv, Rambam, and King David." Most importantly, Kobliner believed that tethering Hebrew to the Jewish and Israeli experience was "not correct." She believed it was a misrepresentation to narrowly categorize Hebrew speakers as a monolithic group and argued that "people use Hebrew to talk about a lot of things, not just about the [Western] Wall, and not just about religion, Ben-Gurion, the Palmach [Jewish military unit during Mandatory Palestine], or the heroism during wars." In this way, NETA offered a distinct contrast to Tal Am in its religious and Israel framing. Additionally, the NETA team departed from approaches that framed Hebrew primarily as a tool for communicative competence. Even when parents of day school students advocated for greater emphasis on fluency, Kobliner resisted these demands on pragmatic grounds. In her view, American children visiting Israel should speak English—"it will be better for them," she explained, noting that "they won't get taken advantage of" when ordering in a restaurant in Israel. For Kobliner, the success of a Hebrew program was not measured by functional language skills but by the richness of its ideas and themes in the texts—one in which even an Israeli Hebrew-speaking child could read and think, "This is interesting."[39]

It is important to take a step back and see Tal Am and NETA in terms of each other.[40] Both were funded by AVI CHAI during the same period, were intended for day school settings, and provided a sequential curriculum, extensive pedagogical material, and teacher training and pedagogical workshops. Nonetheless, there was little overlap in their production, their pedagogical approach, or learning goals. Nor did the writing teams interact with one another. The main coordination rested in the learners they served. To make sure the programs did not compete against each other and confuse prospective schools seeking out Hebrew curricular programs, AVI CHAI limited the development of Tal Am to

K–5 grades, while NETA served middle and high school grades. The two Hebrew curricular programs also differed philosophically in regard to Hebrew educational goals for American youth. Tal Am fashioned itself as a Hebrew program that provided a deeper understanding of Judaism. NETA, in contrast, understood its Jewish content as only one component that would lead students to develop a love for Hebrew. Despite these diverging priorities, both programs rejected explicit grammar teaching and grammatical exercises. They also both prioritized the creation of classroom material, which they believed would compensate for the challenges of underqualified and transient day school Hebrew teachers who were left to their own devices to find classroom material. Relatively quickly, however, the programs' different philosophical underpinnings and the lack of compatibility in scope and sequence proved problematic. The lack of curricular alignment between the programs resulted in an achievement gap as students transitioned between the programs. Kobliner recalled being surprised to discover that elementary school graduates got to middle school at only the beginner Hebrew level in the NETA curriculum. Naomi Stillman, a NETA team member, shared stories of incoming students who did not score well on the NETA placement tests, a situation that she remembered "created a lot of discomfort all around."[41]

My purpose in examining the incommensurability of Tal Am and NETA is not to judge which program was more or less effective in its pedagogical and curricular aims; that is beyond the scope of this discussion. Rather, my purpose has been to illuminate how these two well-funded and widely adopted initiatives embodied distinct ideologies of Hebrew-language education. While both were deeply invested in advancing Hebrew curricula for Jewish day school students, they offered fundamentally different answers to what Hebrew education should accomplish. Their misalignment reveals how each curricular team prioritized particular dimensions of Hebrew learning to advance divergent visions of Judaism and Jewish life. This also underscores how language programs become ideological arenas in which competing models of Jewish education—and by extension, Jewish life—are negotiated. Their differences notwithstanding, both innovative programs profoundly shaped the landscape of Hebrew education in the early 2000s. By the time the AVI CHAI Foundation concluded its grantmaking in 2019, more than 30,000 children in more than 400 schools were using Tal Am, while more than 20,000 students in 175 schools were enrolled in NETA. As additional stakeholders entered the Hebrew education arena, new and competing ideologies of Hebrew language education emerged, each instrumentalizing Hebrew learning to advance shifting Jewish communal, cultural, and moral priorities.

The Proficiency Turn in Hebrew Education

During the early decades of the 2000s, Tal Am and NETA solidified their place within the Jewish day school ecosystem, with their names becoming identified as Hebrew education itself. At the same time, a growing chorus of communal leaders began calling for Hebrew instruction that would strengthen the ties between American and Israeli Jews. To be clear, the AVI CHAI Foundation prioritized Israel education in its grantmaking. However, neither Tal Am nor NETA emphasized communicative fluency in spoken Hebrew, an outcome that many stakeholders regarded as critical for cultivating enduring connections between these two Jewish communities. The paradigmatic reorientation toward Hebrew fluency repositioned language learning as a central pillar of Israel and Jewish education in the United States. This shift effectively decoupled Hebrew from its traditional association with religious study—centered on Bible, prayer, ritual, and rabbinic texts—and reoriented it toward Israel as the cultural and affective core of contemporary American Jewish life.

A surprising part of this transformation can be traced back to a playdate between two children in 1993. Having recently returned to Boston after several years in Israel, Arnee Winshall was disheartened by what she observed at the Solomon Schechter Day School her daughter attended. Within months, her daughter—once fluent in Hebrew—had stopped speaking and reading the language, and had taken on an American accent. Baffled, Winshall could not understand how a child spending half her day in Hebrew and Jewish studies could be losing her Hebrew altogether. When she began volunteering in the classroom, the problem became clear. The curriculum offered little room for differentiation, and teachers dominated classroom talk. "The teachers were talking much more than the kids were," she recalled, noting that students with stronger

Hebrew skills were "put in the back of the room with headphones on, listening to some kind of tape or something." Frustrated, Winshall asked her daughter's second-grade teacher how the program might better serve advanced students. The teacher's answer—"All I know is to follow the book"—crystallized for Winshall the need for a fundamentally different approach to Hebrew education.[42]

While Winshall's daughter was having one kind of Hebrew experience, her son, who attended a preschool with Hebrew- and English-speaking teachers coteaching the class bilingually, was having a dramatically different one. Learning that he got along well with another Hebrew-speaking child in the class, Winshall set out to bring the children together after school. Arranging a playdate, however, did more than solidify a friendship between the children. It ignited a spark for developing a new way of doing Hebrew education. That is because the other boy's mother was Vardit Ringvald, an Israeli American who at the time was director of Brandeis University's Hebrew program.[43] By the time Winshall and Ringvald met through their sons, Ringvald was already immersed in various Hebrew educational initiatives. In the late 1980s, she had been part of a group of Hebrew educators and scholars from higher education who, working under the leadership of Ruth Golan, had developed the Hebrew Proficiency Guidelines at the American Council on the Teaching of Foreign Languages (ACTFL).[44] By the early 1990s, Ringvald had been a Hebrew consultant at her children's school, had created the first Hebrew pedagogy course at Brandeis, and had secured a Covenant Grant, with educator Linda Echt, to develop Hebrew programming at an afterschool Hebrew-immersive program in Boston. Quickly Ringvald and Winshall discovered their shared interest in developing a program for teaching Hebrew as a spoken language. These discussions led them—along with a small group of parents and generous philanthropic support—to create a new day school, the Jewish Community Day School of Greater Boston (JCDS) in 1995. With its eyes on teaching Hebrew as a "living language in the school with a strong connection to Israel," JCDS copied Winshall's and Ringvald's children's dual-language bilingual preschool model—which meant each class was cotaught by an English- and a Hebrew-speaking teacher.[45]

What immediately struck Ringvald was that Jewish day school educators viewed Hebrew not as a foreign or second language, but rather as a language of Jewishness. As a result, Hebrew teachers were often situated within the Jewish studies department rather than regarded as language instructors. Recognizing the need to introduce Second Language Acquisition (SLA) theory and methodology into Hebrew education, Ringvald quickly realized that many day school educators were unfamiliar with these frameworks. "I never imagined," she admitted, "that talking about second language acquisition would be so difficult." Drawing on her earlier work with ACTFL, she used its discourse of assessment to communicate with Jewish educators. When she began discussing proficiency, "it all started to make sense to people."[46] In contrast to the vague measures of Jewish identity which often revolved around feelings, attitudes, and perceptions, the construct of proficiency concretized the goals of Hebrew education.

Yet, to Ringvald's surprise, the concept of proficiency soon became what she called *mahut hakol*—the essence of everything. Educators, policymakers, and funders rapidly adopted it as the dominant framework for articulating Hebrew education goals. As ACTFL defines it, proficiency describes what individuals "can do with language in terms of speaking, writing, listening, and reading in real-world situations in a spontaneous and non-rehearsed context."[47] The model's appeal lay in its accessibility: It provided a shared vocabulary that merged Jewish educational aims with broader American pedagogical standards. Principals and administrators intuitively connected with the term, Ringvald noted, and "understood it because it looked just like math, and it looked just like science."[48] Although few Hebrew educators received full ACTFL training or implemented its detailed assessment protocols, proficiency became a powerful discursive framework. It became a productive way to articulate measurable objectives for Hebrew language learning—a goal that almost all agreed was in desperate need of standards. In contrast to the ambiguous affective outcomes often used to gauge Jewish identity, the construct of proficiency concretized the goals of Hebrew education by offering clarity and structure. The emerging "proficiency approach," as it came to be known, provided a practical template for scaffolding curriculum and evaluating students' communicative development.

After starting JCDS, Ringvald and Winshall noticed two trends among day school students. First, there were significant gaps among students' speaking, reading, and listening skills. Second, there was noticeable regression among students as they moved from the elementary to middle school grades. Seeing these overlapping phenomena, they noted that teachers did not have the pedagogical tools to address either challenge. As Winshall stated, the main problem was that the Hebrew teachers "weren't trained as language teachers." They knew Hebrew, but "they didn't know how to teach language."[49] In short, they lacked what educational theorist (and Hebraist) Lee Shulman referred to as pedagogical content knowledge: a teacher's capacity to integrate what they know about subject matter with how best to teach it.[50] What Winshall and Ringvald witnessed were teachers being creative, enthusiastic, and engaging but as Winshall noted, the teachers lacked the ability to "empower the students because they didn't understand how language is acquired."[51] Winshall and Ringvald believed that this gap resulted in an overreliance on textbooks. With an initial five-year grant of $250,000 from the Covenant Foundation, matched by the Winshall family, they set out in 2003 to create a professional development program for Hebrew teachers at JCDS, and once developed, to bring it to other day schools. Based on the results of the pilot work, Vardit Ringvald, Sharona Givol (the director of Hebrew at JCDS), and Arnee and Walter Winshall founded Hebrew at the Center (HATC) in 2007.[52] According to A "State of the Field" paper commissioned in 2008, the organization "was established in response to what we see as a dearth of effective Hebrew language teaching and learning opportunities in North America."[53] As Winshall emphasized, HATC's mission was twofold: "to empower the teachers to be adaptive language teachers" and to help teachers "understand what to do when something didn't work, and how to know if it was working."[54]

Hebrew at the Center advanced a new ideology of Hebrew education that placed communication at the heart of language learning and elevated teachers as the key agents in achieving that goal. This represented a notable shift in the field in two main ways. First, HATC redirected attention from curriculum design to teacher professionalization. Whereas Tal Am and NETA had focused on developing "teacher-proof" materials, HATC invested in building the capacity and status of educators themselves. As Rabbi Andrew Ergas, HATC's CEO beginning in 2020, explained, the organization sought to transform the gendered image of the Hebrew teacher from "Shula from Afula"—the stereotypical

Israeli woman teaching Hebrew in America by default rather than by training—into a respected language professional with access to ongoing development and career opportunities.[55] Second, HATC's adoption of the proficiency approach reframed the goals of Hebrew education from textual mastery to communicative competence. In contrast to Tal Am, which viewed Hebrew as a medium for teaching Judaism, and NETA, which integrated Hebrew with Jewish cultural creativity, HATC aimed to prepare a new generation of educators trained to teach Hebrew as a living language through contemporary Second Language Acquisition principles and methodologies. This emphasis on Modern Hebrew and communicative fluency foregrounded Israeli culture and shifted the center of gravity of Hebrew education toward contemporary Israel as a defining axis of Jewish identity and learning.

Extending Proficiency Beyond Day Schools

During the early 2000s, the proficiency approach emerged as shorthand for a new curricular paradigm—one that prioritized communicative Hebrew and engagement with Israeli culture over traditional forms of religious literacy. Its influence soon extended beyond the boundaries of Jewish day schools. Around this time, the Steinhardt Foundation for Jewish Life, founded by philanthropist Michael Steinhardt, began to question the day school movement's ability to expand enrollment among non-Orthodox Jews. As Rabbi David Gedzelman, the foundation's president and CEO, later explained, the organization concluded that the issue was "not exclusively about affordability"—which was often touted as the main obstacle to growing day school enrollment.[56] Rather, the foundation recognized that many American Jews felt that sending their children to schools that were exclusively Jewish conflicted with their sense of themselves as Americans. Seeking new models of Jewish education, the foundation reached out in 2007 to former Florida congressman Peter Deutsch, who had recently founded the Ben Gamla Charter School, the first Hebrew language charter school in the United States.[57] By year's end, Steinhardt saw the potential of this approach to serve Jewish communal goals. "What if we unrolled a nationwide system of Jewish charter schools focusing on Jewish elements, not on religious studies—which appeals only to a minority of Jews anyway—but on the elements of Jewish culture that make us strong?" he asked that fall.[58] Gedzelman noted that the foundation "really liked the idea of bringing Israeli Hebrew into charter schools."[59] The idea gained momentum after the Steinhardt Foundation team observed the "proficiency approach" in practice at JCDS in February 2008. They were struck by how the model cultivated students' communicative Hebrew skills while offering authentic, enjoyable learning experiences grounded in clear standards and assessments. As Gedzelman added, for the foundation, this represented "good education."[60] Seeing this approach in action provided the proof of concept that propelled the Hebrew charter school movement forward.[61]

The Areivim Philanthropic Group, established in 2006 and comprised of the Steinhardt Foundation for Jewish Life along with other family foundations, was critical to the growth of the Hebrew charter school movement.[62] According to Gedzelman, though all Areivim's partners made large contributions to the general Hebrew charter school fund and other educational projects, the Steinhardt Foundation leadership stood at the helm of the project.[63] The exact amount of the Steinhardt subset of this support invested in Hebrew charter schools was not publicly available, although one news article indicated that the foundation gave $3.2 million in seed money to cover meeting state-mandated requirements, renting a building for the schools, creating curriculum, and building a team of administrators and teachers.[64] Peter Deutsch, observing the Steinhardt Foundation's growing investment in New York, understood the transformative impact this funding could have on the Hebrew charter school movement. "If we're the jalopy held together by rubber bands," he told the *Forward*, "they're [Google founder] Sergey Brin's 747."[65] His analogy proved prophetic. The flagship school, the Hebrew Language Academy Charter School (HLA), opened in Brooklyn in 2009 with 150 kindergarten and first-grade students.[66] By 2023 the charter management organization Hebrew Public (originally the Hebrew Charter School Center) had expanded to a network of ten schools, serving more than four thousand students from prekindergarten through eighth grade.

According to Gedzelman, HLA surpassed expectations in teaching both spoken Hebrew and Israeli culture. "The kids were internalizing their sense of their Israeli teachers and Israeli culture and loving Israel through learning Hebrew," he recalled.[67] Yet the initiative faced strong resistance from many Jewish educators. Gedzelman attributed this push-back to day schools' financial investment in programs like Tal Am and NETA, which emphasized literacy and Jewish textual knowledge over spoken fluency and cultural immersion. As he put it, day schools "were committed to the notion that you begin with literacy," a stance that reflected a broader conception of Jewish education rooted in religious study.[68] By contrast, Hebrew Public charter schools prioritized spoken language before literacy, aligning more closely with general educational principles and allowing for a broader exploration of Jewish and Israeli topics.[69] The distinction between day schools and Hebrew charters, however, was more than methodological; it was also epistemological. Teaching spoken Israeli Hebrew placed Israel and its culture at the center, while day schools, as religious institutions, remained focused on sacred texts, rituals, and synagogue practices.

To fully grasp their innovative reach, Hebrew charter schools should also be seen within pedagogical frameworks of public K–12 world language programs, a category that includes Spanish, French, Mandarin, and a host of other languages.[70] One of the central tenets of world language education is the belief that language acquisition is a catalyst for changing people's hearts and minds. These programs rest on a humanistic ideal that learning a language fosters empathy, tolerance, and cross-cultural understanding—skills public schools have long recognized as crucial to living and working in a global and linguistically diverse world. Language learning, in this sense, is not only about communication but about socialization—becoming a competent member of a cultural community through interaction with more experienced speakers, an idea at the core of the language socialization paradigm.[71] Thus everyday interactions not only socialize learners to use a language but also socialize them to a community's beliefs, worldviews, and values.[72] World language classrooms, in this regard, teach learners to speak *in* the target language, as well as *about* the target cultural community's worldviews and perspectives.[73] When this was applied to the Hebrew charter school model, students were not merely learning to speak Hebrew; they were being socialized into an appreciation of Israeli worldviews, values, and cultural perspectives.

Positioning Hebrew charter schools as a form of world language education reinforced a perspective that the Hebrew classroom is also Israel education, a concept defined broadly as an understanding of Israeli history and contemporary Israeli society. Binnie Swislow, director of the Public High School Hebrew Teacher Network at the iCenter, argued that seeing Hebrew as a world language (and not solely as a religious language) offered American youth an opportunity to learn about Israel beyond the headlines in the news: "I think the misunderstanding of what Israel's all about could be remedied if they would be more educated about what Israel is." From her experience working in the Chicago suburbs with high schools that offered Modern Hebrew classes, Swislow concluded that "one of the best outcomes of teaching Hebrew at a public high school is the acceptance of Israel being a nation among nations. It's simply another country out there with a world language."[74] This principle operated as a central plank in the Steinhardt Foundation's efforts. Gedzelman asserted that, similar to other world language programs that seek to build a love for the language and the countries in which the language is used, Hebrew charter schools let their students see that "Israel is Israelis, and the Israelis that they know are vibrant and humane."[75]

This philosophy linked Hebrew education to the idea that students could see themselves as legitimate Hebrew users, regardless of their religious or ethnic background. As Gedzelman noted, "We believe that getting kids to truly transact in the language, to own it and make it part of who they are, connects them to Israel and Israeli culture." For Jewish youth attending the charter schools, this sense of Hebrew ownership was especially "rich and powerful." Gedzelman explained that while theology or religious doctrine can feel abstract or inaccessible to nonobservant Jewish families, speaking Hebrew offered meaningful content students could "master and achieve." "What we see from the Birthright data we have," Gedzelman added, "is that a lot of American Jews [say], 'I'm Jewish but I don't know what to do about that. I don't have stuff or content of that identity.'"[76] In this light, Hebrew can serve as "content area of identity," a concrete skill that anchors a Jewish identity. "You don't have to be theological to master Hebrew," Gedzelman emphasized. "It's something you can achieve and feel proud of."[77] Importantly, Steinhardt Foundation charter schools do not promote Jewish theology. They are not, as some in the past accused, smuggling in Jewish theology through the backdoor of Hebrew education.[78] Rather, they teach Hebrew language and culture through teaching about Israel, where Hebrew is a living, spoken language. By emphasizing Modern Hebrew proficiency, Hebrew charter schools redefine Hebrew education's purpose and shift it from religious instruction to cultural and communicative engagement. In doing so, they reimagine who Hebrew learners can be, what Hebrew learning represents, and how it contributes to evolving forms of identity and connection in different ways for its Jewish and non-Jewish students. For Jewish day schools, Hebrew education remains anchored in a religious context; however, for Hebrew charter schools, removing these religious foundations pushes Hebrew education into new and uncharted territory.

Hebrew and Part-Time Jewish Education

While day schools often dominate discussions about Jewish education, they are not where most American Jewish children learn Hebrew. That distinction belongs to supplementary schools—also called religious, congregational, afterschool, or Hebrew schools—which remain the primary settings for Hebrew and Jewish learning in the United States. Although precise numbers are difficult to determine, a 2019–20 report identified roughly 141,000 students enrolled in 1,458 supplementary schools.[79] About 90 percent of these programs operate under synagogue auspices, offering classes in synagogue buildings after regular school hours or on weekends.[80] Their curricula are wide-reaching and typically include Hebrew language, Bible stories, Jewish history, holidays, the Jewish calendar, rituals, the Holocaust, Israel, and Jewish values. To be sure, teaching about all these topics is a tall order given these programs' constraints. As Jack Wertheimer notes, students generally attend only three to six hours per week—fewer than thirty hours a year—for about five years total.[81] Yet, despite these limitations, supplementary schools play a central role in shaping what kind of educated Jew they aim to cultivate.

Hebrew instruction has long been a tricky proposition for supplementary programs. Even during their so-called heyday in the 1950s and early 1960s, critics questioned the quality of Hebrew learning. In 1969, educator Walter Ackerman delivered a scathing assessment of Reform supplementary schools, saying "when judged by even the least demanding standard of what it means to be an educated Jew, it is hard to avoid the feeling that the academic aspirations of the one-day-a-week school are either a joke or an act of cynical pretentiousness." Conservative programs fared little better, producing graduates, he argued, with "only the most infantile notions of biblical thoughts and ideas, a capability in Hebrew which hardly goes beyond monosyllabic responses to carefully worded questions."[82]

It is fair to ask what transpired between the Benderly Hebrew education revolution of the early 1900s and Walter Ackerman's trenchant critique in the late 1960s. Part of the answer lies in the expanded role of the synagogue in post–World War II American Jewish life.[83] As historians note, beginning in the late 1940s, second- and third-generation American Jews entered the middle class and moved from urban centers to the suburbs, where they often felt isolated from the close-knit communities they had come to rely on in the cities.[84] To recreate that sense of communal belonging, they built a large number of synagogues between 1945 and 1965—so many, some argue, that the synagogue itself became the defining emblem of postwar American Judaism.[85] This construction boom fueled the growth of the Conservative (and later Reform) movements and dramatically increased enrollment in synagogue-based educational programs, as parents turned to these institutions to help instill Jewish identity in their children.[86]

Once built, however, synagogues needed a reliable base of dues-paying members to sustain their operations and ensure the building's upkeep. Hebrew education was swept up in efforts to guarantee congregants' long-term financial commitment to synagogue coffers. Historian Stuart Schoenfeld observed that, already in the 1930s, synagogue leaderships were pressuring "otherwise reluctant North American Jews to become more involved" by linking synagogue membership to the bar mitzvah ceremony, which was growing in popularity among an American Jewry increasingly comfortable with public displays of Jewishness.[87] By the late 1940s and early 1950s, the bat mitzvah had gained significant traction, especially in Conservative congregations.[88] Synagogue leadership identified the b'nai (plural of bar and bat) mitzvah ceremony (and Confirmation service in the Reform movement) as a constant revenue stream for synagogue operations and required children to be registered in congregational schools for a certain amount of days and hours a week over a prescribed number of years.[89] Yet, as Jewish education scholar Isa Aron argues, this policy was a "Faustian bargain." With Jewish learning tied to bar and bat mitzvah preparation, supplementary schooling came to be seen primarily as a means to an end. Supplemental schooling "became inextricably linked (in the minds of parents, synagogue leaders, and even some synagogue professionals) with preparation for bar (and later bat) mitzvah," which resulted in significant attrition among post-bar-mitzvah-aged teenagers.[90] Once the milestone was achieved, many teens disengaged. This shift transformed Jewish education from a lifelong pursuit of Jewish knowledge and values into a once-in-a-lifetime event. It also defined Jewish education as the acquisition of a particular set of skills, rather than the orientations, values, and sensibilities comprising Jewish learning and life.

The connection between b'nai mitzvah and required synagogue membership dramatically impacted Hebrew education and, specifically, the type of Hebrew taught. Aron writes that, because most of the children attending supplementary schools did not have any exposure to the register of the prayerbook Hebrew at home, supplementary schools turned to teaching decoding skills. This decision ensured that pre–b'nai mitzvah children could recite their prayers, even if they lacked the vocabulary to understand what they were reading or the religious concepts underlying the words. From Aron's perspective, the Hebrew curriculum was "held hostage" to the b'nai mitzvah complex, reducing Hebrew studies to decoding exercises and prayer reading, with plenty of blame to be spread around: "The rabbis were asleep at the switch. The families were happy, so why should they worry? The cantors, if they were involved, were unhappy, but not talking about it. The bar mitzvah tutors were talking about it, but they didn't have a whole lot of power, and educators were also asleep at the switch. . . . No one was rocking the boat."[91]

Congregational school leaders were not the only drivers of the atomization of the Hebrew curriculum. Jewish educational publishing houses aided in this implementation of Hebrew educational policy by supplying textbooks and workbooks focusing solely on letter-sound relationships. The reigning Hebrew language ideology was that it was enough to decode the letters and be able to chant the prayers; no comprehension was needed. Between working parents' logistical difficulties in getting their children to and from the synagogue in the afternoon and children's increasingly crowded afterschool and weekend commitments to sports teams, music lessons, and other extracurricular interests, many supplemental school administrators in the past two decades have had to downsize their programs to a handful of hours a week or one-day-a-week lessons. As a result, difficult allocation questions have ensued. Should supplementary educators dedicate resources to acquiring Hebrew decoding or to educating about ritual observance, synagogal practices, Jewish holidays, the Holocaust, Jewish history, and Israel? Should they teach specific Hebrew and religious competencies, or should they create powerful and memorable moments that build positive and heartfelt emotional attachments to being Jewish?

The joint examination of congregational schooling by Aron and Nachama Moskowitz, former director of curricular resources at the Jewish Education Center of Cleveland, put these tensions into stark relief.[92] They found that though many congregational schools believed that five years of instruction were needed to prepare students for their b'nai mitzvah, they saw that many sixth graders were still learning decoding skills even after years of religious school attendance. To their surprise, they heard Jewish educators openly admit that they were struggling to teach Hebrew—even at the decoding level. These findings led Aron and Moskowitz, along with other congregational school leaders, to convene a meeting in 2011; its agenda, entitled "Hebrew Meeting in NYC," aimed to develop an action plan for rethinking the role of Hebrew education in supplementary schooling. Once convened, the group wrestled with a central question: What dispositions, knowledge, and skills are truly needed for meaningful participation in Jewish life—especially in worship and prayer? Over the course of their discussions, participants agreed that Hebrew education had to move beyond rote decoding, toward teaching the meaning and significance of prayers. Yet they also recognized the scale of the challenge before them. As Isa Aron recalled, everyone present understood that reimagining Hebrew education required confronting the centrality of the b'nai mitzvah ritual. "To talk about changing the nature of Hebrew instruction without talking about b'nai mitzvah preparation," the meeting notes observed, "was to ignore the 500-pound gorilla in the room."[93] In essence, transforming Hebrew education meant a wholesale rethinking around what it meant to be an "educated Jewish child" beyond the b'nai mitzvah ritual.

These conversations culminated in two groundbreaking initiatives launched at the 2011 Union for Reform Judaism Biennial. The first, developed by Isa Aron and Rabbi Brad Solmsen, was the B'nai Mitzvah Revolution (BMR), which sought to deepen Jewish learning by redefining the b'nai mitzvah not as the endpoint of Jewish education but as an entry into lifelong communal engagement.[94] The second, #OnwardHebrew, founded in 2017 by Rabbi Nicki Greninger, Moskowitz, and other educators, challenged the long-held belief that Hebrew instruction had to begin with decoding.[95] Instead, it promoted a *sound-to-print* model: Children first develop comfort with spoken Hebrew before learning to read it in later grades. By shifting time away from early decoding drills, #OnwardHebrew sought to open space for more meaningful Jewish learning. "When Hebrew is put in its place," Moskowitz explained, and no longer takes up so much of the precious available hours, Jewish educators "have time for more compelling Jewish education—the big ideas, the things that touch one's heart."[96] To be clear, #OnwardHebrew did not seek to deprioritize Hebrew or look to erase it from the Jewish supplemental school curriculum. Rather, it embraced an alternative ideological and pedagogical approach to Hebrew education that envisioned Hebrew learning as a window into meaningful Jewish learning.

Still, the shift faced resistance from parents uneasy about children's Hebrew literacy. Greninger observed, "People have a really weird hangup specifically around decoding Hebrew, like somehow, if you can decode Hebrew, you're an educated Jew." While some of this concern, Greninger noted, stemmed from anxiety about b'nai mitzvah preparation, she also believed deeper issues were at play—namely, how Jewish literacy itself is defined. "I keep coming back to the word *barometer*," she reflected. "What's the measure of success Jewishly—the floor or the ceiling?" Although she recognized that decoding Hebrew carries emotional weight for many parents (and their children), Greninger argued that it can represent an "empty victory." Simply pronouncing Hebrew words without understanding or connection, she said, does not cultivate a meaningful Jewish life. "Sounding out a bunch of nonsense syllables isn't the same as living richly as a Jew." It was "missing the forest for the trees."[97] What is needed, she insisted, was a rethinking of Hebrew knowledge as part of broader spiritual and communal growth. From this perspective, #OnwardHebrew educators understood that debates over Hebrew reading were not merely pedagogical disputes but functioned as proxies for a larger set of questions: What defines a robust Jewish education? What role should prayer play? And what was the role of Hebrew learning in nurturing lifelong Jewish engagement and identity?

Taken together, ideological debates about Hebrew in supplementary schooling reveal how Hebrew education has been instrumentalized in efforts to shape the next generation of synagogue congregants. When Jewish educators question the primacy of the b'nai mitzvah ceremony and reconsider the role of decoding within Hebrew instruction, they engage in deeper conversations about what it truly means to "know" Hebrew and how that knowledge enables children to live and express their Jewish identities. Viewed in this way, Hebrew literacy is not simply a pedagogical goal but a reflection of broader assumptions about the kinds of Jews these programs aim to cultivate, and importantly, the competencies, dispositions, and forms of belonging that Hebrew education is designed to produce.

The Instrumentalization of Hebrew

Jewish day schools, Hebrew language charter schools, and supplementary schools constitute a palette of Hebrew educational contexts in the United States, and each in its own way is engaged in debates that articulate and define the significance of Hebrew for American Jewish life. If it is true that Jewish education is "the vehicle through which we train successive generations of Jews to negotiate their own way as Jews in the American arena," it seems notable that this negotiation involves a lack of consensus about what this education should include, both in the content it covers and the affective feelings it produces.[98] Questions about what Hebrew to teach, how to teach it, and for what purposes speak to the incommensurability of views in regard to definitions of the educated Jew. What is clear is that Hebrew education is never simply concerned with the acquisition of literacy or communicative skills. Rather, choices about why teach Hebrew, what Hebrew to teach, and how to do it effectively are embedded in high-stakes decisions about Jewish life. They also put a spotlight on the stakeholders involved in these decisions. The sociolinguist Deborah Cameron admonishes us to "treat with the gravest suspicion all claims to the effect that a certain linguistic practice should be supported, or opposed, in the interests of 'language itself'; for languages cannot have interests. . . . It is we, the human inheritors and agents of language, who have interests."[99] Taking these words seriously, we might want to think about whose religious, cultural, and political interests different curricular and pedagogical choices serve, even if at times similar types of curricular decisions serve contradictory aims.[100] When we do this, we can see that decisions to prioritize Textual Hebrew for synagogue participation or Modern Hebrew for Israel connections are projections of the community's values, hopes, and concerns. Whether it is to promote cultural or religious Judaism, or a combination of both, the instrumentalization of Hebrew education to reach desired goals underscores a fundamental belief that Hebrew can and will make a difference to the future of American Jews.

This chapter has focused on three groundbreaking and ambitious Hebrew initiatives that emerged during the first two decades of the 2000s. However, the story is far from complete. Efforts to harness Hebrew education in service of broader Jewish communal goals continue to evolve. For example, the Jewish Education Project's 2023 *From Census to Possibilities: Designing Pathways for Jewish Learners* noted that the dramatic decline in supplementary school enrollment in the past fifteen years may prompt supplemental schools to adopt more experiential and culturally oriented models of Jewish learning to sustain and renew Jewish engagement: "Today's Jewish families seek experiences that support a cultural approach to Jewish identity, exploring shared history, language, and peoplehood as foundational curricular components. In some cases, this means shifting the focus of educational content away from prayer and worship, perhaps instead focusing on Modern Hebrew."[101]

The Jewish Education Project's proposal to leverage Modern Hebrew as a solution to broader challenges reflects a familiar and recurring pattern in Hebrew educational discourse. As this chapter has demonstrated, contemporary Hebrew education initiatives have repeatedly mobilized Hebrew instruction to address specific communal concerns and cultivate particular forms of Jewish knowledge. Hebrew is once again being called upon to do consequential Jewish communal work. Historian Jonathan

Sarna once noted that schools are sites in which the "central drama of American Jewish life is introduced and rehearsed."[102] To the degree schools remain sites of Jewish formation, Hebrew—with all the ideological weight it carries—will continue to stand at the center of that drama, scripting not only what students learn but who they become as Jews.

CONCLUSION

New Directions

Even Ye (the rapper previously known as Kanye West) seems to understand the power of mobilizing Hebrew in the American Jewish context. In his December 26, 2023, posting on Instagram, the highly influential artist, producer, and fashion designer atoned for his virulent rant, in which he had made conspiratorial insinuations about Jewish power and compared himself to Adolf Hitler and Jesus. Facing backlash from his corporate sponsors, he issued the following apology: "I sincerely apologize to the Jewish community for any unintended outburst caused by my words or actions. It was not my intention to hurt or demean, and I deeply regret any pain I may have caused. I am committed to starting with myself and learning from this experience to ensure greater sensitivity and understanding in the future. Your forgiveness is important to me, and I am committed to making amends and promoting unity."[1]

Perhaps not unexpectedly, this act of atonement was greeted by American Jews with measured skepticism. The Anti-Defamation League spoke about the "untold damage" he had done over the years to "poison countless minds with vicious antisemitism and hate," but noted that "ultimately, actions will speak louder than words."[2] Other public figures, such as then-second gentleman Doug Emhoff, called for people to "step up" and talk about antisemitism and recognize the "awesomeness" of being Jewish.[3] Yet for many people paying attention to this media event, what caught their attention was not the apology's content. Rather it was the form in which it was written: in Hebrew, with no English translation. While some commented that the use of a translation app was most likely responsible for the text being aligned to the left margin (given that

Hebrew is read from right to left), others noted that the posting was written in error-free Hebrew. Ye had done the unexpected; for one day in America popular culture, the topic of Hebrew was trending.

It would be naive to assume that Ye's decision to apologize in Hebrew was anything but an intentional choice to irrevocably tie Hebrew and Jews together. Bypassing English, Ye was able to single out his intended audience and strengthen the pragmatic potency of his words. Did the posting achieve its aim? The American Jewish Committee noted in its response to the posting that Ye's chosen language may have undermined these intentions: "Beyond being bizarre and possibly a ploy to gain more attention, the Hebrew apology—posted without translation—is inaccessible to most American Jews who do not speak the language." AJC simply pointed out that, as a matter of fact, most American Jews cannot read and understand Modern Hebrew. "To be sure," the organization added, "using Hebrew to communicate with the Jewish community intentionally denies most American Jews—and, consequently, non-Jews—the ability to directly see Kanye's apology."[4] There is no way of fully knowing the degree of Ye's sincerity or cynicism. Either way, writing in Hebrew meant that only a chosen few of "the chosen people" could comprehend the original text. But that may have been beside the point. Posting in Hebrew undoubtedly amplified its reach to hundreds of millions who saw the posting.

Arguably, there are plenty of valid reasons to label Ye a virulent antisemite and to question the sincerity of his apology. What is more complicated is denying the performative value this act achieved in reaffirming the tie between Hebrew and Jewishness. Paradoxically, Ye's use of Hebrew not only further cemented a connection between American Jews and Hebrew but also put him in the company of many Jewish educators and communal leaders who have worked to establish this irreducible link between language and Jewish identity.[5] When seen as such, Ye's use of Hebrew is a prime example of the mutually constitutive relationship among identity, language, and religion—and it is precisely this relationship that this book has sought to illuminate. I highlight Ye's posting because it serves as a fitting heuristic for thinking about the broader questions this book has centered: how and why Hebrew is mobilized to perform meaning and identity for American Jews individually and collectively, despite so few American Jews knowing or using the language.

By turning the assumption that Hebrew is irrelevant to American Jews on its head and framing it as a defining feature of American Jewish life, I was able to examine what Hebrew signifies for Jews outside Israel, what motivates American Jewish adults to pursue Hebrew learning, and how educators and other stakeholders leverage Hebrew education to cultivate ongoing Jewish engagement and commitment.

One of this book's key interventions has been to move beyond traditional measures of language competence—that is, what someone knows in order to communicate effectively—and instead consider what Hebrew *does* for American Jews as individuals and as a community. This shift directs attention to discourse about Hebrew, which includes what people say about the language and the ideologies shaping how language learning and knowledge are understood. Taking this theoretical approach reveals that, even if we are more likely to hear American Jews talking *about* Hebrew than hear them speak *in* the language, Hebrew's presence is nonetheless a crucial part of the debates about American Jewishness. Attending to discourse, we can see how Hebrew gets mobilized as foundational to Jewish peoplehood and linked to ideas about Jewish adaptability and resiliency. We can see how deficiency models of illiteracy frame lack of Hebrew knowledge as a pressing communal concern, while at the same time position Hebrew education as a remedy. This perspective also clarifies how Hebrew learning is leveraged in cultivating committed and knowledgeable Jewish adults. And finally, it highlights how the Hebrew-accented American speaker plays into homeland–diaspora dynamics, raising questions of authenticity and belonging. Taking all these factors into account, this book argues that discourse about Hebrew reverberates with American Jews' desires, concerns, aspirations, fears, and hopes about its current and future state.

The Power of American Hebrew

My hope in writing this book has been to encourage readers to think of Hebrew as an American Jewish language not solely in terms of the number of speakers or their linguistic proficiency, but through the discourse surrounding the language and the ways it shapes broader concerns within the American Jewish community. While this project cannot address every aspect of Hebrew engagement, it offers several meaningful contributions to our understanding of American Jewish life. First, it calls for greater attention to adult language-learning beliefs and practices, particularly outside formal religious institutions. Sociologist Peter Berger's observation that "there is a lot of religion that cannot be studied by looking under 'churches' in the Yellow Pages of the phone book" inspired me to look beyond synagogue-based Hebrew exposure and examine how adults engage with the language at home, in meetups, and in diverse learning contexts.[6] This is not to suggest that the adult Hebrew learners I studied were entirely removed from formal Jewish educational spaces. Rather, their stories reveal how Hebrew shapes their sense of religious and Jewish identity in ways that transcend conventional categories of belief and practice. As such, the book advances a more nuanced understanding of language as a marker of American Jewishness. While scholars debate whether Jewish identity is religious, ethnic, national, or cultural, Hebrew enthusiasts are less concerned with these categories. They do not necessarily define themselves as believers or nonbelievers, often eschewing the language of faith, creed, or theology, and vary widely in their engagement with communal life and halachic practice. Some are highly affiliated; others intentionally remain on the margins. Yet across these differences what stands out is their commitment to Hebrew as an expression of their Jewish identity. Learning Hebrew, in this sense, provides a path for engaging with liturgy, cultivating spiritual connection, building community with other Jewish adults, and grappling with personal and ongoing relationships to Israel. Acting as both compass and map, Hebrew becomes a navigational tool, allowing learners to locate themselves Jewishly—in all the richness and complexity that entails.

Second, using language as a lens for understanding American Jews illuminates the power dynamics embedded within American Jewish life. Hebrew language ideologies concerned with the value of the language, the status of its speakers, the spaces in which it is used, and its desired outcomes are deeply intertwined with questions of authority. Examining beliefs about Hebrew's centrality to Jewish collectivity, the link between American Jews' Hebrew illiteracy and communal survival, the perceived inferiority of English translation, and the definitions of Jewish authenticity raises critical questions: Who benefits from these perspectives? Whose interests do they serve? And what kinds of knowledge are considered essential in Jewish life? In this way, I join scholars who connect power with the production and transmission of Jewish knowledge. Drawing on Michel Foucault, education scholar Ari Kelman observes that notions of the "educated Jew" are inseparable from determinations about "what is knowable, what kinds of knowledge are valuable, who is the reliable bearer of that knowledge, and who is not."[7] These questions are especially salient when examining how Hebrew education is mobilized to shape ideals of the educated Jew. By attending to the ideologies underpinning Hebrew initiatives, we see that Hebrew education is seen as reproductive—preserving knowledge, transmitting heritage, and ensuring continuity—and instrumental, entangled in debates over which forms of Jewishness and Judaism should be prioritized. Decisions about what type of Hebrew to teach and which language proficiencies to cultivate are never neutral. They are, instead, reflective of broader struggles over authority, legitimacy, and the direction of Jewish communal life.

Power dynamics also shape the learning experiences of adult Hebrew enthusiasts. Choosing to study a language that is both difficult and largely impractical in the broader American context needs to be taken seriously. Unlike other serious and committed hobbyists, Hebrew enthusiasts are not necessarily motivated by special rewards or benefits, the promise of flow, or a career path.[8] Yet their engagement represents meaningful acts of intellectual discovery, social connection, and personal enjoyment. If the sociology of leisure offers any insight here, it is that individuals choosing how to spend their "free time" do not act mechanically in predetermined ways. Nobody is forcing adult Hebrew learners to undertake these efforts, and there is no guarantee of specific outcomes. They could be studying any other language, taking up another interest, or for that matter doing nothing at all. By choosing Hebrew, however, they actively shape their identities in both American and Jewish terms. This dynamic is particularly evident in learners' ambivalence toward fluency. Many are unconcerned with perfect grammar, and their approach to pronunciation reflects independence. While they may joke about their accents, wish for greater sophistication when speaking, or feel frustrated when Israelis refuse to speak Hebrew with them, they do not let these feelings silence them. If a recurring theme of this book is the tension between American and Israeli Jews, along with the hierarchies embedded in homeland–diaspora relationships, it becomes clear that

American Jews have their own relationship with Hebrew which allows them to reshape the language to fit local needs and values. In doing so, they create a version of Hebrew that intertwines their Americanness and Jewishness, making the language both a tool and a reflection of their complex identities.

One of the most visible examples is American Jews' efforts to create and use gender-inclusive, gender-neutral, and nonbinary forms of Hebrew.[9] While I hesitate to adopt Orit Bershtling's description of Hebrew as "one of the most sex-manic languages out there," it is true that, like many languages, Hebrew relies on gendered forms for nouns, verbs, and adjectives.[10] Modifying its morphological and syntactic structures is therefore a substantial linguistic, cultural, and political undertaking. Nonetheless, there have been recent initiatives to accommodate genderqueer and nonbinary speakers. In 2016, Habonim Dror, a Jewish socialist-Zionist cultural youth movement, pioneered a gender-neutral Hebrew at its seven North American summer camps. Arguing that "we can't wait around" for Israel or American Jewish educators to act, camp leadership implemented morphological changes with the hope of "setting an example that Hebrew-speakers worldwide might someday follow."[11] A similar effort occurred in 2018 at Kehilat Hadar, an independent egalitarian synagogue in New York City. Responding to members' calls for gender-neutral language, synagogue leaders developed guidelines for a gender-neutral Hebrew prayer option alongside traditional masculine and feminine forms, framing this as "an important step toward making Kehilat Hadar a fully welcoming space to all."[12] These initiatives allow particular Jewish communities to express their progressive values in a distinctly Jewish register.[13] They also expose a rich irony. By pushing Hebrew to evolve for contemporary inclusivity, American Jews are drawing on a long-standing Hebrew ideology of adaptability—one that early Zionist ideologues used to reshape the language in pursuit of a new national identity. In other words, today's gender-neutral Hebrew can be seen as part of a tradition of diaspora Jews bending the language to fit their own vision of Jewish life.

If being the theme of an academic conference is any indication of this topic's importance, we can see this issue taking center stage at the March 2022 Gender-Inclusive and Nonbinary Hebrew: Innovations and Classroom Applications gathering sponsored by the School of Languages,

Literatures, and Cultures at the University of Maryland. At this online event, ten educators and experts in Hebrew came together to discuss the topic of gender-neutral Hebrew in speech and orthography as a way of creating a safe and inclusive space for American Hebrew learners.[14] With an eye toward Hebrew praxis, conference participants spoke about gender inclusivity in the Hebrew language classroom as setting "the stage for a shift in power dynamics in which students have a seat at the linguistic table and have an opportunity to create and change forms, like the native speaker."[15] Conference organizer and Hebrew education scholar Avital Karpman noted the paradox that the American Hebrew classroom may be more conducive to this type of experimentation than Israeli society, where such changes would require a wholesale modification of the entire grammar system and societal buy in: "It's easier to create language alternatives," she noted when discussing Hebrew in the United States, "when the scope of language is so limited and not really related to interlocution."[16] Others underscored the potential benefits of offering American Hebrew learners some control over the language's look and sound. It can provide "intrapersonal means to move closer to their Judaism and authentic identities" and transforms the Hebrew classroom into a space of American Jewish empowerment.[17]

It is difficult to assess how widely these conversations are taking place in Hebrew classrooms across the United States or what their greater impact will be. The 2022 "State of the Field" report by Hebrew at the Center observed that "gender-neutral Hebrew is likely to make its way into Jewish day school Hebrew classrooms in order to ensure that Hebrew is the language of 'belonging' and one that is inclusive for all varieties of learners in our schools."[18] Esty Gross, chief of staff and director of education at HATC, elaborated that this paradigm shift aligns with models of student-centered learning: "If we believe our students are agents of change, they can influence the language. It's not just the language dictating the rules; students can shape it, and we want them to see themselves in Hebrew."[19] Whether or not Hebrew classrooms fully adopt these strategies or if they will have appeal beyond progressive Jewish spaces, the very existence of this discussion of Hebrew as a locally meaningful, particularistic, and distinctly American Jewish practice upends assumptions about the preeminence of Israeli Hebrew in American Hebrew classrooms.[20] It also underscores a central point that weaves across the chapters of this book. For American Jews, Hebrew is more than a language. It is a resource for exploring who they are, what they value, and how they envision their Jewish futures.

Coda: Hebrew in the Post-October 7 World

The Hamas terrorist attack in Israel on October 7, 2023, profoundly changed the world. The onslaught that killed more than 1,200 people in Israel and saw 253 hostages abducted into Gaza and the subsequent war between Israel and Gaza was a seismic event in an already decades-old conflict between Israelis and Palestinians. For American Jews, these events triggered a host of disorienting questions about their relationship to the State of Israel and their position as an ethnoreligious minority group in the United States. For many it was the first time they were confronted with explicit antisemitic acts and violence rooted in Jewish hate. So much is still up in the air as I write this conclusion in August 2025, but preliminary data indicate notable shifts in Jewish life in the United States, including an increase in conversions to Judaism, a spike in funding to combat antisemitism, an increase in synagogue attendance, an upturn in Jewish day school enrollment, and a rise in participation in Jewish cultural and educational events.[21] At the same time, the data show that the fault lines among American Jews have never been more visible and fragile. Families, synagogues, communities, and Jewish institutions have been pulled apart, particularly along generational and denominational lines.[22] Writing more than half a year after the initial attack, rabbi and scholar of American Jews Steven Windmueller captured the unprecedented degree of uncertainty pulsing through all aspects of American Jewish life:

> We are reminded how these past seven months have profoundly altered our beliefs and actions. Just as Israel is undergoing a significant transformation, many American Jews are feeling personally and collectively the impact of these events on their lives. How we see ourselves as part of America, as well as how we understand our connections with Israel and the global Jewish community, are being refashioned. We are now redefining our identities as

> we revisit our political standing, communal priorities, and cultural moorings. We are encountering a totally different moment in our Jewish consciousness. Physically and emotionally, we find ourselves in an uncomfortable and uncertain place as we awaken to the full impact of this tsunami of hate and political disruption that is transforming the Jewish people.[23]

If writing this book has taught me anything, it is that the conversations about Hebrew knowledge often surface alongside feelings of Jewish misgiving, doubt, and concern. It was therefore not surprising to see Hebrew once again emerge in public discourse amid the growing uncertainty about the Jewish future in both the United States and Israel. In the immediate aftermath of the October 7, 2023, Hamas terrorist attack, Hebrew became a visible marker of solidarity and identity. Within days, American Jews began adding *Am Yisrael Chai* ("the People of Israel Live")—in Hebrew script and transliteration—to their social media profiles. A week later, on October 16, *Forward* correspondent Arno Rosenfeld noted on X (formerly Twitter) a statement issued by the organization If Not Now—a group that calls for "an end to U.S. support for Israel's apartheid system and demands equality, justice, and a thriving future for all Palestinians and Jews"—regarding its use of Hebrew at a Washington, DC, rally protesting Israel's Gaza military incursion, which began on October 27, 2023.[24] The statement read: "Now a disclaimer for the use of Hebrew at this event: We are using Hebrew because it is our lineage. . . . We refuse to let this violent bloodthirsty regime take that away from us."[25] With this declaration, If Not Now made two distinct discursive moves. It reaffirmed its Jewish lineage through the use of Hebrew, while simultaneously claiming ownership of a language used by the Israeli government to carry out what they believed were immoral acts. A similar dynamic unfolded months later when Jewish Voice for Peace (JVP), a progressive antizionist organization, incorporated Hebrew into a seder plate image painted on a large fabric banner displayed at a university anti-Israel encampment during Passover 2024. Yet the Hebrew words on the banner were inadvertently written backward, rendering them unintelligible. The resulting social media ridicule over the orthographic error allowed pro-Israel commentators to mock JVP's linguistic blunder and question the group's Jewish authenticity.[26] If organizations such as JVP and If Not Now mobilized Hebrew to make overt political statements, others turned to the language in more personal ways. Many American Jews began wearing necklaces engraved with their Hebrew names as visible affirmations of Jewish belonging or solidarity with Israel.[27] From opposing ideological standpoints, American Jews harnessed Hebrew to express their visions of Jewishness, articulate moral and political commitments, and negotiate their relationships to Israel.[28]

Hebrew enthusiasts, too, began to activate new forms of engagement with the language in the wake of the October 7, 2023, attack. Before that seismic event, many had been careful to sidestep Israeli politics or to frame Hebrew learning as detached from contentious political debates. After the attack, however, this posture shifted noticeably. By mid-October, members of one Hebrew meetup group broke their long-standing, though unstated, policy of avoiding talk about Israeli leadership or political affairs. An email thread beginning on October 19, 2023, revealed members exchanging resources that directly addressed the war. One participant circulated a Hebrew vocabulary list of about twenty words related to the conflict—*azaka* (siren), *ason* (disaster), *gvul* (border), *dover Tzahal* (Israel Defense Forces spokesperson), and *bet kvarot* (cemetery). Another member shared the Hebrew text of the "Prayer for the Welfare and Return of Israel's Captured and Missing," while yet another posted links to Hebrew songs written in the aftermath of the attack, including "Moledet" ("Homeland") by Hanan Ben Ari and "The 7th of October" by Israeli rapper Erez Sharon (known as EZ). Both songs conveyed poignant emotions of grief, loss, and fragile hope for Israel's future. Ahead of the group's November online session, one participant circulated an article profiling a survivor of the Nova Music Festival massacre. For a community that had previously gone to great lengths to steer clear of politically charged or emotionally fraught material, this crowd-sourced content marked a decisive departure—a redefinition of what counted as legitimate Hebrew engagement.[29]

In some instances the enterprise of Hebrew education was explicitly mobilized in support of Israel. In early November 2023, HebrewToday, publisher of popular simplified newspapers for Hebrew learners, launched a special "Chai18" promotion offering 18 percent off all online products. The campaign's banner, "Strengthen Your Connection with Israel," was accompanied by a closing message that read: "Thank you for your support. Our nation is strong, our spirit is strong, and our strength is in our unity." Thus Hebrew learning was framed not simply as a linguistic pursuit but as a form of collective solidarity and national patriotism. A similar logic was at work in an essay by Sara Steinhardt Bloom, vice chair of the board of the Steinhardt Foundation for Jewish Life. In the essay, published on November 5, 2023, Steinhardt Bloom decried "the rot in the university system" that had allowed antisemitism to flourish. She urged American Jews to channel their energy into "the rebirth of a strong, forceful, pride-infused Jewish life in America." Among the six priorities she proposed, one directly called for mobilizing Hebrew as a response to rising Jewish hate: "What if," she asked, "we built vibrant, exciting ulpans in major American cities, so young adults returning from gap years or Birthright trips could learn to speak Hebrew and enjoy Israeli music, food, and film?"[30] A similar call for educational renewal came from Jewish education scholar Alex Pomson, who, in a June 15, 2024, opinion piece, advocated for a reimagined Israel education situated within "a larger Jewish educational project." He urged Jewish communities to "double down on building Jewish communities supported by Hebrew literacy, an appreciation for Jewish values, and the capacity to create Jewish culture for ourselves and for others."[31] Although Steinhardt Bloom and Pomson may not have had the same kinds of initiatives in mind, both articulated a shared Hebrew language ideology. In the post–October 7 context, American Jews needed to urgently rethink Hebrew education—not only as a means of teaching about Israel, but as a vital resource for revitalizing Jewish life in America.

Not all post–October 7 advocates for Hebrew, however, operated from the same political or educational playbook. Echoing the impulses of If Not Now and JVP, journalist Lux Alptraum described Hebrew learning as a subversive act in her January 31, 2024, article. Born in Israel but raised in the United States in a non-Hebrew-speaking home, Alptraum wrote that the Israel–Gaza war "threw [her] Hebrew practice into overdrive." Feeling "surrounded by messaging about the evils of modern Hebrew—about the symbolic violence that Hebrew had done, not just against Palestinians, but against Jews themselves," she described an almost counterintuitive drive to study the language as a form of resistance: "I felt compelled to embrace it, if only to prove to myself that Hebrew could be more than a language of right-wing nationalism." Learning

Hebrew, she concluded, allowed her to "take more control over it" and demonstrate "that being Israeli and speaking Hebrew did not inherently require [her] to support apartheid, oppression, or nationalism."[32] What stands out in this reflection is that while Hebrew study enabled Alptraum to affirm her personal convictions as an American Jew, she could never fully untether Hebrew from its Israeli roots—or from her own inescapable relationship to the country.

These examples represent just a handful of the Hebrew language ideologies at play, yet together they offer a complex portrait of how Jewish individuals and communities are navigating the post–October 7 landscape through their relationship to Hebrew. Collectively, they reveal that Hebrew ideologies are surfacing and evolving in unpredictable ways, as familiar patterns acquire new layers of meaning and resonance. They also validate a central argument of this book: American Jews' beliefs and practices surrounding Hebrew profoundly shape how they understand their lives, their religious identities, and the world around them. As in earlier periods, Hebrew language ideologies both question and provide coherency to American Jewish life. To speak about Hebrew, then, is to engage in a conversation that is at once timely and timeless. If anything, the moment of crisis and reconfiguration in post–October 7, 2023, American Jewish life has made this conversation more vital than ever.

This book has sought to trace where and how Hebrew appears in discourse, the familiar and novel registers it assumes, who learns it and to what ends, and how Hebrew learning spaces delineate the boundaries of Jewish belonging. Attending to these dynamics carves out a new way to think about how American Jews project their identities, anxieties, values, and aspirations through their engagements with the language. In the spirit of centering talk about Hebrew as a revelatory lens for understanding this dynamic, it seems fitting to give the last word to journalist Aviya Kushner, who writes frequently about language in the Jewish press: "Take a moment to notice Hebrew making appearances in unexpected places. Long live this trend."[33] As American Jewish life continues to evolve in unpredictable directions, Hebrew will undoubtedly be involved in giving voice to the unfinished story of what it means to be Jewish in the United States.

NOTES

Preface

1 Mendoza-Denton, *Homegirls*, 1.

2 Though I am aware of the problematics of this dichotomy, I mostly follow sociological convention and use *Judaism* to refer Jewish faith or religion and *Jewishness* to refer to Jewish cultural identity.

3 Years later I studied this linguistic phenomenon and coauthored a scholarly book on Hebrew usage in American Jewish summer camps. See Benor, Krasner, and Avni, *Hebrew Infusion*.

Chapter 1

1 The World Zionist Organization is a non-governmental organization whose mission is to promote Zionism and Israel.

2 Ovadia Luski does not address multilingualism in Israel. See Walters et al., "Sociolinguistics in Israel," 278–88; Spolsky and Shohamy, *The Languages of Israel*.

3 Ovadia Luski, "Hebrew Language Day." The sociological term for American Jewry has for decades been "the Jewish community." This is insufficient and reductive, and yet absent another or better term to describe the diversity internal to American Jews, I will follow sociological convention and use "American Jews" or "the American Jewish community" as a shorthand. When writing about American Jews, American Jewry, and the American Jewish community, this book is referring to the "liberal" spectrum of American Jewry—Reform, Conservative,

Modern Orthodox, religiously unaffiliated, and secular Jews. This book does not look at Orthodox or ultra-Orthodox/Haredi sectors. It also does not focus on Israeli Americans. When writing about Israelis, this book is referring to Jewish Israelis, unless otherwise noted. When writing about American Jews, this book also recognizes that not every American Jew has or wants a connection with Israel or Hebrew, and that American Jews acquire other Jewish languages. This was true historically for pockets of Yiddish-speaking socialists and other immigrant individuals, many of whom sought to preserve Yiddish as the Jewish vernacular.

4 Ovadia Luski, "Hebrew Language Day."

5 Ovadia Luski, "Hebrew Language Day."

6 The historiographic and linguistic scholarship on the evolution of Hebrew is quite extensive. Scholars debate whether Hebrew was ever dead as a spoken language, how Modern Hebrew relates to historical forms of Hebrew, and how Hebrew was revived as a modern language. These and other disputes are traced and discussed in these works: Sáenz-Badillos, *A History of the Hebrew Language*; Hoffman, *In the Beginning: A Short History of the Hebrew Language*; Schniedewind, *A Social History of Hebrew: Its Origins Through the Rabbinic Period*; Glinert, *The Story of Hebrew*; Fellman, *The Revival of a Classical Tongue*. For a discussion of the role media technologies played in the revitalization and modernization of Hebrew, see Ramati, *Lingua Ex Machina*.

7 Mintz, "Foreword," in *American Hebrew Literature*, by Michael Weingrad, xii. The German poet Heinrich Heine called the Torah the Jews' "portable homeland," while historian Daniel Boyarin identifies the Babylonian Talmud as the "traveling homeland" that defined diasporic Judaism as a distinctive Jewish textual, interpretive community. Boyarin, *A Traveling Homeland: The Babylonian Talmud as Diaspora*.

8 Zerubavel, *Recovered Roots*, 32, 22–36.

9 Zerubavel, *Recovered Roots*, 26–28; Spiegel, *Embodying Hebrew Culture*; Even-Zohar, "The Emergence of a Native Hebrew Culture in Palestine: 1882–1948," 167–84.

10 Ovadia Luski, "Hebrew Language Day."

11 Mintz, ed., *Hebrew in America*, 24.

12 Weingrad, "Robert Whitehill-Bashan and the Prospects for a New American Hebrew Literature," 205.

13 Berg, "The Anxiety of Authenticity: Hebrew, Sushi, and Suspicious Objects," 63.
14 Zerubavel, *Recovered Roots*, 32, 22–36.
15 Diner, *A New Promised Land*, ix.
16 In 1857, the Reform movement published its prayerbook, *Minhag America*, which included Hebrew texts and English translations. The Conservative movement's prayerbook, *Shabbat and Festival Prayer Book*, published in 1947, included English translations and transliterated texts. For the role of Hebrew in Reform and Conservative Judaism, see Gordis, "A Jewish Prayer Book for the Modern Age," 3; Friedland, *Were Our Mouths Filled with Song*; Meyer, *Response to Modernity: A History of the Reform Movement in Judaism*; Wertheimer, *The New American Judaism*. More recent publications that use English translations of religious texts have also shaped the Orthodox denomination. Jeremy Stolow shows how the decision in the 1970s by ArtScroll, one of the world's largest Orthodox Jewish publishing houses, to introduce English-translated prayerbooks, Bibles, rabbinic commentaries, self-help books, and cookbooks had significant effects on Hebrew literacy in the Orthodox community. Stolow, *Orthodox by Design*.
17 Mintz, ed., *Hebrew in America*, 29–67.
18 Fellman, "Concerning the 'Revival' of the Hebrew Language," 250–57.
19 Pelli, "Ideology and Reality."
20 Weingrad, *American Hebrew Literature*, xvii–xxv.
21 Mintz, "The Erosion of the Tarbut Ivrit Ideology in America and the Consequences for the Teaching of Hebrew in the University," 52.
22 Kirsch, "The Temple Mount in New York," *New Republic*, March 9, 2024.
23 Marcus, *United States Jewry, 1776–1985*, 372.
24 Asscher, *Reading Israel, Reading America*; Whitfield, *In Search of American Jewish Culture*; and Wirth-Nesher, *Call It English*.
25 Weingrad, *American Hebrew Literature*, 228–34.
26 Weingrad, *American Hebrew Literature*, xxiii.
27 Asscher argues that while Kaplan believed in the importance of studying Hebrew, he also celebrated American Jews' use of English and did not think a lack of Hebrew would pose a challenge to what he called the religious literacy needed for the study and practice of Judaism. Asscher, "Language Ideology in American Jewish Thought," 384–408.

28 Myers and Ravid, *Between Babylon and Jerusalem*, 14.
29 Kaplan, *Judaism as a Civilization*, 193, 452.
30 Kaplan, *Communings of the Spirit*, 210–11.
31 Mintz, "Hebrew in America: A Memoir," 212. For a contemporary discussion on the use of the term "Hebrew School," see Bunin Benor, Avineri, and Greninger, *Let's Stop Calling It "Hebrew School": Rationales, Goals, and Practices of Hebrew Education in Part-Time Jewish Schools.*
32 Spolsky and Shohamy, *The Languages of Israel.*
33 Sokoloff and Berg, eds., *What We Talk About When We Talk About Hebrew*, 17.
34 Other texts that explore American Jews' language practices include Bunin Benor, *Becoming Frum: How Newcomers Learn the Language and Culture of Orthodox Judaism*; Fader, *Mitzvah Girls: Bringing Up the Next Generation of Hasidic Jews in Brooklyn*; Shandler, *Adventures in Yiddishland: Postvernacular Language and Culture.*
35 Wuthnow, "Taking Talk Seriously: Religious Discourse as Social Practice," 1–21.
36 Ammerman, *Studying Lived Religion: Contexts and Practices.*
37 Eichler-Levine, *Painted Pomegranates and Needlepoint Rabbis*; Gross, *Beyond the Synagogue.*
38 Bercovitch, "The Problem of Ideology in American Literary History," 1–3.
39 Pew Research Center, *Modeling the Future of Religion in America*, September 13, 2022.
40 Pew Research Center, *Jewish Americans in 2020*, May 11, 2021.
41 Pew Research Center, *Jewish Americans in 2020*; Phillips, "Expanding Our Definitions of and Questions for American Jewry," 237–39; Kelman et al., "The Social Self: Toward the Study of Jewish Lives in the Twenty-First Century," 53–79.
42 Auerbach, *Are We One? Jewish Identity in the United States and Israel*, 103–5; Rosenthal, *Irreconcilable Differences? The Waning of the American Jewish Love Affair with Israel*; Beinart, *The Crisis of Zionism*, 160–77; Waxman, *Trouble in the Tribe: The American Jewish Conflict over Israel*, 49–54; Gordis, *We Stand Divided: The Rift Between American Jews and Israel*; Alterman, *We Are Not One: A History of America's Fight over Israel*; Wertheimer, *A People Divided: Judaism in Contemporary America*, 193–94; Sasson, *The New American Zionism.*

43 Ribak, "Israelis Are from Mars, American Jews Are from Venus?" 231.
44 For the origin of this remark, see Gordis, *We Stand Divided.*
45 Gray, *Men Are from Mars, Women Are from Venus.*
46 Schnur, "In a Time of Division, Bridge-Building Must Begin in the Jewish Community." https://jewishjournal.com/commentary/opinion/343651/in-a-time-of-division-bridge-building-must-begin-in-the-jewish-community/.
47 Schieffelin, Woolard, and Kroskrity, eds., *Language Ideologies: Practice and Theory.*
48 Cameron, *Verbal Hygiene*, vii.
49 Cameron, *Verbal Hygiene*, 82.
50 Bloomfield, *Language*, 29.
51 Avni, "Hebrew in the North American Linguistic Landscape: Materializing the Sacred"; Bunin Benor, "Bivalent Writing: Hebrew and English Alphabets in Jewish English," 108–57.
52 Pew Research Center, *A Portrait of Jewish Americans*, October 1, 2013.
53 Pew Research Center, *Jewish Americans in 2020.*
54 See "Adam Sandler and Howard Stern Sing a Torah Blessing Together," *Howard Stern Show*, September 26, 2018; and Ethan and Joel Coen's film *A Serious Man* (2009); *Fleishman Is in Trouble*, a television drama based on author Taffy Brodesser-Akner's 2019 popular novel of the same name and streamed on Hulu in 2023, showed a short scene in which a university student is cringingly flirting with an Israeli woman at an off-campus party.

Chapter 2

1 Shulsinger, "Hebrew Camping: The Creator of a Hebrew World, Jewish Education," 6–14.
2 Wisse, "The Hebrew Imperative," 273.
3 Irvine, "When Talk Isn't Cheap: Language and Political Economy," 248–67.
4 The term "sitings" is borrowed from Kathryn Woolard, who uses it to designate the multiple locations—language practices, explicit metalinguistic discourse, and implicit metapragmatic cues—across which language ideologies become observable and available for

analysis. Woolard, "Introduction: Language Ideology as a Field of Inquiry."

5 Following the lead of linguistic anthropologist Kathlyn Woolard, I distinguish between ideologies and discourses, using the former to refer to beliefs and the latter to refer to "the actual representations of language" in printed or digital media. Kathryn Woolard, *Singular and Plural*, 16.

6 American Jewish public figures, communal leaders, journalists, and scholars represent the majority of voices presented in this chapter. However, I also included some Israeli authors or American authors living in Israel if their pieces were written for English-speaking audiences in the United States. A review of Hebrew language ideologies in Israel appears in Asscher, *Reading Israel, Reading America*, 158–84.

7 The iCenter board announced in February 2026 that the organization was winding down its operations.

8 Sagarin, "Modern Hebrew: Culture and Identity," 60.

9 Anderson, *Imagined Communities*; Fox, "J. G. Herder on Language."

10 Wisse, "The Hebrew Imperative," 274 (italics in original).

11 Pianko, *Jewish Peoplehood: An American Innovation*, 36.

12 Pianko, *Jewish Peoplehood*, 29.

13 Pianko, *Jewish Peoplehood*, 51, 56.

14 Pianko, *Jewish Peoplehood*, 34.

15 Ergas, "American Jews Should Learn Hebrew."

16 Mintz, "Seven Theses on Hebrew and Jewish Peoplehood."

17 DellaPergola, "World Jewish Population, 2023," 9.

18 Gringas, "Jewish World: We Should Stop Hugging Israel and Start Wrestling."

19 Cohen and Kelman, *Beyond Distancing*; Muchnick and Kamarck, "The Generation Gap in Opinions Toward Israel"; Sasson, "Understanding Young Adult Attachment to Israel"; Waxman, "Young American Jews and Israel."

20 Horowitz, "A New Balancing Act? Teaching About Israel and Diaspora Jewish Communities in Unsettled Times," 31.

21 Asscher, "Language Ideology in American Jewish Thought," 384–408.

22 Mintz, "Seven Theses."

23 Hazony, "Memo to American Jews: Learn Hebrew."

24 Loeffler, "Should American Jews Speak Hebrew?"

25 Asscher also notes that this is a common sentiment among some Israeli intellectuals as well. Asscher, *Reading Israel, Reading America*, 173–76.
26 Loeffler, "Should American Jews Speak Hebrew?"
27 Gedzelman, "The Possibilities and Potential," 4.
28 Israel American Council, "About IAC."
29 Journalist Ben Sales acknowledges that it was not the referential meaning of the words that was the problem. Rather, Israeli Americans and Americans were "speaking two different metaphorical, or cultural languages." Sales, "At IAC Conference, Jewish Leaders Ponder How to Integrate Israeli-Americans into Their Communities."
30 Shufutinsky, "Learning Hebrew Can Save American Judaism." https://blogs.timesofisrael.com/learning-hebrew-can-save-american-judaism/.
31 Beinart, "Yavne: A Jewish Case for Equality in Israel-Palestine"; "I No Longer Believe in a Jewish State."
32 Gordis, "End the Jewish State? Let's Try Some Honesty, First."
33 Schiff, *The Mystique of Hebrew: An Ancient Language in the New World*, 143.
34 Schiff, *The Mystique of Hebrew*, 27; Schiff, "The Significance of Hebrew Language for Jewish Education," 2.
35 Schiff, "How Crucial Is Hebrew for Jewish Continuity and the Effectiveness of Jewish Education?" 8.
36 Mintz, ed., *Hebrew in America: Perspectives and Prospects*, 14.
37 Yosef Klausner in Harshav, *Language in Time of Revolution*, 210.
38 Glinert, *The Story of Hebrew*, 1.
39 Browning, *Medieval and Modern Greek*.
40 Ozick, *The Puttermesser Papers*, 5.
41 Lowin, *Hebrew Matters*, preface.
42 Schiff, "How Crucial Is Hebrew for Jewish Continuity and the Effectiveness of Jewish Education?" 8.
43 Glinert, *The Joys of Hebrew*, 3.
44 Benstein, *Hebrew Roots, Jewish Routes*, 193.
45 Benstein, *Hebrew Roots, Jewish Routes*, 193.
46 Glinert, *The Story of Hebrew*, 248.
47 Asscher provides a typology of Hebrew primacy that includes romantic, symbolic, and practical perspectives. *Reading Israel, Reading America*, 182–83.

48 Bartal, "From Traditional Bilingualism to National Monolingualism," 141–50.

49 Spolsky, *The Languages of the Jews: A Sociolinguistic History*, xi.

50 Glinert, *Hebrew in Ashkenaz: A Language in Exile*.

51 Seidman, *Faithful Renderings*, 14–15.

52 Asscher, "A Translation Hypothesis for the Development of Migration Communities into Enduring Diasporas," 6.

53 Chomsky, *Hebrew: The Eternal Language*, 213.

54 Shaked, "Judaism in Translation: Thoughts on the Alexandria Hypothesis," 280.

55 Wisse, "The Hebrew Imperative," 272.

56 Wisse, "The Hebrew Imperative," 272.

57 Mintz, "Seven Theses."

58 Halkin, "A Culture Loses Its Flavor," 6–7.

59 Glinert, *The Story of Hebrew*, 246. Journalist Rochelle Furstenberg takes up this claim in her article discussing Tanakh RAM, a translated version of the Bible from Biblical Hebrew to Modern Hebrew intended for Israeli students who cannot read the original text. Furstenberg, "Israeli Life: Translating the Bible into Hebrew."

60 Shaked, "Judaism in Translation: Thoughts on the Alexandria Hypothesis," 285.

61 Asscher makes the point that beliefs that authentic Jewish works of literature can be written only in Hebrew go back to the early revivalists, who insisted on Hebrew monolingualism as a central component of nation-building. Asscher, *Reading Israel, Reading America: The Politics of Translation Between Jews*, 159. Connections between translation and Jewish authenticity also emerge in debates about how Israeli Jewish authors living in the United States and Israel deploy forms of Hebrew-English multilingualism. See Wirth-Nesher, *Call It English*, 8; Weininger, *Beyond the Land*; Peleg, "A New Hebrew Literary Diaspora? Israeli Literature Abroad," 321–38.

62 Halkin, "A Culture Loses Its Flavor," 6. Halkin may have had his uncle, the poet and novelist Simon Halkin, in mind. American born and later appointed head of the department of Hebrew literature at the Hebrew University in Jerusalem in 1949, Simon Halkin insisted that literature had to be written in Hebrew to be considered

Jewish, even though this effectively foreclosed the American English-reading audience from reading his works. Halkin, "My Uncle Simon."

63 Horn, "Living in Hebrew: On Jealousy and Creativity," 35.
64 Benstein, *Hebrew Roots, Jewish Routes*, 185.
65 Levinson, "Entering the Heart of a Language," 2–3.
66 Loeffler, "Should American Jews Speak Hebrew?"
67 Wieseltier, "Language, Identity, and the Scandal of American Jewry," 22.
68 Halkin, "A Culture Loses Its Flavor," 6.
69 Charendoff, "Publisher's Note."
70 Horn, "My First Hebrew Test."
71 Weingrad, "Robert Whitehill-Bashan," 204–5.
72 Weingrad, "Can't or Won't Learn Hebrew?" https://jewishstudies.washington.edu/hebrew-humanities/american-jews-hebrew-active-resistance/.
73 Weingrad, "Can't or Won't Learn Hebrew?"
74 Weingrad, "Robert Whitehill-Bashan," 205.
75 Kelman and Levisohn, *Beyond Jewish Identity*.
76 Kravel-Tovi and Dash Moore, eds., *Taking Stock: Cultures of Enumeration in Contemporary Jewish Life*.
77 Urla, "Cultural Politics in an Age of Statistics: Numbers, Nations, and the Making of Basque Identity," 818–43.
78 Duchêne and Heller, eds. *Discourses of Endangerment: Ideology and Interest in the Defence of Languages*, 4.
79 Porter, *Trust in Numbers: The Pursuit of Objectivity in Science and Public Life*.
80 Shandler, "Keepers of Accounts: The Practice of Inventory in Modern Jewish Life," https://www.fulcrum.org/concern/monographs/rv042w44t.
81 Kravel-Tovi, "Language of Continuity: Crisis and the Work of Care Among the Organized American Jewish Community," 141–42.
82 Pew Research Center, *A Portrait of Jewish Americans*, October 1, 2013; Pew Research Center, *Jewish Americans in 2020*, May 11, 2021.
83 Silow-Carroll, "Putting Pew's New Survey into Context: How Similar Studies Have Shaped 3 Decades of Jewish Life."
84 Pew Research Center, *A Portrait of Jewish Americans*.
85 Loeffler, "The Death of Jewish Culture."

86 American Jewish Committee, "AJC 2021 Survey of American Jewish Opinion."

87 Kushner, "No One's Studying Hebrew Anymore: That's a Big Problem."

88 Spolsky, "Language Policy and the Teaching of Hebrew," 166.

89 Cameron, *Verbal Hygiene*, 82.

90 Duchêne and Heller, *Discourses of Endangerment*, 4.

91 For the perspective that Modern Hebrew is a Slavic language, see Wexler, *The Schizoid Nature of Modern Hebrew*.

92 Zuckermann, "Hebrew Revivalists' Goals Vis-à-Vis the Emerging Israeli Language," 68–84.

93 Zuckermann, "Hybridity Versus Revivability: Multiple Causation, Forms and Patterns," 47.

94 Zuckermann, "A New Vision for Israeli Hebrew," 5.

95 An abundance of academic research on the historiography of the Hebrew language refutes Zuckermann's controversial claims that Modern Hebrew represents a fundamental linguistic break from historical Hebrew. See Angel Sáenz-Badillos, *A History of the Hebrew Language*.

96 Philologos, "Are Biblical Hebrew and Modern Hebrew the Same Language, or Two Different Ones?" https://ideas.tikvah.org/mosaic/observations/are-biblical-hebrew-and-modern-hebrew-the-same-language-or-two-different-ones. The argument between Halkin (Philologos) and Zuckermann dates back to a series of pieces in 2004. Philologos, "Hebrew vs. Israeli"; Zuckermann, "The Genesis of the Israeli Language: A Brief Response to 'Philologos.'"

97 Lest we think that this choice is made only by non-Jewish authors, Pulitzer Prize–winning novelist Michael Chabon wrote in an email to the Associated Press that "as a proudly Jewish writer who wants Israel to survive and thrive, and (and therefore) supports the Palestinian people in their struggle for equality, justice and human rights, I say yasher koach (Hebrew for 'Good job' or 'More power to you') to Rooney." https://www.pbs.org/newshour/arts/sally-rooney-holds-off-on-hebrew-translation-of-new-novel.

98 Sales, "Sally Rooney: Israeli Publishers Can't Put Out My New Book for Now, but Hebrew Translation 'Would Be an Honour.'" Later Rooney clarified that while she wanted to make her work available to Hebrew readers, she was unwilling to sell the translation rights to

an Israel-based publisher unless they were compliant with the BDS guidelines.

99 Knight, "Sally Rooney Novels Pulled from Israeli Bookstores After Translation Boycott."

100 Rudolph, "American Jewry Must Reclaim Hebrew."

101 Sales, "Sally Rooney."

102 Charter schools are publicly funded schools that by law cannot espouse or promote religious beliefs.

103 Bass, "Hebrew Language Charter School Proposed."

104 Bass, "Hebrew Language Charter School Proposed."

105 Historian Liora Halperin reminds us that, around the turn of the twentieth century, Zionist leaders also promoted "the language's universalist bona fides" by tying Hebrew to human values, which allowed them to celebrate Modern Hebrew as a secular, modern language that reflected "civilizational advancement, power, and global reach and associated with western Europe." Halperin, "Modern Hebrew, Esperanto, and the Quest for a Universal Language," 3. Halperin reminds us that Hebrew's signification as universal predates modern Zionism. Over centuries, Christian seminaries, theologians, and scholars considered Hebrew universal, but only as the key to the universal truth of the Christian Bible and Christian scripture. For more on the relationship between Christianity and Hebrew Scripture, see Sharp, *Wrestling the Word: The Hebrew Scriptures and the Christian Believer*; Lapide, *Hebrew in the Church: The Foundations of Jewish-Christian Dialogue*.

106 Bass, "Hebrew Language Charter School Proposed."

107 Hebrew Public, "FAQs." Accessed August 20, 2025. https://hebrewpublic.org/faq/.

108 Bass, "Hebrew Language Charter School Proposed."

109 Avni, "The Meanings of Hebrew," 188–202.

110 Benor, Krasner, Avni, *Hebrew Infusion*, 126.

Chapter 3

1 "Cheder Ivrit" is a pseudonym for a monthly Hebrew meetup group in New York City.

2 All names of Hebrew enthusiasts are pseudonyms except for the public figures, educators, and communal leaders who gave consent for my using their names. All interviews were conducted over Zoom unless otherwise noted.

3 Bialik wrote most of his poetry using Ashkenazi pronunciation, and not the Sephardic diction adopted by the revivalists. As a result, reading a Bialik poem aloud results in some incongruities in meter, stress, and rhyme, though the group was unaware of this difference.

4 "I know a forest and, in that forest / I know a hidden pool / In the denseness of the void, isolated from the world / In the shades of a lofty oak, blessed by light and accustomed to storm / Alone she dreams dreams of an inverted world / And spawns, secretly, her golden fish—But no one knows what is in her heart." Translation taken from https://www.posenlibrary.com/entry/pool.

5 Heilman, *The People of the Book: Drama, Fellowship and Religion.*

6 Aberbach, *Bialik.*

7 For a description of Bialik's six-month visit to the United States in 1926 on behalf of Keren Hayesod (the fundraising arm of the Zionist movement) and his changing views regarding American Jews, see Safit, "When Poet Bialik Visited America."

8 Brown, "Waste Land with Promise: Chaim Nachman Bialik's America," 54.

9 Segal, *A New Sound in Hebrew Poetry: Poetics, Politics, Accent*, 139–48. Famously, Bialik is known for his metaphor denouncing the inferiority of translation, which he compares to kissing a bride through a handkerchief.

10 Brown, "Waste Land with Promise," 51–56.

11 Sokoloff and Berg, eds., *What We Talk About When We Talk About Hebrew (and What It Means to Americans)*, 5.

12 I took people's commitment to Hebrew at face value; I did not evaluate their Hebrew proficiency, nor did I ask them to self-assess their proficiency.

13 Sokoloff and Berg, eds., *What We Talk About When We Talk About Hebrew (and What It Means to Americans)*, 7.

14 Prell, "Developmental Judaism: Challenging the Study of American Jewish Identity in the Social Sciences," 39.

15 Orsi, "Is the Study of Lived Religion Irrelevant to the World We Live In?" 172.

16 Tickton Schuster, *Portraits of Adult Jewish Learning: Making Meaning at Many Tables.*

17 To be sure, I have contributed to this bias in my own scholarship, which has focused primarily on children and teenagers at Jewish day schools, congregational schools, and summer camps.

18 The individuals I observed and interviewed were not engaged in activities or careers that required knowledge of the language. Though a few worked in Jewish organizations, I limited my analysis by design to those who did not use Hebrew in their work, did not grow up in a home in which Hebrew was spoken, and did not have any intentions of living in Israel.

19 Several of the Gen Z participants mentioned that their ability to engage in Hebrew was a direct result of the pandemic. As a result of the strong response to online programming during the pandemic, JCCs and synagogues offered online educational programming, which included reduced-price Hebrew classes. Ariel, a twenty-four-year-old woman, told me that it was her local JCC's social media outreach, along with its reduced tuition plan, that prompted her to sign up for the weekly Hebrew class. "I couldn't open Facebook or Instagram without seeing ads for *ulpan* at the JCC. And so finally, I was just like, it's the pandemic, I literally have, quite frankly, nothing else going on really because I'm stuck inside all day, I might as well try *ulpan*."

20 Chug Ivrit's founder—author and educator Philip Birnbaum, who had been staying at the home of Rabbi Jacob Kraft from Congregation Beth Shalom—thought it would be a good idea to gather a group of locals who loved Hebrew. Starting in 1946, Harry Bluestone, former director of the Wilmington, Delaware, Jewish Community Center, and about a dozen others began to meet at people's homes.

21 One long-running meetup group in New York City had two participants get married, though the couple initially hid their romantic relationship from the others so they wouldn't disturb the dynamics of the group.

22 Oldenburg, *The Great Good Place: Cafes, Coffee Shops, Bookstores, Bars, Hair Salons, and Other Hangouts at the Heart of a Community*, 1999.

23 This detachment must be seen in light of other efforts Israeli American families make to ensure their children maintain their Hebrew. See Kober, "A Fraying Connection: Israeli-American Perspectives on Diasporic Hebrew Learning Through and Beyond Jewish Education"; Kattan, "'Because She Doesn't Speak Real Hebrew': Accent and the Socialization of Authenticity Among Israeli Shlichim."
24 Glinert, "Hebrew from Symbol to Substance," 227–50.
25 SLA is an interdisciplinary field focused on the social, psychological, cognitive, linguistic, and cultural complexities of acquiring an additional language.
26 Lewis Glinert interview, July 25, 2019.
27 Alexandra Jaffe talks about similar adult Corsican learners in Corsica: "Defining the New Speaker," 41.
28 Dan Siegel's poem in which he playfully acknowledges that his Israeli friend's dog knows more Hebrew than he does even after years of studying captures this sentiment. https://blogs.timesofisrael.com/there-are-many-roads-to-the-holiness-of-hebrew/. Accessed September 2, 2025.

Chapter 4

1 Heilman, *Portrait of American Jews*, 135.
2 Pew Research Center, *Religious "Nones" in America*, January 24, 2024.
3 Gold, "A Sketch of the Linguistic Situation in Israel Today," 370.
4 Philologos, "Are Biblical Hebrew and Modern Hebrew the Same Language, or Two Different Ones?"
5 "Lech Lecha" is a Torah portion from Genesis 12:1–17:27 which recounts Abram's (Abraham's) encounter with God, the birth of his son Ishmael, and the covenant God makes with him to make his descendants a great nation.
6 In the Coen brothers' 2009 movie, *A Serious Man*, a rabbi tells the story about a dentist in the congregation who, after taking impressions of "a goy's teeth," found letters behind several teeth spelling out the Hebrew word *hoshieni*. Perturbed by the mysterious message, he takes the *gematria* of the letters, adds up their numerical significance, and arrives at the telephone number of a grocery store, which unsurprisingly offers him no revelations.

7 According to SVARA's website, "SVARA's mission is to empower queer and trans people to expand Torah and tradition through spiritual practice of Talmud study." https://svara.org/mission-vision/.

8 This expression is found in Deuteronomy 21:10–14. It affirms the right of the Israelite soldier to have sex with the non-Israelite woman war prisoner and stipulates the conditions under which a soldier can marry his captive. Rabbinic and scholarly commentaries are divided over the law, with some arguing that it legitimizes rape and others claiming it minimizes the abuse a woman would experience as a result of being held captive in war.

9 "Off the *derech*" refers to formerly devout Orthodox Jews who have left the path of traditional observance and taken on a secular, non-Jewish, or less observant form of Judaism.

10 Stavans, *Resurrecting Hebrew*, 201.

11 While a majority of American Jews report some emotional connection to Israel, a significant minority explicitly rejects identification with the Jewish state, reflecting broader generational, political, and ideological divides. See Pew Research Center, *Jewish Americans in 2020*, May 11, 2021; Waxman, *Trouble in the Tribe: The American Jewish Conflict over Israel*, 2016.

12 In my interviews, I did not hear anyone question Israel's right to exist as a sovereign Jewish state. However, there was a spectrum of political opinions about Israeli government leaders, religious policies, and military actions.

13 Shaul Kelner describes Israel homeland tourism as a category of travel that seeks to foster a transnational attachment to Israel among Jews living in the diaspora. Kelner, "Historical Perspectives on Diaspora Homeland Tourism: 'Israel Experience' Education in the 1950s and 1960s," 99–113. It is important to note that Zionism was not always widely embraced by American Jews. In the early 1900s, there was fear that Zionist beliefs might impede Jews' movement into the American mainstream or raise questions about their political loyalties. The establishment of Israel in 1948 and the Holocaust's impact on European Jewry pushed Israel to the top of the communal, political, and philanthropic agenda. Katz, *Bringing Zion Home: Israel in American Jewish Culture, 1948–1967.*

14 Boym, *The Future of Nostalgia*, xviii.

15 Sachar, *A History of Israel*; Segev, *1967: Israel, the War, and the Year That Transformed the Middle East*.
16 Diner, *The Jews of the United States, 1654 to 2000*.
17 This optimistic reaction was not monolithic. Segments of the American and Israeli Jewish public expressed ambivalence and voiced concerns about Israeli militarism and the implications of occupation.
18 Wertheimer, "American Jews and Israel: A 60-Year Retrospective."
19 Elazar, *Community and Polity: The Organizational Dynamics of American Jewry*, 107. Woocher, "Sacred Survival: American Jewry's Civil Religion."
20 The Temple Mount is considered the holiest site in Judaism, revered as the location of the ancient Temples and the site of the Binding of Isaac (Akedah), as well as other Bible events. Muslims refer to the Temple Mount as the Haram al-Sharif (the Noble Sanctuary), the site of Muhammad's ascent to heaven. Today, Al-Aqsa Mosque and the gold-topped Dome of the Rock occupy the site.
21 Boym, *The Future of Nostalgia*, 14.
22 Shaul Kelner interview, July 19, 2019.
23 Shaul Kelner, personal email, March 8, 2022.
24 This line is taken from Israeli poet and songwriter Naomi Shemer's famous 1980 song, "Al Kol Eleh" (For All These Things), which reads like a prayer asking God to protect the Jewish people in good and bad times. It makes use of an expression found in Midrash (a body of commentaries on the Bible) to speak to Israel's growing pains.
25 Pew Research Center, *Jewish Americans in 2020*. Orthodox Jews had the strongest attachment to Israel, with 60 percent saying they were very attached to the Jewish state. Approximately 72 percent of those who identified as Republicans were very or somewhat attached to Israel, in comparison to about half of those who identified as Democrats. Younger Jews were less attached to Israel than their older counterparts, with two-thirds of Jews ages sixty-five and older saying they were very or somewhat emotionally attached to Israel, in comparison with 48 percent of those aged eighteen to twenty-nine. American Jews sixty-five and older were more likely than younger Jews to say that caring about Israel was essential to what being Jewish meant to them. For a look at young Jewish adults and their attachments to

Israel and Hebrew, see Graizbord, *The New Zionists: Young American Jews, Jewish National Identity, and Israel*, 195.

26 Kelman and Zvi Baron, "Framing Conflict: Why American Congregations Cannot Not Talk About Israel."

27 Hebrew music has served as a crucial means through which many American Jews engaged in aspects of Zionism and Hebrew national culture. See Eli Sperling, *Singing the Land*.

28 Speaker of the US House of Representatives Nancy Pelosi quoted the last line of "Ein Li Eretz Acheret" in Congress after the January 6, 2021, insurrection at the Capitol.

29 For more on the Israeli radio stations' scheduling of time to mark everyday life and times of commemoration and emergencies, see Kaplan, "The Songs of the Siren: Engineering National Time on Israeli Radio."

30 For the role of popular music in projecting and navigating a nation's history and future, see Neiger, Meyers, and Zandberg, "Tuned to the Nation's Mood: Popular Music as a Mnemonic Cultural Object."

31 Squires, "From TV Personality to Fans and Beyond: Indexical Bleaching and the Diffusion of a Media Innovation."

32 Notably, in July 2023, after the Israeli parliament passed a watershed bill to significantly limit the Supreme Court's ability to review government decisions, group members were upset by the events and asked each other how they were handling it at the beginning of the class. I mentioned that I could not recall us discussing anything political in previous meetings. Nobody responded to my comment, and the class members immediately started the reading for the evening, which was a recipe.

33 Mac Ginty, "Everyday Peace: Bottom-Up and Local Agency in Conflict-Affected Societies."

34 Mac Ginty, "Everyday Peace: Bottom-Up and Local Agency in Conflict-Affected Societies," 553.

35 Katriel, *Talking Straight: Dugri Speech in Israeli Sabra Culture*.

36 For more on politeness theory in American English, see Leech, *The Pragmatics of Politeness*.

37 Mac Ginty, "Everyday Peace," 554.

38 Vieira, "The Concept of Utopia," 3.

39 Shandler, *Yiddish: Biography of a Language*, 150–64.

40 Shandler, *Yiddish: Biography of a Language*, 36. *Doikayt* continues to be a topic that resonates among American Jewish Yiddish speakers, with all of its politically left-wing connotations and commitments to diaspora Jewish life. See Bardi, "Doikayt: The Jewish Left Is Here"; Tracy, "Is Israel Part of What It Means to Be Jewish?"; and Boyarin, *The No-State Solution: A Jewish Manifesto*, 33–34, 90–91.
41 Brenner, "Hebrew and Yiddish: The Language War."
42 See Stavans and Lambert, eds., *How Yiddish Changed America and How America Changed Yiddish*.
43 The largest Yiddish-speaking communities in the United States and in Israel are made up of *haredim*, who use Yiddish as their everyday form of communication to intentionally draw religious, spatial, social, and linguistic boundaries between themselves and "secular" non-Haredi Jews and non-Jews, as well as to maintain the sanctity of Hebrew as a sacred tongue.
44 It might be the case that American Jews unfamiliar with either language are not always able to tell the difference between the two. Over the years people have shown me photos or sent me images of words written in Hebrew letters, asking me if it was Hebrew or Yiddish. It is worth noting that Yiddish, much like Hebrew, is not widely known or used by non-Haredi American Jews today.
45 Bennett, *Sacred Languages of the World: An Introduction*, 117. For a look at the sanctification of Yiddish in history, see Fishman, "The Holiness of Yiddish: Who Says Yiddish Is Holy and Why?"
46 Shandler, *Adventures in Yiddishland: Postvernacular Language and Culture*, 4.
47 Wex, *Born to Kvetch: Yiddish Language and Culture in All Its Moods*.
48 Shandler, *Adventures in Yiddishland*, 87. The connection between Yiddish and queerness is also discussed in Boyarin et al., eds., *Queer Theory and the Jewish Question*, and Seidman, *A Marriage Made in Heaven: The Sexual Politics of Hebrew and Yiddish*.
49 Shaul Kelner interview, July 19, 2019.
50 Stavans, "Yiddish Is Having a Moment."
51 Seidman, *Faithful Renderings*; Stavans, "Yiddish Is Having a Moment."

Chapter 5

1 Avni, "Effie the Sassy Gym Bubbe and Her Very Special Hebrish."

2 "Effie Hercky with Ittay Flescher and Benji Lovitt (Video)."

3 "Effie's Firsts and Favorites in Israel," *Bagels*, accessed May 25, 2021. https://bagels.tv/effies-firsts-and-favorites-in-israel/.

4 "Bubbly 81-Year-Old Is Israel's Favorite New Celebrity," *United with Israel*.

5 Yehudah Dov, "Anglo-Israeli Grandma Goes Viral After Hilarious Interview with Israeli Anchor Rafi Rashef," *VINnews*, March 2, 2021.

6 "Let Effie Hercky Light an Independence Day Torch," Change.org.

7 For reading on Nordau's notion of the Jewish body and Jewish regeneration, see Presner, "Clear Heads, Solid Stomachs, and Hard Muscles: Max Nordau and the Aesthetics of Jewish Regeneration," 269–96.

8 The gender dynamics that emerge in the Hertzke episode are beyond the scope of this chapter but warrant a separate analysis. Gender was arguably a main dynamic in the creation of Hebrew and the Israeli sound prior to the establishment of the state, especially in the rejection of Yiddish, which was depicted as the feminine and weak language of diasporic Jews. For more about Hebrew and gender, see Segal, *A New Sound in Hebrew Poetry*.

9 Bourdieu, *Language and Symbolic Power*.

10 Trilling, *Sincerity and Authenticity*.

11 Lindholm, "The Theory and History of Authenticity," 11.

12 Charmé, "Varieties of Authenticity in Contemporary Jewish Identity," 138.

13 Charmé, *Authentically Jewish: Identity, Culture, and the Struggle for Recognition*.

14 Charme, "Varieties of Authenticity in Contemporary Jewish Identity," 134.

15 About Israel-diaspora symbolic boundaries, authenticity, and language, see Asscher and Shiff, "Diasporic Stances, Homeland Prisms," and Schweid, "The Rejection of the Diaspora in Zionist Thought: Two Approaches."

16 Dobozy, "The Holocaust as Fiction: Derrida's *Demeure* and the Demjanjuk Trial in Philip Roth's *Operation Shylock*," 41.

17 Woolard, *Singular and Plural*, 22.
18 Accent has always been central to the idea of a speech community, whose theoretical origins derived from nineteenth-century nationalist yearnings for political and social unity through linguistic homogeneity.
19 Lippi-Green, "Accent, Standard Language Ideology, and Discriminatory Pretext in the Courts," 165.
20 Agha, *Language and Social Relations*; Coupland, *Style: Language Variation and Identity*; Johnstone and Kiesling, "Indexicality and Experience: Exploring the Meanings of /aw/-Monophthongization in Pittsburgh." Examples of intentional accent changes also show up in the popular press; see "David and Victoria Beckham 'Getting Posher,' Study Finds," *BBC.com*, April 7, 2013.
21 Yildiz, *Beyond the Mother Tongue: The Postmonolingual Condition*, 11–14.
22 We can hear echoes of Stephen Krashen's influential acquisition-learning hypothesis, which differentiates between language acquisition (unconscious learning) and language learning (explicit language instruction). Krashen, *Second Language Acquisition and Second Language Learning*.
23 Woolard, *Singular and Plural*, 32.
24 Kaplan, *French Lessons: A Memoir*, 55.
25 Harshav, *Language in Time of Revolution*, 166.
26 For more on the role of media technologies in the revitalization of the Hebrew accent, see Ramati, *Lingua Ex Machina: Media in the Revitalization of Modern Hebrew*.
27 It is important to note that there were many Sephardi Hebrew dialects, just as there were many Ashkenazi Hebrew dialects. The Jews of Italy, Morocco, Turkey, Iran, and Yemen all sounded different when they pronounced Hebrew. For the contemporary implications of the social and linguistic distinction between the Ashkenazi and Mizrachi sound, see Gafter's doctoral dissertation, "The Most Beautiful and Correct Hebrew: Authenticity, Ethnic Identity and Linguistic Variation in the Greater Tel Aviv Area."
28 Harshav, *Language in Time of Revolution*, 157.
29 Segal, *A New Sound in Hebrew Poetry*, 4.
30 Kahlenberg, "How the Locals Grew an Accent," 107. This article goes on to probe Mizrachi and Sephardic Jews' roles in the

revernacularization process and their quest to achieve "vocal capital." Kahlenberg also writes about how Palestinians took part in debates about the stakes of the Hebrew accent. For the role of Arab-Palestinian people in the construction of Modern Hebrew, see Mendel and Ranta, *From the Arab Other to the Israeli Self: Palestinian Culture in the Making of Israeli National Identity*.

31 Harshav, *Language in Time of Revolution*, 153–66.

32 Harshav, *Language in Time of Revolution*, 155.

33 Segal, *A New Sound in Hebrew Poetry*, vii.

34 Di Giulio, "Protecting the Jewish Throat: Hebrew Accent and Hygiene in the Yishuv," 153–75.

35 Di Giulio also points out that some "hygienists" imagined the throat as feminine—a cavity lined with vulnerable tissue—and thus requiring protection from the harsh usage of certain phonemes, which could, when articulated, act as "sexual stimulus" for its speakers.

36 Linguist Roey Gafter shows that the two pharyngeal phonemes—the voiceless pharyngeal fricative /ħ/ and the voiced pharyngeal approximant /ʕ/, which signify defining features of "Mizrachi Hebrew" in contemporary Israeli society—are stigmatized, associated with lower socioeconomic status, and perceived as liabilities. Yet he also shows that these sounds retain authenticity as the true and correct sounds used in official Israeli ceremonies. Gafter, "What's a Stigmatized Variant Doing in the Word List? Authenticity in Reading Styles and Hebrew Pharyngeals," 31–58.

37 I thank Tuvi Voorhees for his help analyzing the features of the American Hebrew accent. I draw on Shlomy Kattan's thorough analysis of the contrasts in American English and Israeli Hebrew phonetic inventories. For more details than I provide here, see Kattan's doctoral dissertation, "Language Socialization and Linguistic Ideologies Among Israeli Emissaries in the United States."

38 Despite Hebrew enthusiasts' comments about the Israeli Hebrew accent, it is important to note that there is no single Israeli Hebrew accent. Israeli society is made up of immigrants, refugees, and people of different religions and ethnicities, which results in a spectrum of Hebrew accents.

39 Feelings of inferiority extended to those who wrote in Hebrew. Author Dan Siegel recounted a correspondence he had with Michael

Oren, an American-born Israeli historian, author, statesman, and politician. As Siegel recalls, Oren expressed regret that he could not write Hebrew literature: "Here was the guy that was the ambassador from Israel in the United States. It's one thing to be a diplomat, and it's another thing to be able to be a literary person in Hebrew. He's written all kinds of communication, everything, but to do literature [in Hebrew] is something else." Dan Siegel interview, February 9, 2021.

40 Mintz, "Hebrew in America: A Memoir," 211–26.

41 For critiques of the American-Hebrew accent in Israeli media, see Martin, "Why Can't the Anglos Learn to Speak?"; Spiegel, "American Accent? You'll Never Be a 'Real' Israeli." For negative depictions of characters speaking with an American Hebrew accent on popular Israeli television shows, see *Shtisel* (season 2, episode 5), *Srugim* (season 3, episode 12, and season 1, episode 1), and *Eretz Nehederet* (January 23, 2012). Interviewees brought up these examples, finding them both funny and insulting.

42 Agha, *Language and Social Relations*, 80.

43 Blommaert and Varis, "Enough Is Enough: The Heuristics of Authenticity in Superdiversity," 1–13.

44 Labov, "Hypercorrection by the Lower Middle Class as a Factor in Linguistic Change."

45 Gloria was not making a broader statement about Hebrew and gender here. In follow-up conversations she clarified that she simply found the male conjunction system easier to use.

46 For an understanding of present-day Israeli plurilingualism and the demographic changes in the country, see Walters et al., "Sociolinguistics in Israel: From Hebrew Hegemony to Israeli Plurilingualism," 278–88.

47 Berg, "The Anxiety of Authenticity: Hebrew, Sushi, and Suspicious Objects," 53–71.

48 Berg, "The Anxiety of Authenticity," 64.

49 Wineberg interview, June 30, 2020 (in Hebrew; translation mine). Wineburg noted in the interview that Israelis "do not know Americans who know the language like me unless they live in the country," which might be true, but may not be fully accurate. I know many American Hebrew-speakers who have lived in Israel for decades, as

well as many Israeli-born and raised Hebrew-speakers who are not at his level.

50 Loeffler, "Should American Jews Speak Hebrew?" https://www.tabletmag.com/sections/arts-letters/articles/ben-gurion-hebrew-revolution.

Chapter 6

1 Golda Meir Jewish Day School is a pseudonym. Jewish day schools are private, sectarian K–12 schools that offer secular and religious studies. Within this category are schools affiliated with the Modern Orthodox, Conservative, and Reform denominations. They are also pluralistic community schools. Jewish day schools are not centralized, and the curriculum of a school will vary according to its affiliation and the community it serves. Day schools serving the Orthodox and ultra-Orthodox communities are called yeshiva. As Pomson et al. argue, Jewish day schools are spaces of organized Jewish life, and their assumption is that graduates will "play a leading role in Jewish life when they come of age." Pomson, Wertheimer, Hacohen-Wolf, *Hearts and Minds: Israel in North American Jewish Day Schools*, 35.

2 The ethnographic study of the Hebrew classes at this school was funded by the Moshe and Sylvia Ettenberg Award Fund.

3 Pomson and Wertheimer, *Hebrew for What?* Benor, Avineri, and Greninger found that decisions about which Hebrew to teach and for what religious and educational purposes were prevalent in supplemental schooling. Benor, Avineri, and Greninger, *Let's Stop Calling It "Hebrew School": Rationales, Goals, and Practices of Hebrew Education in Part-Time Jewish Schools.*

4 Zelkowicz, "Jewish Educators Don't Make Jews," 150.

5 Zelkowicz, "Jewish Educators Don't Make Jews," 163.

6 *Visions of Jewish Education* was an influential publication in which a select group of eight Jewish religious leaders and scholars expounded on three questions: What is an educated Jew? What does an educated Jew need to know? And what is a successful Jewish education? Fox, Scheffler, and Marom, eds. *Visions of Jewish Education.*

7 Peshkin, *God's Choice: The Total World of a Fundamentalist Christian School*, 60.
8 Kelman, *Jewish Education*.
9 Pinar, *What Is Curriculum Theory?*, xvii.
10 See Avni, "Hebrew Education in the United States: Historical Perspectives and Future Directions."
11 Krasner, *The Benderly Boys and American Jewish Education*, 41.
12 Ashton, *Rebecca Gratz: Women and Judaism in Antebellum America*. Yares, *Jewish Sunday Schools: Teaching Religion in Nineteenth-Century America*.
13 Sarna, *American Judaism*.
14 Krasner, "American Jewry at Risk: 'A Time to Act' and the Prioritization of Jewish Education."
15 Ruskay and Rubin-Kurshan, "American Jewry's Focus on Continuity—At Ten Years."
16 Commission on Jewish Education in North America, *A Time to Act: The Report of the Commission on Jewish Education in North America*, 5.
17 Krasner, "American Jewry at Risk," 119.
18 Krasner, "American Jewry at Risk," 85.
19 Krasner, "On the Origins and Persistence of the Jewish Identity Industry in Jewish Education," 61. For insight into the link between Jewish education and the identity-driven outcomes, see Kelman and Levisohn, eds., *Beyond Jewish Identity: Rethinking Concepts and Imagining Alternatives*.
20 Zisenwine and Schers, eds., *Present and Future: Jewish Culture, Identity and Language*; Schiff, "How Crucial Is Hebrew for Jewish Continuity and the Effectiveness of Jewish Education?"
21 Ruth Wisse interview, July 30, 2020.
22 Due to space limitations, this chapter does not cover other innovative programs used at day schools, including *Nitzanim* and *Chaverim b'Ivrit* or other Hebrew textbooks published by private publishers. It also does not discuss AVI CHAI's funding of the Ivriyon Immersion Program, a summer course at the Jewish Theological Seminary intended for Jewish studies teachers wishing to further their Hebrew proficiency.
23 AVI CHAI, "Mission."
24 Fleishman, *Within Our Lifetime: A Reflection on the Spend-Down of the AVI CHAI Foundation*.

25 Lesley Littman interview, July 27, 2020.
26 Susan Kardos interview, July 30, 2020.
27 Joel Einleger interview, July 17, 2020.
28 According to the AVI CHAI 1999 Annual Report, NETA received $195,000 for a study grant, and then an additional $500,000 the following year. Tal Am was allocated $715,000 in 1999 and then another $1,000,000 in 2000.
29 When the foundation began its sunsetting agenda, it secured long-term sustainability for both programs. Tal Am merged with the for-profit educational technology firm Compedia in 2011. Additional funding came from the Gruss Life Monument Fund and the Azriela Foundation. See AVI CHAI Foundation, *A Case Study of a Foundation as Social Enterprise Investor: The Creation of iTaLAM*. Tal Am developed into iTalAm, a digital blended-learning environment. NETA merged with Israel's nonprofit Center for Educational Technology in 2012 and is now known as Bishvil Ha-Ivrit. In the early 2010s, both programs shifted into the digital arena and away from tangible workbooks and classroom material.
30 Einleger interview, July 17, 2020. See Birkner, "The New Look of Hebrew Instruction," for more about how this neglect was understood.
31 It is important to note that the renewed focus on Hebrew education spoke to the hearts of several members of the AVI CHAI leadership, including Ruth Wisse and Leah Meir, who had grown up in Hebraist families and held strong attachments to Hebrew. This was also the case for Harlene Appelman, head of the Covenant Foundation, who noted that Hebrew "seemed a reasonable piece of the jigsaw puzzle of Jewish education across North America. For me, it was a personal quest, quite frankly, I was in." Appelman interview, July 29, 2020.
32 Shimon worked as a Hebrew and Jewish history teacher in Israeli elementary and high schools, was an instructor of Hebrew pedagogy at McGill University, and served as director of curriculum development and implementation at the Jewish Education Council of Greater Montreal (JEC).
33 Interview with Tova Shimon, September 3, 2020. Interview was conducted in Hebrew; English translation is mine. In 1979 Tova Shimon developed Tal Sela, the precursor to Tal Am, with her

husband, Shlomo Shimon, a Jewish educator and director of the Education Resource Centre (ERC) at the Jewish Education Council of Greater Montreal, which was renamed the Bronfman Jewish Education Centre (BJEC) in 2000. It secured seed funding from the Multiculturalism Directorate of the Secretary of State of Canada and BJEC. Additional funding later came from the Covenant Foundation. Tova Shimon recounted her chance encounter in the 1980s, at a Jewish education conference in Toronto, with Magda Winter, a writer of Hebrew educational material for supplemental schools at the publisher Behrman House; the two women later met again for dinner at Winter's home. At that time Shimon introduced her work to Nathan Winter, a Benderly scholar and then educational consultant to the United Synagogue of America. Shimon recalled that Winter was enthusiastic about this new Hebrew curricular program and suggested that the Solomon Schechter schools in New Jersey—the network of day schools then affiliated with the Conservative movement—might be interested in implementing it. Solomon Schechter's adoption led other day schools using the material, and it became one of the most popular Hebrew curricula used in Jewish day schools across the country.

34 Tova Shimon interviews, September 3 and 21, 2020.

35 Yossi Prager interview, July 22, 2020.

36 Joel Einleger interview, July 7, 2020.

37 Ruth Wisse interview, July 30, 2020.

38 Hila Kobliner interview, July 20, 2020. Original interview conducted in Hebrew; English translation is mine.

39 Hila Kobliner, interview, July 20, 2020.

40 Though beyond the scope of this chapter, it is important to note that a handful of Hebrew educators indicated that both programs had been "outsourced" to Israeli educators and not developed by American Jewish educators.

41 Naomi Stillman interview, July 13, 2020.

42 Arnee Winshall interview, July 6, 2020.

43 Ringvald was also director of Arabic, Japanese, Mandarin, and Romance languages at Brandeis.

44 ACTFL is an organization that provides assessment tools for measuring speaking, writing, listening, and reading proficiency and performance

in a wide range of languages taught in K–12 and higher educational settings.

45 Arnee Winshall interview, July 6, 2020. According to Winshall, the school adopted Tal Am at first in order to have a structured curriculum.

46 Vardit Ringvald interview, August 12, 2020. Original interview conducted in Hebrew; English translation is mine. ACTFL uses the vocabulary of proficiency as a general framework for organizing instruction and curriculum to assess language learners on a graded scale of language mastery in different skills.

47 ACTFL Proficiency Guidelines Overview. Accessed August 20, 2020. https://www.actfl.org/proficiency-guidelines-overview.

48 Vardit Ringvald interview, August 12, 2020.

49 Arnee Winshall interview, July 6, 2020.

50 Shulman, "Those Who Understand: Knowledge Growth in Teaching," 9.

51 Arnee Winshall interview, July 6, 2020.

52 In 2008, Hebrew at the Center became an independent 501(c)(3) organization.

53 Hebrew at the Center, "State of the Field: Hebrew Teaching and Learning," unpublished document, 2008. Copy in possession of the author.

54 Arnee Winshall interview, July 6, 2020.

55 Rabbi Andrew Ergas interview, July 6, 2019.

56 David Gedzelman interview, August 10, 2020.

57 Charter schools are state-funded but privately operated. They can teach about a religion but are constitutionally barred from proselytizing or promoting any particular religious beliefs. Peter Deutsch noted that the idea came to him after learning about the success of Greek language charter schools. Peter Deutsch interview, August 12, 2020.

58 Weiss, "Mega-Donor Throws Clout Behind Hebrew Charter School." https://forward.com/news/13482/mega-donor-throws-clout-behind-hebrew-charter-scho-01941/.

59 David Gedzelman interview, August 10, 2010.

60 David Gedzelman interview, August 10, 2010.

61 Areivim also supported the creation of Kayitz Kef (translation: fun summer)/Hebrew at Camp, a Hebrew immersive program for children attending Jewish summer camps. In August 2023, Kayitz Kef

became part of the Consortium for the Teaching of Hebrew Language and Culture at Brandeis, directed by Vardit Ringvald.

62 In this section, "Hebrew-language charter schools" refers to the schools in the Hebrew Public network, which were originally funded by Areivim and led by the Steinhardt Foundation for Jewish Life. Lack of space prevented me from including the network of schools in Florida.

63 Areivim started and funded the Hebrew Charter School Center (HCSC) in 2009, and all support for the growing network of schools went through HCSC. HCSC later became a 501(c)3, the National Center for Hebrew Language Charter School Excellence and Development (d/b/a "Hebrew Public").

64 Phillips, "Hebrew School." The school also received funding from New York City and New York State.

65 Weiss, "Mega-Donor Throws Clout."

66 The original HLA plan called for science and social studies to be taught in English. Math, music, art, and physical education, as well as a daily period of Hebrew, were to be taught in Hebrew. This formula has undergone change over the years. Cohler-Esses and Slutsky, "Steinhardt Seeks Hebrew Charter School Here."

67 David Gedzelman interview, August 10, 2010.

68 David Gedzelman interview, August 10, 2010.

69 Gedzelman noted that the choice to focus on spoken language first was premised on language-acquisition research that shows young children naturally learn languages through exposure to oral language and only later begin to interact with the written word and literacy activities. David Gedzelman interview, August 10, 2010.

70 For more about Hebrew in public schooling, see Avni and Karpman, *Mapping Hebrew Education in Public Schools: A Resource for Jewish Educators.*

71 Schieffelin and Ochs, *Language Socialization Across Cultures.*

72 Language socialization theorists are careful to point out that socialization does not always work in predictable or desirable ways. See Kulick and Schieffelin, "Language Socialization," 349–68.

73 Duff, "Second Language Socialization," 564–86.

74 Binnie Swislow interview, July 16, 2019.

75 David Gedzelman interview, August 10, 2010.

76 David Gedzelman interview, August 10, 2010.

77 David Gedzelman interview, August 10, 2010.

78 When Hebrew charters started, there was great concern among Jewish educators that Hebrew charters would redefine Hebrew education as a secular endeavor—a move many Jewish educators and leaders believed would challenge the importance of the language in building Jewish identity. For background into how the Jewish press covered the emergence of the Hebrew charter school movement, see Avni, "Negotiating Language Ownership: Hebrew Charter Schools and the American Jewish Press."

79 Winer, *A Census of Jewish Supplementary Schools in North America, 2019–2020*, 20. Reports indicate a downward enrollment pattern over the past two decades.

80 For an overview of the congregational schools' range of structural arrangements and curricular approaches, see Aron, "Upending the Grammar of the Conventional Religious School."

81 Wertheimer, *Learning and Community*, ix.

82 Ackerman, "Jewish Education—For What?," 22.

83 Kaufman, *Shul with a Pool*.

84 Sarna, *American Judaism*, 283.

85 Sarna, *American Judaism*, 279.

86 Sarna, *American Judaism*, 282–85.

87 Schoenfeld, "Folk Judaism, Elite Judaism and the Role of the Bar Mitzvah," 72.

88 Sarna, *American Judaism*, 287.

89 *B'nai mitzvah* can refer to a ceremony for two or more people or serve as a generic term for both bar and bat mitzvah. More recently, the gender-neutral term *b-mitzvah* is being used.

90 Aron, "Congregational Schools," 693.

91 Isa Aron interview, July 28, 2020.

92 Aron and Moskowitz were paired together as part of a broader group of six teams tasked with studying what was working in ten highly regarded part-time educational programs. Findings from this project were published in Wertheimer, *Learning and Community*, 236–76.

93 Committee Notes, Hebrew Meeting in NYC, "BM Discussion Qs," June 30, 2011.

94 B'nai Mitzvah Revolution was a joint project of URJ's Campaign for Youth Engagement and HUC-JIR's Rhea Hirsch School of Education and its Experiment in Congregational Education. See Bien, "B'nai Mitzvah Revolution."

95 Nachama Moskowitz interview, November 12, 2019. Moskowitz was influenced by her mentor, Lifsa Schachter, who at Cleveland College of Jewish Studies had developed Hebrew through Movement (HTM), a program used in congregational schools in the 1980s that emphasized the use of physical activity for learning Jewish life words. Hebrew Through Movement was an adaptation of Total Physical Response (TPR)—a pedagogical method created by the American psychologist Dr. James Asher in the 1960s.

96 Nachama Moskowitz, email, May 6, 2024.

97 Nicki Greninger interview, August 21, 2019. Greninger also raised the idea that perhaps it is the forest itself that is undergoing change. She noted that knowing how to read the Hebrew letters had become less critical with the advent of new technologies. Apps providing recorded texts were letting children chant Torah or read prayers without needing to read. She also noted that "the cat is out of the bag" regarding the use of transliterated texts. It is no longer seen as an inferior form of Hebrew literacy. Translator and scholar Joel Hoffman also argues for the value of transliteration as a form of Jewish religious literacy. Hoffman, "The Role of Transliteration in the Synagogue."

98 Sarna, "American Jewish Education in Historical Perspective," 9.

99 Cameron, *Verbal Hygiene*, 227.

100 Wertheimer and Pomson found that the leadership at a Modern Orthodox K–8 Hebrew-intensive school saw Hebrew as a tool to ensure "that Israel, and especially Israeli culture, is close to the heartbeat of the school," but did not see Hebrew proficiency as its primary goal. Wertheimer and Pomson, *Inside Jewish Day Schools: Leadership, Learning, and Community*, 33.

101 Jewish Education Project, *From Census to Possibilities: Designing Pathways for Jewish Learners*, 23.

102 Sarna, *American Jewish Education*, 10.

Conclusion

1 Chris Williams, "Kanye West Apologizes to the Jewish Community—in Hebrew—in Curiously Generic Message," *Variety*, December 26, 2023. https://variety.com/2023/music/news/kanye-west-apologizes-jewish-community-hebrew-message-1235850532/.

2 Kuo, "Ye Apologizes for Antisemitic Comments with Post in Hebrew."

3 Robertson, "Ye Posts Hebrew-Language Apology to Jewish Community."

4 Sherman, "Kanye West, Now Known as Ye, Posts Hebrew Apology After Antisemitic Comments."

5 The centrality of machine translation in Ye's use of Hebrew and non-Hebrew speakers' ability to read this posting raises a host of questions about the future role of machine translation in homeland–diaspora dynamics. See Asscher, "The Position of Machine Translation in Translation Studies: A Definitional Perspective."

6 Berger, "Foreword," in *Everyday Religion*, ed. Ammerman, v–viii.

7 Kelman, *Jewish Education*, 131.

8 Stebbins and Sachsman, *Serious Leisure: A Perspective for Our Time*.

9 Moehlman, "Can Hebrew Be Gender-Neutral?"

10 Orit Bershtling, quoted in Benaim, "Does the Hebrew Language Have a Gender Problem?" In her *Forward* piece in support of gender-neutral Hebrew, Aviya Kushner notes that the Israeli poet Yona Wallach used the expression "Hebrew is a sex maniac" in the poem "Hebrew." Aviya Kushner, "Why Making Hebrew Nonbinary Is So Crucial."

11 Zauzmer, "A Camp Tries to Reinvent the Hebrew Language, so Transgender Kids Can Fit In." This language policy involved changing the gendered suffixes in Hebrew nouns from *-im* (plural masculine) and *-ot* (plural feminine) to a newly created suffix: *-imot*. As a result, campers are no longer called *chanichim* but rather *chanichimot*.

12 Kehilat Hadar, *Kehilat Hadar Gender Inclusive Ritual Guidelines*.

13 See Sass Orol's poem "Grammar Lesson" (2021), in which they take on the topic of gender-neutral Hebrew as a form of resistance to native-speaker hegemony: "When I make [שושנות] into a word / I hope it bitchslaps the fluent listener / as it does now." Sass Orol, *The Shortest Skirt in Shul*, 54.

14 Karpman, "Gender-Inclusive and Nonbinary Hebrew: Innovations and Classroom Applications; Summary of a March 13, 2022, Conference," 185–90.

15 Karpman, "Mapping Grassroots," 60.

16 Personal communication with Avital Karpman, June 19, 2024. For more on efforts to adopt a gender-neutral form of Hebrew in Israel, see Kershner, "In Israel, a Biblical Tongue Meets Gender Politics."

17 Karpman, "Mapping Grassroots," 57.

18 Britt Gale, "The State of the Field Report: Hebrew Education in North American Jewish Day Schools."

19 Esty Gross interview, February 20, 2023. Esty Gross was the former education director for Bishvil Ha-Ivrit (formerly NETA-CET).

20 Asscher, "Language Ideology in American Jewish Thought," 21.

21 Maltz, "'Time to Take the Plunge': How October 7 Sparked a Huge Wave of Jewish Conversions."

22 Goldberg and Tracy, "Jewish American Families Confront a Generational Divide over Israel."

23 Windmueller, "In the Wake of October 7: Reflections on the American Jewish Community."

24 If Not Now, "Homepage," accessed February 28, 2026. https://www.ifnotnowmovement.org/.

25 Rosenfeld (@ArnoRosenfeld), Twitter, October 16, 2023, https://x.com/ArnoRosenfeld/status/1713962651569582449.

26 Doherty, "Anti-Israel Jewish Group Writes Backwards Hebrew on Seder Plate for Gaza."

27 Olefson, "My Hebrew Necklace: What Judaism Means to Me."

28 For more on Hebrew materiality and lettering in the American linguistic landscape, see Avni, "Hebrew in the North American Linguistic Landscape: Materializing the Sacred," 208–25.

29 I stopped attending gatherings in early fall of 2023 but continued to receive all email communications.

30 Steinhardt Bloom, "New Priorities for American Jews."

31 Pomson, "When the Price of Loving Israel Is Ostracism."

32 Alptraum, "I Started Learning Hebrew for My Father. I Became Obsessed with It After Oct. 7."

33 Kushner, "Why Hebrew Is Showing Up in Unexpected Places—And Why That Matters."

BIBLIOGRAPHY

Aberbach, David. *Bialik*. Vol. 1. Halban Publishers, 2020.

Ackerman, Walter. "Jewish Education—For What?" *American Jewish Year Book* 70 (1969): 3–36.

Agha, Asif. *Language and Social Relations*. Cambridge University Press, 2007.

Alptraum, Lux. "I Started Learning Hebrew for My Father. I Became Obsessed with It After Oct. 7." *Forward*, January 31, 2024. https://forward.com/opinion/578274/learning-hebrew-father-war/.

Alterman, Eric. *We Are Not One: A History of America's Fight over Israel*. Basic Books, 2022.

American Jewish Committee. "AJC 2021 Survey of American Jewish Opinion." June 14, 2021. https://www.ajc.org/news/survey2021.

Ammerman, Nancy. *Studying Lived Religion: Contexts and Practices*. New York University Press, 2021.

Anderson, Benedict. *Imagined Communities: Reflections on the Origin and Spread of Nationalism*. Rev. ed. Verso, 2016.

Aron, Isa. "Congregational Schools." In *International Handbook of Jewish Education*, ed. Helene Miller, Lisa Grant, and Alex Pomson, 693–710. Springer, 2011.

———. "Upending the Grammar of the Conventional Religious School." *Journal of Jewish Education* 80, no. 3 (2014): 193–228.

Aronson, Cole. "Why Can't the Jews Teach Their Children How to Speak Hebrew?" *Mosaic*, September 30, 2024. https://mosaicmagazine.com/observation/jewish-world/2024/09/why-cant-the-jews-teach-their-children-how-to-speak-hebrew/.

Ashton, Diane. *Rebecca Gratz: Women and Judaism in Antebellum America*. Wayne State University Press, 1997.

Asscher, Omri. *Reading Israel, Reading America: The Politics of Translation Between Jews*. Stanford University Press, 2019.

——. "Translation as a Probe into Homeland-Diaspora Relations." *Translation Studies* 14, no. 1 (2021): 36–50.

——. "Language Ideology in American Jewish Thought." *Religion* 52, no. 3 (2022): 384–408.

——. "A Translation Hypothesis for the Development of Migration Communities into Enduring Diasporas." In *The Routledge Handbook of Translation and Migration*, ed. Brigid Maher, Loredana Polezzi, and Rita Wilson, 6–20. Routledge, 2024.

Asscher, Omri, and Ofer Shiff. "Diasporic Stances, Homeland Prisms: Representing Diaspora in the Homeland as Internal Negotiation of National Identity." *Diaspora Studies* 13, no. 1 (2020): 1–15.

Auerbach, Jerold. *Are We One? Jewish Identity in the United States and Israel.* Rutgers University Press, 2001.

AVI CHAI Foundation. *A Case Study of a Foundation as Social Enterprise Investor: The Creation of iTaLAM*. March 2019. Accessed April 6, 2025. https://avichai.org/knowledge_base/a-case-study-of-a-foundation-as-social-enterprise-investor-the-creation-of-italam/.

——. "Mission." Accessed February 26, 2026. https://avichai.org/about-us/81-2/.

Avni, Sharon. "Hebrew Education in the United States: Historical Perspectives and Future Directions." *Journal of Jewish Education* 80, no. 3 (2014): 256–86.

——. "Hebrew in the North American Linguistic Landscape: Materializing the Sacred." In *Challenges for Language Education and Policy: Making Space for People*, ed. Bernard Spolsky, Ofra Inbar-Lourie, and Michal Tannenbaum, 208–25. Routledge, 2014.

——. "The Meanings of Hebrew: Defining Bilingual Education in a Dual-Language Charter School." *International Journal of Bilingual Education and Bilingualism* 18, no. 2 (2015): 188–202.

——. "Negotiating Language Ownership: Hebrew Charter Schools and the American Jewish Press." *Language & Communication* 45 (2015): 83–95.

——. "Effie the Sassy Gym Bubbe and Her Very Special Hebrish." *Times of Israel*, February 25, 2021. https://www.jta.org/2021/02/24/ideas/our-beloved-israeli-gym-bubbe-has-a-thick-american-accent-and-thats-a-great-thing.

Avni, Sharon, and Avital Karpman. *Mapping Hebrew Education in Public Schools: A Resource for Jewish Educators*. Consortium for Applied Studies in

Jewish Education, 2019. Accessed February 22, 2025. https://www.casje.org/resources/mapping-hebrew-education-public-schools.

Bardi, Jennifer. "Doikayt: The Jewish Left Is Here." *Moment*. April 11, 2024. https://momentmag.com/jewish-word-doikayt/.

Bartal, Israel. "From Traditional Bilingualism to National Monolingualism." *Hebrew in Ashkenaz: A Language in Exile* (1993): 141–50.

Bass, Paul. "Hebrew Language Charter School Proposed." *New Haven Independent*, November 10, 2022. https://www.newhavenindependent.org/2022/11/10/hebrew_language_charter_school_proposed/.

Beinart, Peter. *The Crisis of Zionism*. Melbourne University Publishing, 2012.

———. "Yavne: A Jewish Case for Equality in Israel-Palestine." *Jewish Currents*, July 7, 2020. https://jewishcurrents.org/yavne-a-jewish-case-for-equality-in-israel-palestine.

———. "I No Longer Believe in a Jewish State." *New York Times*, July 8, 2020. https://www.nytimes.com/2020/07/08/opinion/israel-annexation-two-state-solution.html.

Benaim, Rachel D. "Does the Hebrew Language Have a Gender Problem?" *Forward*, November 9, 2015. https://forward.com/life/324205/degendering-hebrew/.

Bennett, Brian. *Sacred Languages of the World: An Introduction*. John Wiley & Sons, 2017.

Benor, Sarah Bunin. *Becoming Frum: How Newcomers Learn the Language and Culture of Orthodox Judaism*. Rutgers University Press, 2012.

———. "Bivalent Writing: Hebrew and English Alphabets in Jewish English." *Journal of Jewish Languages* 8, nos. 1–2 (2020): 108–57.

Benor, Sarah Bunin, Jonathan Krasner, and Sharon Avni. *Hebrew Infusion: Language and Community at American Jewish Summer Camps*. Rutgers University Press, 2020.

Benor, Sarah Bunin, Neta Avineri, and Nicki Greninger. *Let's Stop Calling It "Hebrew School": Rationales, Goals, and Practices of Hebrew Education in Part-Time Jewish Schools*. AVI CHAI Foundation and Jim Joseph Foundation, July 2020.

Benstein, Jeremy. *Hebrew Roots, Jewish Routes: A Tribal Language in a Global World*. Behrman House, 2019.

Bercovitch, Sacvan. "The Problem of Ideology in American Literary History." *Critical Inquiry* 12, no. 4 (1986): 631–53.

Berg, Nancy. “The Anxiety of Authenticity: Hebrew, Sushi, and Suspicious Objects.” In *What We Talk About When We Talk About Hebrew (and What It Means to Americans)*, ed. Naomi Sokoloff and Nancy Berg, 53–71. University of Washington Press, 2018.

Berger, Peter. “Foreword.” In *Everyday Religion: Observing Modern Religious Lives*, ed. Nancy Ammerman, v–viii. Oxford University Press, 2007.

Bien, Julie. “B’nai Mitzvah Revolution.” *Jewish Journal*, December 18, 2013. https://jewishjournal.com/judaism/125485/.

Birkner, Gabrielle. “The New Look of Hebrew Instruction.” *Jewish Telegraphic Agency*, July 8, 2005. https://www.jta.org/2005/07/08/ny/the-new-look-of-hebrew-instruction.

Blanc, Haim. *The Israeli Koine as an Emergent National Standard*. John Wiley & Sons, Inc., 1968.

Blom, Sara Steinhardt. “New Priorities for American Jews.” *Sapir*, November 5, 2023. https://sapirjournal.org/war-in-israel/2023/11/new-priorities-for-american-jews/.

Blommaert, Jan, and Piia Varis. “Enough Is Enough: The Heuristics of Authenticity in Superdiversity.” *Tilburg Papers in Culture Studies* 2 (2011): 1–13.

Bloomfield, Leonard. *Language*. Holt, 1933.

Bourdieu, Pierre. “The Economics of Linguistic Exchanges.” *Social Science Information* 16, no. 6 (1977): 645–68.

———. *Language and Symbolic Power*. Harvard University Press, 1991.

Boyarin, Daniel. *A Traveling Homeland: The Babylonian Talmud as Diaspora*. University of Pennsylvania Press, 2015.

———. *The No-State Solution: A Jewish Manifesto*. Yale University Press, 2023.

Boyarin, Daniel, et al., eds. *Queer Theory and the Jewish Question*. New York: Columbia University Press, 2003.

Boym, Svetlana. *The Future of Nostalgia*. Basic Books, 2008.

Breger, Sarah. “Can Hebrew Be Gender-Neutral?” *Moment*, August 22, 2022. https://momentmag.com/from-the-newsletter-can-hebrew-be-gender-neutral/.

Brenner, Naomi. “Hebrew and Yiddish: The Language War.” In *Routledge Handbook on Zionism*, 1st ed., ed. Colin Schindler. London: Routledge, 2024.

Britt Gale, Tal. “The State of the Field Report: Hebrew Education in North American Jewish Day Schools.” Hebrew at the Center, May 2022. https://hebrewatthecenter.org/research/#sof.

Brown, Michael. “Waste Land with Promise: Chaim Nachman Bialik’s America.” *Jewish Political Studies Review* 6, nos. 3/4 (1994): 51–56.

Browning, Robert. *Medieval and Modern Greek*. Cambridge University Press, 1983.

"Bubbly 81-Year-Old Is Israel's Favorite New Celebrity." *United with Israel*, March 2, 2021. https://unitedwithisrael.org/watch-bubbly-81-year-old-is-israels-favorite-new-celebrity/.

Cameron, Deborah. *Verbal Hygiene*. London: Routledge, 2012.

Cavanaugh, Jillian. "Accent Matters: Material Consequences of Sounding Local in Northern Italy." *Language & Communication* 25, no. 2 (2005): 127–48.

Charendoff, Mark. "Publisher's Note." *Sapir* 6 (Summer 2022). https://sapirjournal.org/education/2022/08/publishers-note-education/.

Charles Lindholm. "The Theory and History of Authenticity." *Social Media & the Self: An Open Reader*, ed. J. Pooley (2007), mediastudies.press. Accessed August 5, 2025. https://doi.org/10.32376/3f8575cb.5a28f280.

Charmé, Stuart. "Varieties of Authenticity in Contemporary Jewish Identity." *Jewish Social Studies* 6, no. 2 (2000): 133–55.

———. *Authentically Jewish: Identity, Culture, and the Struggle for Recognition*. Rutgers University Press, 2022.

Chomsky, William. *Hebrew: The Eternal Language*. New York: Jewish Publication Society of America, 1957.

Cohen, Steven M., and Arnold Eisen. *The Jew Within: Self, Family, and Community in America*. Indiana University Press, 2000.

Cohen, Steven M., and Ari Kelman. *Beyond Distancing: Young Adult American Jews and Their Alienation from Israel*. Andrea and Charles Bronfman Philanthropies, 2007.

Cohler-Esses, Larry, and Carolyn Slutsky. "Steinhardt Seeks Hebrew Charter School Here." *Jewish Telegraphic Agency*, May 28, 2008. https://www.jta.org/2008/05/28/ny/steinhardt-seeks-hebrew-charter-school-here.

Commission on Jewish Education in North America. *A Time to Act: The Report of the Commission on Jewish Education in North America*. University Press of America, 1990.

Coupland, Nikolas. *Style: Language Variation and Identity*. Cambridge University Press, 2007.

"David and Victoria Beckham 'Getting Posher,' Study Finds." *BBC.com*, April 17, 2013.

DellaPergola, Sergio. "World Jewish Population, 2023." In *American Jewish Year Book 2024*, ed. Arnold Dashefsky and Ira M. Sheskin, 309–422. Springer Nature, 2024.

Di Giulio, Marco. "Protecting the Jewish Throat: Hebrew Accent and Hygiene in the Yishuv." *Journal of Israeli History* 35, no. 2 (2016): 153–75.

Diner, Hasia. *A New Promised Land: A History of Jews in America*. Oxford University Press, 2003.

———. *The Jews of the United States, 1654 to 2000*. University of California Press, 2004.

Dobozy, Tamas. "The Holocaust as Fiction: Derrida's *Demeure* and the Demjanjuk Trial in Philip Roth's *Operation Shylock*." *Philip Roth Studies* 1, no. 1 (2005): 41–59.

Doherty, Rosa. "Anti-Israel Jewish Group Writes Backwards Hebrew on Seder Plate for Gaza." *Jewish Chronicle*, April 30, 2024. https://www.thejc.com/news/usa/jewish-voice-peace-la-usc-gaza-seder-plate-hebrew-blunder-qp7jod6v.

Dov, Yehudah, "Anglo-Israeli Grandma Goes Viral After Hilarious Interview with Israeli Anchor Rafi Rashef." *VINnews*, March 2, 2021.

Duchêne, Alexandre, and Monica Heller, eds. *Discourses of Endangerment: Ideology and Interest in the Defence of Languages*. A&C Black, 2008.

Duff, Patricia. "Second Language Socialization." In *The Handbook of Language Socialization*, ed. Alessandro Duranti, Elinor Ochs, and Bambi B. Schieffelin, 564–86. Blackwell, 2011.

"Effie Hercky with Ittay Flescher and Benji Lovitt (Video)." *Life in Israel*, March 17, 2021. http://lifeinisrael.blogspot.com/2021/03/effie-hercky-with-ittay-flescher-and.html.

"Effie's Firsts and Favorites in Israel." *Bagels*, April 18, 2021. https://bagels.tv/effies-firsts-and-favorites-in-israel/.

Eichler-Levine, Jodi. *Painted Pomegranates and Needlepoint Rabbis: How Jews Craft Resilience and Create Community*. Where Religion Lives. University of North Carolina Press, 2020.

Elazar, Daniel. *Community and Polity: The Organizational Dynamics of American Jewry*. Jewish Publication Society, 1995.

Ergas, Andrew. "American Jews Should Learn Hebrew." *Jerusalem Post*, April 8, 2019. https://www.jpost.com/opinion/american-jews-should-learn-hebrew-586145.

Even-Zohar, Itamar. "The Emergence of a Native Hebrew Culture in Palestine: 1882–1948." In *Essential Papers on Zionism*, ed. Yehuda Reinharz and Anita Shapira, 727–44. New York University Press, 1996.

Fader, Ayala. *Mitzvah Girls: Bringing Up the Next Generation of Hasidic Jews in Brooklyn*. Princeton University Press, 2009.

Fellman, Jack. "Concerning the 'Revival' of the Hebrew Language." *Anthropological Linguistics* (1973): 250–57.

———. *The Revival of a Classical Tongue: Eliezer Ben Yehuda and the Modern Hebrew Language*. Mouton, 1973.

Fishman, Joshua. "The Holiness of Yiddish: Who Says Yiddish Is Holy and Why?" *Language Policy* 1 (2002): 123–41.

Fleishman, Joel L. *Within Our Lifetime: A Reflection on the Spend-Down of the AVI CHAI Foundation*. Center for Strategic Philanthropy and Civil Society, Sanford School of Public Policy at Duke University, August 2020. https://avichai.org/#spend-down-reports.

Fox, Russell. "J. G. Herder on Language and the Metaphysics of National Community." *Review of Politics* 65, no. 2 (2003): 237–62.

Fox, Seymour, Israel Scheffler, and Daniel Marom, eds. *Visions of Jewish Education*. Cambridge University Press, 2003.

Friedland, Eric. *Were Our Mouths Filled with Song: Studies in Liberal Jewish Liturgy*. Hebrew Union College Press, 1997.

Furstenberg, Rochelle. "Israeli Life: Translating the Bible into Hebrew." *Hadassah Magazine*, February–March 2012. https://www.hadassahmagazine.org/2012/02/28/israeli-life-translating-bible-hebrew/.

Gafter, Roey. "The Most Beautiful and Correct Hebrew: Authenticity, Ethnic Identity and Linguistic Variation in the Greater Tel Aviv Area." PhD diss., Stanford University, 2014.

———. "What's a Stigmatized Variant Doing in the Word List? Authenticity in Reading Styles and Hebrew Pharyngeals." *Journal of Sociolinguistics* 20, no. 1 (2016): 31–58.

Gedzelman, David. "The Possibilities and Potential of Hebrew in America." *Contact Magazine: The Steinhardt Foundation for Jewish Life* 13, no. 2 (Spring 2011): 3–4.

Glinert, Lewis. *The Joys of Hebrew*. Oxford University Press, 1992.

———. "Hebrew from Symbol to Substance." In *Hebrew in America: Perspectives and Prospects*, ed. Alan Mintz, 227–50. Wayne State University Press, 1993.

———. *Hebrew in Ashkenaz: A Language in Exile*. Oxford University Press, 1993.

———. *The Story of Hebrew*. Princeton University Press, 2017.

Gold, David. "A Sketch of the Linguistic Situation in Israel Today." *Language and Society* 18, no. 3 (1989): 370.

Goldberg, Emma, and Marc Tracy. "Jewish American Families Confront a Generational Divide over Israel." *New York Times*, December 5, 2023. https://www.nytimes.com/2023/12/05/us/jewish-american-israel-gaza-generation-gap.html.

Gordis, Daniel. *We Stand Divided: The Rift Between American Jews and Israel.* Ecco, 2019.

———. "End the Jewish State? Let's Try Some Honesty, First." *Times of Israel*, July 8, 2020. https://blogs.timesofisrael.com/end-the-jewish-state-lets-try-some-honesty-first/.

Gordis, Robert. "A Jewish Prayer Book for the Modern Age." *Conservative Judaism* 2, no. 1 (1945): 1–20.

Graizbord, David. *The New Zionists: Young American Jews, Jewish National Identity, and Israel.* Lexington Books, 2020.

Gray, John. *Men Are from Mars, Women Are from Venus.* Harper Collins, 1992.

Gringras, Robbie. "Jewish World: We Should Stop Hugging Israel and Start Wrestling." Accessed July 20, 2023. https://www.haaretz.com/2008-08-17/ty-article/jewish-world-we-should-stop-hugging-israel-and-start-wrestling/0000017f-e109-d7b2-a77f-e30f32840000.

Gross, Rachel B. *Beyond the Synagogue: Jewish Nostalgia as Religious Practice.* North American Religions. New York: New York University Press, 2021.

Halkin, Hillel. "A Culture Loses Its Flavor." *Sh'ma: A Journal of Jewish Ideas* 35, no. 619 (2005): 6–7.

———. "My Uncle Simon." *Commentary*, May 2005.

Halperin, Liora. "Modern Hebrew, Esperanto, and the Quest for a Universal Language." *Jewish Social Studies: History, Culture, Society* 19, no. 1 (2012): 1–33.

———. *Babel in Zion: Jews, Nationalism, and Language Diversity in Palestine, 1920–1948.* Yale University Press, 2015.

Harshav, Benjamin. *Language in Time of Revolution.* Stanford University Press, 1993.

Hary, Benjamin, and Sarah Bunin Benor. *Languages in Jewish Communities, Past and Present.* De Gruyter, 2018.

Hazony, David. "Memo to American Jews: Learn Hebrew." *Forward*, April 19, 2012. https://forward.com/opinion/154253/memo-to-american-jews-learn-hebrew/.

Heilman, Samuel. *Portrait of American Jews: The Last Half of the 20th Century.* University of Washington Press, 1995.

——. *The People of the Book: Drama, Fellowship and Religion*. Routledge, 2017.

Hoffman, Joel. *In the Beginning: A Short History of the Hebrew Language*. NYU Press, 2004.

——. "The Role of Transliteration in the Synagogue." December 9, 2009, https://blog.joelmhoffman.com/2009/12/09/the-role-of-transliteration-in-the-synagogue.

Horn, Dara. "Living in Hebrew: On Jealousy and Creativity." In *What We Talk About When We Talk About Hebrew (and What It Means to Americans)*, ed. Naomi Sokoloff and Nancy Berg, 35–42. University of Washington Press, 2018.

——. "My First Hebrew Test." Accessed February 22, 2026. https://jewishstudies.washington.edu/personal-history/dara-horn-my-first-hebrew-test/.

Horowitz, Bethamie. "A New Balancing Act? Teaching About Israel and Diaspora Jewish Communities in Unsettled Times," 30–33. *Peoplehood Papers* 33: The Relations Between Peoplehood Education and Israel Education. Accessed August 25, 2023. https://old.jpeoplehood.org/wp-content/uploads/2023/09/Peoplehood-Papes-33-final.pdf.

If Not Now. "If Not Now Homepage." Accessed February 28, 2026. https://www.ifnotnowmovement.org/.

Irvine, Judith. "When Talk Isn't Cheap: Language and Political Economy." *American Ethnologist* 16, no. 2 (1989): 248–67.

Israel American Council. "About IAC." Accessed April 5, 2024. https://www.israeliamerican.org/about-us.

Jacobs, Benjamin. "Socialization into a Civilization: The Dewey–Kaplan Synthesis in American Jewish Schooling in the Early 20th Century." *Religious Education* 104, no. 2 (2009): 149–65.

Jacobs, Paula. "The Changing Landscape of Hebrew Education." *Tablet*, December 16, 2022. https://www.tabletmag.com/sections/community/articles/changing-landscape-hebrew-education.

Jaffe, Alexandra. "Defining the New Speaker: Theoretical Perspectives and Learner Trajectories." *International Journal of the Sociology of Language* 2015, no. 231 (2015): 21–44.

Jewish Education Project. *From Census to Possibilities: Designing Pathways for Jewish Learners*. April 2023. https://educator.jewishedproject.org/content/census-possibilities.

Johnstone, Barbara, and Scott F. Kiesling. "Indexicality and Experience: Exploring the Meanings of /aw/-Monophthongization in Pittsburgh." *Journal of Sociolinguistics* 12, no. 1 (2008): 5–33.

Kahlenberg, Caroline. "How the Locals Grew an Accent: The Sounds of Modern Hebrew in Early Twentieth-Century Palestine." *Jewish Social Studies* 28, no. 3 (2023): 105–42.

Kaplan, Alice. *French Lessons: A Memoir*. University of Chicago Press, 2018.

Kaplan, Danny. "The Songs of the Siren: Engineering National Time on Israeli Radio." *Cultural Anthropology* 24, no. 2 (2009): 313–45.

Kaplan, Mordecai. *Judaism as a Civilization: Toward a Reconstruction of American-Jewish Life*. Macmillan Company, 1934.

———. *Communings of the Spirit: The Journals of Mordecai M. Kaplan, 1913–1934*, ed. Mel Scult, 210–11. Detroit: Wayne State University Press, 2002.

Karpman, Avital. "Gender-Inclusive and Nonbinary Hebrew: Innovations and Classroom Applications; Summary of a March 13, 2022, Conference." *Hebrew Higher Education* 24 (2022): 185–90.

———. "Mapping Grassroots Initiatives in the Creation of Gender-Inclusive and Nonbinary Hebrew." *Journal of the National Council of Less Commonly Taught Languages* 34 (2023): 8–20.

Katriel, Tamar. *Talking Straight: Dugri Speech in Israeli Sabra Culture*. Cambridge University Press, 1986.

Kattan, Shlomy. "'Because She Doesn't Speak Real Hebrew': Accent and the Socialization of Authenticity Among Israeli Shlichim." *Crossroads of Language, Interaction, and Culture* 7 (2009): 65–94.

———. "Language Socialization and Linguistic Ideologies Among Israeli Emissaries in the United States." PhD diss., University of California, Berkeley, 2010.

Katz, Emily. *Bringing Zion Home: Israel in American Jewish Culture, 1948–1967*. State University of New York Press, 2015.

Kaufman, David. *Shul with a Pool: The "Synagogue-Center" in American Jewish History*. University Press of New England, 1999.

Kehilat Hadar. *Kehilat Hadar Gender Inclusive Ritual Guidelines*. Accessed April 5, 2024. https://www.kehilathadar.org/gender-inclusive-ritual-guidelines.

Kelman, Ari Y. *Jewish Education*. Rutgers University Press, 2024.

Kelman, Ari Y., and Ilan Zvi Baron. "Framing Conflict: Why American Congregations Cannot Not Talk About Israel." *Contemporary Jewry* 39, nos. 3/4 (September–December 2019): 497–522.

Kelman, Ari Y., Tobin Belzer, Ziva Hassenfeld, Ilana Horwitz, and Matthew Casey Williams. "The Social Self: Toward the Study of Jewish Lives in the Twenty-First Century." *Contemporary Jewry* 37, no. 1 (2017): 53–79.

Kelman, Ari Y., and Jon Levisohn, eds. *Beyond Jewish Identity: Rethinking Concepts and Imagining Alternatives*. Academic Studies Press, 2019.

Kelner, Shaul. "Historical Perspectives on Diaspora Homeland Tourism: 'Israel Experience' Education in the 1950s and 1960s." *Diaspora, Indigenous, and Minority Education* 7, no. 2 (2013): 99–113.

Kershner, Isabel. "In Israel, a Biblical Tongue Meets Gender Politics." *New York Times*, August 1, 2022. https://www.nytimes.com/2022/08/01/world/middleeast/israel-hebrew-gender.html.

Kirsch, Adam. "The Temple Mount in New York." *New Republic*, March 9, 2024.

Knight, Lucy. "Sally Rooney Novels Pulled from Israeli Bookstores After Translation Boycott." *Guardian*, November 5, 2021.

Kober, Hannah. "A Fraying Connection: Israeli-American Perspectives on Diasporic Hebrew Learning Through and Beyond Jewish Education." *Journal of Jewish Education* 89, no. 3 (2023): 210–44.

Krashen, Stephen. *Second Language Acquisition and Second Language Learning*. Pergamon Press, 1981.

Krasner, Jonathan. *The Benderly Boys and American Jewish Education*. Brandeis University Press, 2011.

———. "American Jewry at Risk: 'A Time to Act' and the Prioritization of Jewish Education." *Contemporary Jewry* 36 (2016): 85–123.

———. "On the Origins and Persistence of the Jewish Identity Industry in Jewish Education." In *Beyond Jewish Identity*, ed. Ari Y. Kelman and Jon A. Levisohn, 61–88. Academic Studies Press, 2019.

Kravel-Tovi, Michal. "Language of Continuity: Crisis and the Work of Care Among the Organized American Jewish Community." In *Taking Stock: Cultures of Enumeration in Contemporary Jewish Life*, ed. Michal Kravel-Tovi and Deborah Dash Moore, 141–60. Indiana University Press, 2016.

Kravel-Tovi, Michal, and Deborah Dash Moore, eds. *Taking Stock: Cultures of Enumeration in Contemporary Jewish Life*. Indiana University Press, 2016.

Kuo, Christopher. "Ye Apologizes for Antisemitic Comments with Post in Hebrew." *New York Times*, December 26, 2020. https://www.nytimes.com/2023/12/26/arts/music/kanye-west-apology-antisemitism.html.

Kulick, Don, and Bambi B. Schieffelin. "Language Socialization." In *A Companion to Linguistic Anthropology*, ed. Alessandro Duranti, 347–68. Blackwell, 2004.

Kushner, Aviya. "Why Making Hebrew Nonbinary Is So Crucial." *Forward*, January 24, 2019. https://forward.com/culture/417978/why-making-hebrew-nonbinary-is-so-crucial/.

———. "No One's Studying Hebrew Anymore: That's a Big Problem." *Forward*, July 11, 2019. https://forward.com/culture/427477/no-ones-studying-hebrew-anymore-thats-a-big-problem/.

———. "Why Hebrew Is Showing Up in Unexpected Places—And Why That Matters." *Forward*, June 6, 2024. https://forward.com/culture/620155/hebrew-language-jessica-jacobs-toby-lloyd-yael-van-der-wouden/.

Labov, William. "Hypercorrection by the Lower Middle Class as a Factor in Linguistic Change." *Sociolinguistics* 84 (1966): 84–113.

Lapide, Pinchas. *Hebrew in the Church: The Foundations of Jewish-Christian Dialogue*. Eerdmans, 1984.

Leech, Geoffrey N. *The Pragmatics of Politeness*. Oxford University Press, 2014.

"Let Effie Hercky Light an Independence Day Torch." Change.org, March 15, 2021. https://www.change.org/p/israeli-ministry-of-culture-let-effie-hercky-light-an-independence-day-torch-representing-anglo-olim.

Levinson, Julian. "Entering the Heart of a Language." *Sh'ma: A Journal of Jewish Ideas* 4, no. 674 (2010): 2–3.

Lindholm, Charles. "The Theory and History of Authenticity." *Social Media & the Self: An Open Reader*, 2007.

Lippi-Green, Rosina. "Accent, Standard Language Ideology, and Discriminatory Pretext in the Courts." *Language in Society* 23, no. 2 (1994): 163–98.

———. *English with an Accent: Language, Ideology and Discrimination in the United States*. London: Routledge, 2011.

Loeffler, James. "The Death of Jewish Culture." *Mosaic*, May 2014. https://ideas.tikvah.org/mosaic/essays/the-death-of-jewish-culture.

———. "Should American Jews Speak Hebrew?" *Tablet*, July 30, 2019. https://www.tabletmag.com/sections/arts-letters/articles/ben-gurion-hebrew-revolution.

Lowin, Joseph. *Hebrew Matters: 110 Hebrew Roots; the Roads They Take; the Stories They Tell*. GCRR Press, 2022.

Mac Ginty, Roger. "Everyday Peace: Bottom-Up and Local Agency in Conflict-Affected Societies." *Security Dialogue* 45, no. 6 (2014): 548–64.

Maltz, Judy. "'Time to Take the Plunge': How October 7 Sparked a Huge Wave of Jewish Conversions." *Haaretz*, June 2, 2024. https://www.haaretz.com/jewish/2024-06-02/ty-article-magazine/.premium/time-to-take-the-plunge-how-oct-7-sparked-a-huge-wave-of-jewish-conversions-in-america/0000018f-d964-d5bc-a1bf-df7408700000.

Marcus, Jacob Rader. *United States Jewry, 1776–1985*. 4 vols. Wayne State University Press, 1989.

Martin, Noga. "Why Can't the Anglos Learn to Speak?" *Times of Israel*, July 7, 2012.

Mendel, Yonatan, and Ronald Ranta. *From the Arab Other to the Israeli Self: Palestinian Culture in the Making of Israeli National Identity*. Routledge, 2016.

Mendoza-Denton, Norma. *Homegirls: Language and Cultural Practice Among Latina Youth Gangs*. Wiley, 2008.

Meyer, Michael. *Response to Modernity: A History of the Reform Movement in Judaism*. Wayne State University Press, 1995.

Mintz, Alan. "The Erosion of the Tarbut Ivrit Ideology in America and the Consequences for the Teaching of Hebrew in the University." *Shofar* (1991): 50–54.

———. "Seven Theses on Hebrew and Jewish Peoplehood." *Contact Magazine: The Steinhardt Foundation for Jewish Life*, Spring 2008. https://steinhardtfoundation.org/contact/spring_2008/spring_2008-mintz.html.

———. "Hebrew in America: A Memoir." In *What We Talk About When We Talk About Hebrew (and What It Means to Americans)*, ed. Naomi Sokoloff and Nancy Berg, 211–26. University of Washington Press, 2018.

Mintz, Alan. ed. *Hebrew in America: Perspectives and Prospects*. Wayne State University Press, 1993.

Moehlman, Lara. "Can Hebrew Be Gender-Neutral?" *Moment*, October 8, 2018. https://momentmag.com/can-hebrew-be-gender-neutral/.

Muchnick, Jordan, and Kamarck, Elaine. "The Generation Gap in Opinions Toward Israel." Brookings Institution, August 20, 2024. https://www.brookings.edu/articles/the-generation-gap-in-opinions-toward-israel/.

Myhill, John. *Language in Jewish Society: Towards a New Understanding*. Multilingual Matters, 2004.

Myers, David, and Ravid, Benjamin. *Between Babylon and Jerusalem*. Vandenhoeck & Ruprecht, 2020.

Neiger, Motti, Oren Meyers, and Eyal Zandberg. "Tuned to the Nation's Mood: Popular Music as a Mnemonic Cultural Object." *Media, Culture & Society* 33, no. 7 (2011): 971–87.

Oldenburg, Ray. *The Great Good Place: Cafes, Coffee Shops, Bookstores, Bars, Hair Salons, and Other Hangouts at the Heart of a Community*. Da Capo Press, 1999.

Olefson, Rachel. "My Hebrew Necklace: What Judaism Means to Me." *Inkling News*, November 3, 2023. https://www.inklingsnews.com/opinions/2023/11/03/from-a-symbol-of-faith-to-question-of-safety-unpacking-the-meaning-of-my-hebrew-necklace/.

Orol, Sass. *The Shortest Skirt in Shul*. Ben Yehudah Press, 2021.

Orsi, Robert A. "Is the Study of Lived Religion Irrelevant to the World We Live In? Special Presidential Plenary Address, Society for the Scientific Study of Religion, Salt Lake City, November 2, 2002." *Journal for the Scientific Study of Religion* 42, no. 2 (2003): 169–74.

Ovadia Luski, Ifat. "Hebrew Language Day." *Jerusalem Post*, January 5, 2021. https://www.jpost.com/opinion/hebrew-language-day-654334.

Ozick, Cynthia. *The Puttermesser Papers*. New York: Knopf, 1997.

Peleg, Yaron. "A New Hebrew Literary Diaspora? Israeli Literature Abroad." *Studia Judaica* 18, no. 36 (2015): 321–38.

Pelli, Moshe. "Ideology and Reality: The American Hebrew Movement in Its Inception—In Search of Identity." *Hebrew Studies* 36, no. 1 (1995): 73–85.

Peshkin, Alan. *God's Choice: The Total World of a Fundamentalist Christian School*. University of Chicago Press, 1988.

Pew Research Center. *A Portrait of Jewish Americans: Findings from a Pew Research Center Survey of American Jews*. October 1, 2013.

———. *Jewish Americans in 2020*. May 11, 2021.

———. *Modeling the Future of Religion in America*. September 13, 2022.

———. *Religious "Nones" in America: Who They Are and What They Believe*. January 24, 2024.

Phillips, Anna. "Hebrew School." *Tablet*, March 9, 2011. https://www.tabletmag.com/sections/community/articles/hebrew-school.

Phillips, Bruce A. "Expanding Our Definitions of and Questions for American Jewry." *Contemporary Jewry* 42, no. 2 (2022): 237–39.

Philologos. "Hebrew vs. Israeli." Forward, December 24, 2004. https://forward.com/news/4052/hebrew-vs-israeli/.

———. "Are Biblical Hebrew and Modern Hebrew the Same Language, or Two Different Ones?" *Mosaic*, February 5, 2020. https://ideas.tikvah.org/mosaic/observations/are-biblical-hebrew-and-modern-hebrew-the-same-language-or-two-different-ones.

Pianko, Noam. *Jewish Peoplehood: An American Innovation*. Rutgers University Press, 2015.

Pinar, William F. *What Is Curriculum Theory?* 3rd ed. New York: Routledge, 2019.

Pomson, Alex. "When the Price of Loving Israel Is Ostracism." *Times of Israel*, June 13, 2024. https://blogs.timesofisrael.com/when-the-price-of-loving-israel-is-ostracism/.

Pomson, Alex, and Jack Wertheimer. *Hebrew for What? Hebrew at the Heart of Jewish Day Schools*. AVI CHAI Foundation, 2017.

Pomson, Alex, Jack Wertheimer, and Hagit Hacohen-Wolf. *Hearts and Minds: Israel in North American Jewish Day Schools*. AVI CHAI Foundation, 2014.

Porter, Theodore. *Trust in Numbers: The Pursuit of Objectivity in Science and Public Life*. Princeton University Press, 1995.

Prell, Riv-Ellen. "Developmental Judaism: Challenging the Study of American Jewish Identity in the Social Sciences." *Contemporary Jewry* 21, no. 1 (2000): 33–54.

Presner, Todd. "Clear Heads, Solid Stomachs, and Hard Muscles: Max Nordau and the Aesthetics of Jewish Regeneration." *Modernism/modernity* 10, no. 2 (2003): 269–96.

Rajak, Tessa. *Translation and Survival: The Greek Bible of the Ancient Jewish Diaspora*. Oxford University Press, 2009.

Ramati, Ido. *Lingua Ex Machina: Media in the Revitalization of Modern Hebrew*. University of Pennsylvania Press, 2025.

Ribak, Gil. "Israelis Are from Mars, American Jews Are from Venus? Cultural Differences and Rivalry in American Jewish Attitudes Toward Israel." *Israelis* 10 (2021): 209–36.

Robertson, Nick. "Ye Posts Hebrew-Language Apology to Jewish Community." WKRG.com, December 26, 2023. https://www.wkrg.com/national/ye-posts-hebrew-language-apology-to-jewish-community/?utm_source=t.co+&utm_medium=referral&utm_campaign=socialflow.

Rosenthal, Steven T. *Irreconcilable Differences? The Waning of the American Jewish Love Affair with Israel*. Brandeis University Press, 2003.

Rudolph, Ari. "American Jewry Must Reclaim Hebrew." *Jewish Telegraphic Agency*, March 23, 2014. https://www.jta.org/2014/03/23/opinion/op-ed-american-jewry-must-reclaim-hebrew.

Ruskay, John S., and Lisa Rubin-Kurshan. "American Jewry's Focus on Continuity—At Ten Years." *Journal of Jewish Communal Service* (Fall–Winter 1999): 81–88.

Sachar, Howard M. *A History of Israel: From the Rise of Zionism to Our Time.* Knopf, 2007.

Sáenz-Badillos, Angel. *A History of the Hebrew Language.* Cambridge University Press, 1996.

Safit, Ilan. "When Poet Bialik Visited America." *NY Jewish Week*, January 5, 2010.

Sagarin, Lori. "Modern Hebrew: Culture and Identity." Accessed August 25, 2023. https://theicenter.org/aleph_bet/modern-hebrew-culture-and-identity/.

Sales, Ben. "Sally Rooney: Israeli Publishers Can't Put Out My New Book for Now, but Hebrew Translation 'Would Be an Honour.'" *Jewish Telegraphic Agency*, October 12, 2021.

——. "At IAC Conference, Jewish Leaders Ponder How to Integrate Israeli-Americans into Their Communities." *eJewishPhilanthropy*, January 20, 2023. https://ejewishphilanthropy.com/at-iac-conference-jewish-leaders-ponder-how-to-integrate-israeli-americans-into-their-communities/.

Sarna, Jonathan. "American Jewish Education in Historical Perspective." *Journal of Jewish Education* 64, nos. 1–2 (1998): 8–21.

——. *American Judaism: A History*. Yale University Press, 2004.

Sasson, Theodore. *The New American Zionism*. New York University Press, 2013.

——. "Understanding Young Adult Attachment to Israel: Period, Lifecycle and Generational Dynamics." *Contemporary Jewry* 34, no. 1 (2013): 67–84.

Scheinberg, Robert. "Al Kol Eleh—'For All These Things': Thoughts on Israel's 70th Birthday." April 19, 2018. https://rabbischeinberg.blogspot.com/2018/04/al-kol-eleh-for-all-these-things.html.

Schieffelin, Bambi B., and Elinor Ochs, eds. *Language Socialization Across Cultures*. Cambridge University Press, 1986.

Schieffelin, Bambi B., Kathryn A. Woolard, and Paul V. Kroskrity, eds. *Language Ideologies: Practice and Theory*. Vol. 16. Oxford University Press, 1998.

Schiff, Alvin. "The Significance of Hebrew Language for Jewish Education." *Journal of Jewish Education* 49, no. 2 (1981): 2–3.

——. *The Mystique of Hebrew: An Ancient Language in the New World*. Academic Press, 1998.

——. "How Crucial Is Hebrew for Jewish Continuity and the Effectiveness of Jewish Education?" *Journal of Jewish Education* 62, no. 3 (2006): 8–14.

Schniedewind, William M. *A Social History of Hebrew: Its Origins Through the Rabbinic Period*. Yale University Press, 2013.

Schnur, Dan. "In a Time of Division, Bridge-Building Must Begin in the Jewish Community." *Jewish Journal*, December 29, 2021.

Schoenfeld, Stuart. "Folk Judaism, Elite Judaism and the Role of the Bar Mitzvah in the Development of the Synagogue and Jewish School in America." *Contemporary Jewry* 9 (1987): 67–85.

Schuster, Diane Tickton. *Portraits of Adult Jewish Learning: Making Meaning at Many Tables*. Wipf & Stock, 2022.

Schweid, Eliezer. "The Rejection of the Diaspora in Zionist Thought: Two Approaches." *Studies in Zionism* 5, no. 1 (1984): 43–70.

Segal, Miryam. *A New Sound in Hebrew Poetry: Poetics, Politics, Accent*. Indiana University Press, 2010.

Segev, T. *1967: Israel, the War, and the Year That Transformed the Middle East*. Metropolitan Books, 2007.

Seidman, Naomi. *A Marriage Made in Heaven: The Sexual Politics of Hebrew and Yiddish*. University of California Press, 1997.

———. *Faithful Renderings: Jewish-Christian Difference and the Politics of Translation*. University of Chicago Press, 2010.

Shaked, Gershon. "Judaism in Translation: Thoughts on the Alexandria Hypothesis." In *Hebrew in America: Perspectives and Prospects*, ed. Alan Mintz, 280–90. Wayne State University Press, 1993.

Shandler, Jeffrey. *Adventures in Yiddishland: Postvernacular Language and Culture*. University of California Press, 2005.

———. "Keepers of Accounts: The Practice of Inventory in Modern Jewish Life." David W. Belin Lecture in American Jewish Affairs, 2010. https://hdl.handle.net/2027/spo.13469761.0017.001.

———. *Yiddish: Biography of a Language*. Oxford, 2020.

Sharim, Yehuda. "The Struggle for Sephardic-Mizrahi Autonomy: Racial Identities in Palestine-Israel, 1918–1948." PhD diss., University of California Los Angeles, 2013.

Sharp, Carolyn. *Wrestling the Word: The Hebrew Scriptures and the Christian Believer*. Westminster John Knox Press, 2010.

Sherman, Maria. "Kanye West, Now Known as Ye, Posts Hebrew Apology After Antisemitic Comments." WCNC.com, December 27, 2020. https://www.wcnc.com/article/news/nation-world/kanye-west-apology-in-hebrew-to-jewish-community/507-da469541-1682-4bb2-b129-c7d4c20638e6.

Shufutinsky, Dmitri. "Learning Hebrew Can Save American Judaism." *Times of Israel*, January 7, 2022.

Shulman, Lee. "Those Who Understand: Knowledge Growth in Teaching." *Educational Researcher* 15, no. 2 (1986): 4–14.

Shulsinger, Shlomo. "Hebrew Camping: The Creator of a Hebrew World, Jewish Education." *Journal of Jewish Education* 37, nos. 1–2 (1967): 6–14.

Siegel, Danny. "There Are Many Roads to the Holiness of Hebrew." *Times of Israel*, May 13, 2016. https://blogs.timesofisrael.com/there-are-many-roads-to-the-holiness-of-hebrew/.

Silow-Carroll, Andrew. "Putting Pew's New Survey into Context: How Similar Studies Have Shaped 3 Decades of Jewish Life." *Forward*, May 11, 2021. https://forward.com/news/469342/new-pew-survey-jewish-america-three-decades/.

Sokoloff, Naomi B., and Nancy E. Berg, eds. *What We Talk About When We Talk About Hebrew (and What It Means to Americans)*. University of Washington Press, 2018.

Sperling, Eli. *Singing the Land: Hebrew Music and Early Zionism in America*. University of Michigan Press, 2024.

Spiegel, Dror. *The Revival of Hebrew: Ideology and Practice*. Magnes Press, 2009.

Spiegel, Nina. *Embodying Hebrew Culture: Aesthetics, Athletics, and Dance in the Jewish Community of Mandate Palestine*. Wayne State University Press, 2012.

Spiegel, Varda. "American Accent? You'll Never Be a 'Real' Israeli." *Times of Israel*, May 27, 2015.

Spolsky, Bernard. "Language Policy and the Teaching of Hebrew." In *Issues in the Acquisition, Learning and Teaching of Hebrew*, ed. Avital Feuer, Sharon Armon-Lotem, and Bernard Cooperman, 155–70. University Press of Maryland, 2009.

———. *The Languages of the Jews: A Sociolinguistic History*. Cambridge University Press, 2014.

Spolsky, Bernard, and Elana Shohamy. *The Languages of Israel: Policy, Ideology, and Practice*. Multilingual Matters, 1999.

Squires, Lauren. "From TV Personality to Fans and Beyond: Indexical Bleaching and the Diffusion of a Media Innovation." *Journal of Linguistic Anthropology* 24, no. 1 (2014): 42–62.

Stavans, Ilan. *Resurrecting Hebrew*. New York: Random House Digital, 2008.

———. "Yiddish Is Having a Moment." *New York Times*, September 2, 2023. https://www.nytimes.com/2023/09/02/opinion/yiddish-language-diaspora.html.

Stavans, Ilan, and Josh Lambert, eds. *How Yiddish Changed America and How America Changed Yiddish*. Restless Books, 2020.

Stebbins, Robert A., and David B. Sachsman. *Serious Leisure: A Perspective for Our Time*. Routledge, 2017.

Stolow, Jeremy. *Orthodox by Design: Judaism, Print Politics, and the ArtScroll Revolution*. University of California Press, 2010.

SVARA. "About SVARA." Accessed September 10, 2025. https://svara.org/.

Syme, Daniel. *A Jewish Home: A Guide for Jewish Living*. Rowman and Littlefield, 2003.

Tannenbaum, Michal, and Elana Shohamy. "Languages and Policy in Israel: History and Present." In *Developing Multilingual Education Policies*, ed. Michal Tannenbaum and Elana Shohamy. Routledge, 2023.

Tene, David. "Israeli Hebrew." *Ariel* 25 (1969): 48–63.

Tracy, Marc. "Is Israel Part of What It Means to Be Jewish?" *New York Times*, January 14, 2024. https://www.nytimes.com/2024/01/14/us/israel-jewish-america-diasporism.html.

Trilling, Lionel. *Sincerity and Authenticity*. Harvard University Press, 2009.

Urla, Jacqueline. "Cultural Politics in an Age of Statistics: Numbers, Nations, and the Making of Basque Identity." *American Ethnologist* 20, no. 4 (1993): 818–43.

Vieira, Fátima. "The Concept of Utopia." In *The Cambridge Companion to Utopian Literature*, ed. Gregory Claeys, 3–27. Cambridge University Press, 2010.

Walters, Joel, et al. "Sociolinguistics in Israel: From Hebrew Hegemony to Israeli Plurilingualism." In *The Routledge Handbook of Sociolinguistics Around the World*, ed. Martin Ball et al., 278–88. Routledge, 2009.

Waxman, Dov. *Trouble in the Tribe: The American Jewish Conflict over Israel*. Princeton University Press, 2016.

———. "Young American Jews and Israel: Beyond Birthright and BDS." *Israel Studies* 22, no. 3 (2017): 177–99.

Weingrad, Michael. *American Hebrew Literature: Writing Jewish National Identity in the United States*. Syracuse University Press, 2011.

———. "Robert Whitehill-Bashan and the Prospects for a New American Hebrew Literature." In *What We Talk About When We Talk About Hebrew (and What It Means to Americans)*, ed. Naomi Sokoloff and Nancy Berg, 196–210. University of Washington Press, 2018.

———. "Can't or Won't Learn Hebrew?" Stroum Center for Jewish Studies. Accessed April 6, 2023. https://jewishstudies.washington.edu/hebrew-humanities/american-jews-hebrew-active-resistance/.

Weininger, Melissa. *Beyond the Land: Diaspora Israeli Culture in the Twenty-First Century*. Wayne State University Press, 2023.

Weiss, Anthony. "Mega-Donor Throws Clout Behind Hebrew Charter School." *Forward*, May 29, 2008. https://forward.com/news/13482/mega-donor-throws-clout-behind-hebrew-charter-scho-01941/.

Wertheimer, Jack. "American Jews and Israel: A 60-Year Retrospective." *American Jewish Year Book* 108 (2008): 3–79.

———. *Learning and Community: Jewish Supplementary Schooling in the Twenty-First Century*. Brandeis University Press, 2009.

———. *The New American Judaism: How Jews Practice Their Religion Today*. Princeton University Press, 2018.

———. *A People Divided: Judaism in Contemporary America*. Brandeis University Press, 2022.

Wertheimer, Jack, and Alex Pomson. *Inside Jewish Day Schools: Leadership, Learning, and Community*. Brandeis University Press, 2022.

Wex, Michael. *Born to Kvetch: Yiddish Language and Culture in All Its Moods*. St. Martin's Press, 2007.

Wexler, Paul. *The Schizoid Nature of Modern Hebrew: A Slavic Language in Search of a Semitic Past*. Otto Harrassowitz Verlag, 1990.

Whitfield, Stephen J. *In Search of American Jewish Culture*. Brandeis University Press, 1999.

Wieseltier, Leon. "Language, Identity, and the Scandal of American Jewry." *Journal of Jewish Communal Service* 86, nos. 1/2 (2011): 14–22.

Williams, Chris. "Kanye West Apologizes to the Jewish Community—in Hebrew—in Curiously Generic Message." *Variety*, December 26, 2023. https://variety.com/2023/music/news/kanye-west-apologizes-jewish-community-hebrew-message-1235850532/.

Windmueller, Steven. "In the Wake of October 7: Reflections on the American Jewish Community." *Jerusalem Center for Public Affairs*, May 20, 2024. https://jcpa.org/in-the-wake-of-october-7-reflections-on-the-american-jewish-community/.

Winer, Amanda. *A Census of Jewish Supplementary Schools in North America, 2019–2020*. Jewish Education Project, April 2023.

Wirth-Nesher, Hana. *Call It English: The Languages of Jewish American Literature*. Princeton University Press, 2005.

Wisse, Ruth. "The Hebrew Imperative." In *Hebrew in America: Perspectives and Prospects*, ed. Alan Mintz, 265–76. Wayne State University Press, 1993.

Woocher, Jonathan S. "Sacred Survival: American Jewry's Civil Religion." *Judaism* 34, no. 2 (1985): 151–62.

Woolard, Kathryn. "Introduction: Language Ideology as a Field of Inquiry." In *Language Ideologies: Practice and Theory*, ed. Bambi B. Schieffelin, Kathryn A. Woolard, and Paul V. Kroskrity, 3–47. Oxford University Press, 1998.

———. *Singular and Plural: Ideologies of Linguistic Authority in 21st Century Catalonia*. Oxford University Press, 2016.

Wuthnow, Robert J. *America and the Challenges of Religious Diversity*. Princeton University Press, 2005.

———. "Taking Talk Seriously: Religious Discourse as Social Practice." *Journal for the Scientific Study of Religion* 50, no. 1 (2011): 1–21.

Yares, Laura. *Jewish Sunday Schools: Teaching Religion in Nineteenth-Century America*. NYU Press, 2023.

Yildiz, Yasemin. *Beyond the Mother Tongue: The Postmonolingual Condition*. New York: Fordham University Press, 2012.

Zauzmer, Julie. "A Camp Tries to Reinvent the Hebrew Language, so Transgender Kids Can Fit In." *Washington Post*, August 11, 2016. https://www.washingtonpost.com/news/acts-of-faith/wp/2016/08/11/what-does-a-gender-neutral-kid-call-themself-in-a-gendered-language/.

Zelkowicz, Tali. "Jewish Educators Don't Make Jews: A Sociological Reality Check About Jewish Identity Work." In *Beyond Jewish Identity: Rethinking Concepts and Imagining Alternatives*, ed. Jon A. Levisohn and Ari Y. Kelman, 144–66. Academic Studies Press, 2019.

Zerubavel, Yael. *Recovered Roots: Collective Memory and the Making of Israeli National Tradition*. University of Chicago Press, 1995.

Zisenwine, David, and David Schers, eds. *Present and Future: Jewish Culture, Identity and Language*. Tel Aviv University Press, 1999.

Zuckermann, Ghil'ad. "The Genesis of the Israeli Language: A Brief Response to 'Philologos.'" *The Mendele Review: Yiddish Literature and Language* 8, no. 13 (December 28, 2004).

——. "A New Vision for Israeli Hebrew: Theoretical and Practical Implications of Analyzing Israel's Main Language as a Semi-Engineered Semito-European Hybrid Language." *Journal of Modern Jewish Studies* 5, no. 1 (2006): 57–71.

——. "Hybridity Versus Revivability: Multiple Causation, Forms and Patterns." *Journal of Language Contact* 2, no. 2 (2009): 40–67.

——. "Hebrew Revivalists' Goals Vis-à-Vis the Emerging Israeli Language." In *Handbook of Language and Ethnic Identity: The Success-Failure Continuum in Language and Ethnic Identity Efforts*, ed. Joshua Fishman and Ofelia Garcia, 68–84. Oxford University Press, 2011.

Zuckermann, Ghil'ad, and Gitit Holzman. "Let My People Know! Towards a Revolution in the Teaching of the Hebrew Bible." *International Journal of the Sociology of Language* 2014, no. 226 (2014): 57–82.

INDEX